Commodity Trading Manual

EM42-10
ISBN0917456041
©Board of Trade of the City of Chicago 1973, 1976, 1977, 1980, 1982, 1985, 1989, 1994.

Commodity Trading Manual
Prepared by the Market Development Department of the Chicago Board of
Trade

Executive Editor	Patrick J. Catania
	Vice President
Project Editors	Peter Alonzi
	Senior Manager
	Christine Depp Stebbins
	Senior Editor
Market Development Subcommittee	Robert J. Pierce, co-chairman;
	Lawrence C. Dorf, co-chairman;
	Avi Goldfeder, vice chairman;
	David M. Berlinghof; R. Franklin
	Cantrell; Anthony P. Danielak III;
	John W. Janney; Lawrence M.
	Latimer; John Pietrzak; Joel R.
	Riechers; Pamela R. Rogers; Jonathan
	Sion; Howard L. Sorkin; Jay S. Sorkin

A book of this scope requires the work of many and the editors thank Jerry
Mastey for contributing to Chapters 17 and 18 and to those Chicago Board
of Trade staff members who helped in the editorial and production of the
Commodity Trading Manual, especially Jenny Garcia, manager publication
services, Nancy Keefer, managing director, Laura Senak, production
coordinator, Dana Kellerman, senior copy editor, and Bruce Andrews,
senior manager.

We express our appreciation to the following people who generously gave their time and effort in reviewing sections of this latest edition of the *Commodity Trading Manual.*

Reviewers

Jeffrey M. Christian, CPM Group; Alan Hanson, Commodity Exchange, Inc.; Nachamah Jacobovits, New York Mercantile Exchange; Mary Irwin, Chicago Mercantile Exchange; Paul Kram, Merrill Lynch; Andrea B. Liebelt, New York Cotton Exchange; Lynda O. Lucker, Philadelphia Board of Trade; Eileen Moccaldi, New York Futures Exchange; James Moser, Federal Reserve Bank of Chicago; Sheldon Natenberg, Chicago Board of Trade member; Laura Oatney, National Futures Association; Kathleen Garcia, Kansas City Board of Trade; Phil Plourd, Coffee, Sugar & Cocoa Exchange; Roger D. Rutz; Kenneth H. Shaleen, Chartwatch; Connie Tsuchiya, Minneapolis Grain Exchange

Chicago Board of Trade Staff Reviewers

Michael Boyle, Pamela Brassel, James S. Chrystal, Dennis Collins, William M. Cullen, Ted Doukas, Paul Draths, Craig Fujibayashi, Sue Goll, Arthur Hitterman, Eileen Klecka, Rita Macellaio, Greg Monroe, Julie Reinert, Mary Beth Rooney, Randall Sheldon, Steve Sural

The Chicago Board of Trade also appreciates the time given by those who have reviewed previous editions: Jin Choi, DePaul University; Anthony P. Danielak III, Harris Futures Corporation; Thomas V. Mauro, Cargill Investor Services; Dennis Dutterer, Board of Trade Clearing Corporation; Dirk Walvoord, Chicago Board of Trade member; Jeffrey Hersh, Richard Jelinek, Terrance Livingston, Patricia Mosley, Eugene Mueller, JoEllen Schroedter, Donald Sternard, Thomas Thompson, Chicago Board of Trade staff.

The *Commodity Trading Manual* holds a special niche among futures market literature. It is a comprehensive textbook/reference guide on the futures industry covering topics from the historical development of futures to a nuts-and-bolts description of the day-to-day operations of a futures exchange. While some books offer more in-depth explanations of specific aspects of futures trading, the *Commodity Trading Manual* is unique in providing the interested novice with a concise, yet readable, overview of the futures industry.

This feat becomes harder to accomplish with each new edition of the *Commodity Trading Manual,* as new contracts emerge and futures markets expand throughout the world. Ironically, it is also the industry's growth that makes it important that this publication exits. It is through literature like the *Commodity Trading Manual* that the public is made aware of the importance of the futures industry to the global economy and learns of our efforts to ensure a vital, responsive marketplace.

In the time span since the last edition, the futures industry has experienced many changes that will surely impact where and how the world trades futures and options on futures for many years to come. Non-U.S. exchanges continue to accelerate both in number and in trading volume. And, the desire for increased volume and market share have become a rallying point for both U.S. and non-U.S. exchanges alike. To meet these challenges, exchanges are developing a new breed of contracts designed to attract a larger customer base. The regulatory environment also is changing, which is bound to affect where customers trade futures and options on futures now and in the years ahead. In addition, advanced computer technology has the potential to radically alter futures trading practices. These topics and more are covered in our newest chapter, "The Future of the Futures Industry."

Also new with this edition is the financial instruments chapter. It has been completely rewritten to give a comprehensive background on the cash markets underlying financial futures products.

Changes in the futures industry are coming rapidly. Frequent revisions have become a necessity to keep this learning tool viable. It is a challenge the Chicago Board of Trade accepted more than 20 years ago, and one we will continue to meet.

Patrick J. Catania
Vice President
Market Development Department
Chicago Board of Trade

Cover illustration by Mark McMahon. Chicago Board of Trade Agricultural Trading Floor during the summer of 1988, when grain prices and trading activity soared due to drought conditions. Book design by Allen Stebbins.

TABLE OF CONTENTS

Today's futures markets and the principles that underlie commodity futures trading evolved from practices that are centuries old.

Dating to the ancient Greek and Roman markets, formalized trading practices began with a fixed time and place for trading, a central marketplace, common barter and currency systems, as well as a practice of contracting for future delivery. At the height of the Roman Empire, trading centers, called *fora vendalia* (sales markets), served as distribution centers for commodities that the Romans brought from the far corners of the empire. The Forum in Rome was initially established as a trading center, while the Agora in Athens served as a commercial market.

Despite the fall of these civilizations, the basic principles of the central marketplace survived. During the Dark Ages, when the widespread flow of commerce was disrupted, products were bought and sold in scattered local markets. Eventually, the practice of preannouncing markets to be held at specific times and places reemerged in the form of medieval fairs. These regional fairs were organized by merchants, craftsmen, and promoters with the aid of political authorities. *Pieds Poudres*, or *men of dusty feet*, as they were known, traveled from town to town arranging and promoting the fairs.

By the 12th century, the medieval fairs of England and France were quite large and complex. And, as specialization developed, certain fairs

DEVELOPMENT OF THE MARKETPLACE

Medieval Markets to Today

1

became the focus of trading between the English and Flemish, Spanish, French, or Italian merchants. During the 13th century, spot (cash) transactions for immediate delivery were most common; but the practice of contracting for later delivery of merchandise, with standards of quality established by samples, had begun.

Among the chief contributions of the medieval fair to modern commerce are the principles of self-regulation and arbitration, and formalized trading practices. In medieval England, a code known as the *Law Merchant* established standards of conduct acceptable to local authorities. In some cases, the standards were minimal, but they formed a basis for common practices in the use of contracts, bills of sale, freight and warehouse receipts, letters of credit, transfer of deeds, and other bills of exchange. Anyone who violated a provision of the Law Merchant could be prohibited from trading by his fellow merchants. This principle of self-regulation, found in England's Common Law and followed in the American colonies, was later adopted by U.S. commodity exchanges.

To arbitrate disputes between buyers and sellers, the English merchant associations obtained the right from local and national authorities to administer their own rules of conduct. The associations were able to enforce judgments with assessments of penalties and awards of damages by establishing *the courts of the fair,* also known as *the courts of the Pieds Poudres.* By the time these courts were officially recognized by English Common Law courts in the 14th century, their jurisdiction superseded that of the local courts. The regional fairs declined in importance with improved transportation and communication and as modern cities developed. Specialized market centers replaced the fairs in many parts of the world. In Europe, the markets were called by the names *bourse, boerse, beurs,* and *bolsa.* The words come from the surname of an 18th-century innkeeper, Van der Beurs, whose establishment in Bruges, Belgium, became a gathering place for local commerce. Initially, these markets were held outdoors, usually in town squares. They later moved inside to teahouses and inns and, finally, found more permanent locations.

The development of the bourses was not limited to England and Europe. At the same time, similar markets were formed in Japan and the United States. Japan's commodity exchanges date back to the 1700s and preceded Japanese securities markets by nearly a century and a half. This pattern is generally the reverse of that in Europe, England, and the United States, where securities markets usually predated commodity markets. Spot, or cash, trading in rice dates from the early 1700s and "forward contracting" of rice on the Dojima Rice Market was implemented in 1730. Forward contracting is a cash transaction in which a buyer and seller agree upon price, quality, quantity, and a future delivery date for some commodity. Since nothing in the contract is standardized, each contract term must be negotiated between the buyer and seller. In addition to the Dojima market, Japanese markets also were established for edible oils, cotton, and precious metals, but their trading volume was small in comparison with that of rice.

Commodity markets in the United States existed as early as 1752 and traded domestic produce, textiles, hides, metals, and lumber. Most transactions were cash transactions for immediate delivery; however, these early markets greatly enhanced the ease and scope of trading all types of goods.

Chicago Board of Trade members pictured on their trading floor during the early 1900s.

The history of modern futures trading began on the Midwestern frontier in the early 1800s. It was tied closely to the development of commerce in Chicago and the grain trade in the Midwest. Incorporated as a village in 1833, Chicago became a city in 1837 with a population of 4,107. Chicago's strategic location at the base of the Great Lakes, close to the fertile farmlands of the Midwest, contributed to the city's rapid growth and development as a grain terminal. Problems of supply and demand, transportation, and storage, however, led to a chaotic marketing situation and the logical development of futures markets.

For producers and processors in the early 1800s, supply and demand chaos was quite common. Farmers, who brought grain and livestock to

Chicago Markets: History of the City

regional markets at a certain time each year, often found that the supply of meat and grain far exceeded the immediate needs of packers and millers. These processors, seeing more than adequate supplies, would bid the lowest price. Often, the short-term demand could not absorb the glut of commodities at any price, however low, and grains were dumped in the street for lack of buyers.

The glut of commodities at harvesttime was only part of the problem. Inevitably, there were years of crop failure and extreme shortages. Even in years of abundant yield, supplies became exhausted, prices soared, and people went hungry. Businesses were faced with bankruptcy because they lacked raw materials to keep their operations going. In this situation, the rural people, although having sufficient food for themselves, had crops they couldn't sell and, therefore, did not have the income to pay for needed manufactured products—tools, building materials, and textiles.

Transportation difficulties and a lack of adequate storage facilities aggravated the problems of supply and demand. Throughout most of the year, snow and rain made the dirt roads from the farmlands to Chicago impassable. Although roads of wooden boards, called *plank roads*, enabled farmers to bring wagonloads of grain to the city, transportation was very expensive. In the 1840s, if a farmer had to haul a load of wheat 60 miles, he would barely break even, because it cost as much to bring the wheat to market as it did to produce it. Once commodities reached the city, buyers were faced with the problem of inadequate storage space. Underdeveloped harbor facilities impeded the shipment of grain to eastern markets and the return of needed manufactured goods to the West.

Reliable transportation was a high priority because it was vital for the further growth of Chicago and the Midwest. When commodity exchanges were organized, they became a major force behind legislative efforts to improve rural roads, build inland waterways, and expand storage and harbor facilities.

In response to the intolerable marketing conditions, farmers and merchants began to contract for forward delivery. Forward contracts in corn were first used by river merchants who received corn from farmers in late fall and early winter but had to store it until the corn reached a low enough moisture to ship and the river and canal were free of ice. Seeking to reduce the price risk of storing corn through the winter, these river merchants would travel to Chicago, where they would contract with processors for delivery of grain in the spring. In this way, they assured themselves of a buyer as well as a price for the grain. The earliest recorded forward contract in corn was made on March 13, 1851. The contract was for 3,000 bushels of corn to be delivered in June at a price of one cent per bushel below the price of corn on March 13.

Forward contracts in wheat developed later than those in corn. For wheat, however, it was the Chicago merchants and processors who faced the price risk of storing grain and, thus, sold wheat through forward contracts to eastern millers and exporters.

As grain trade expanded, a centralized marketplace—the Chicago Board of Trade (CBOT®)—was formed in 1848 by 82 merchants. Their purpose was to promote the commerce of the city and to provide a place where buyers and sellers could meet to exchange commodities. During the exchange's early years, forward contracts were used.

But forward contracts had their drawbacks. They were not standardized according to quality or delivery time, and merchants and traders often did not fulfill these forward commitments. Then, in 1865, the Chicago Board of Trade took a step to formalize grain trading by developing standardized agreements called *futures contracts*. Futures contracts, in contrast to forward contracts, are standardized as to quality, quantity, and time and place of delivery for the commodity being traded.

A margining system was initiated that same year to eliminate the problem of buyers and sellers not fulfilling their contracts. (A margining system requires traders to deposit funds with the exchange or an exchange representative to guarantee contract performance.) Following these monumental steps, most of the basic principles of futures trading as we know them today were in place. But no one could have guessed how this infant industry would change and develop in the next century and beyond.

Emergence of Futures Contracts

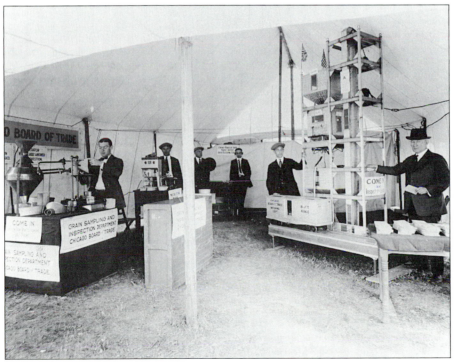

During the early years of the Chicago Board of Trade, grain was inspected to determine its quality.

Growth of the Futures Industry Since 1870

The late 1800s were critical to the scope and efficiency of futures trading. Trading practices were formalized, contracts were standardized, and rules of conduct and clearing and settlement procedures were established.

Trading became more efficient as speculators entered the picture. Lawyers, physicians, and others not connected with the grain trade began to speculate on price and buy and sell futures contracts, hoping to make an honest profit. By purchasing and selling grain that would not otherwise have been traded, speculators made the markets more liquid and helped minimize price fluctuations.

One feature of futures contracts that became standardized was the delivery month. Months were chosen, or gradually agreed upon, by grain merchants based on harvesting and transportation conditions. March was a logical choice because the end of winter made transportation possible once again. May also became an established delivery month because of the cleanup of old-crop oats and wheat (those crops harvested the previous summer). December was selected for the marketing of new-crop corn (harvested in the fall) and was the last month that farmers could move corn to market before winter weather made travel impossible. Quality and quantity standards developed as a more accurate system of weighing bushels of grain replaced measurement, and an inspection process was initiated.

Growth in futures trading increased in the late 19th and early 20th centuries as new exchanges were formed. Many types of commodities were traded on these exchanges, including cotton, butter, eggs, coffee, and cocoa. And, as the United States moved away from an agrarian-based economy, the number and variety of futures contracts grew. In addition to the traditional agricultural futures, trading developed in precious metals, manufactured or processed products, and nonstorable commodities. But the most dramatic growth and successful contracts in the futures industry were yet to come—financial instrument futures contracts.

Financial Instruments

As the world's financial structure changed because of new monetary policies and other reasons, the futures industry expanded its contract offerings so businesses and financial institutions could continue to manage price risks.

Beginning in the 1970s, the first futures contracts in financial instruments were launched with Government National Mortgage Association (GNMA) mortgage-backed certificates and foreign currency futures. GNMAs were a joint effort between the Chicago Board of Trade and members of the mortgage lending industry. Several years of extensive research went into developing the contract, which began trading in October 1975. Futures trading in foreign currencies—British pound, Canadian dollar, Deutsche mark, French franc, Japanese yen, and Swiss franc—was initiated by the Chicago Mercantile Exchange in May 1972.

Since the introduction of these first financial contracts, financial futures trading has been initiated in an increasing number of financial

Chicago Board of Trade price-reporting systems (ABEF). Exchange floor (C). Grain inspecting and weighing (D). circa 1930.

instruments, including U.S. Treasury bond futures, stock index futures, and municipal bond index futures.

By 1982, another market innovation—options on futures—was instituted. In contrast to futures, options on futures allow investors and risk managers to define and limit risk in the form of a premium paid for the right to buy or sell a futures contract. At the same time, options can provide the buyer with unlimited profit potential. Options on Treasury bond futures began trading in October 1982 at the Chicago Board of Trade as part of a government pilot program. The success of this contract opened the way for options on agricultural and other financial futures, beginning with options on soybean and corn futures contracts in 1984 and 1985, respectively.

Even before options on futures were introduced, the Chicago Board of Trade formed the Chicago Board Options Exchange, which trades stock options. One of the unique trading aspects adopted from the futures exchanges by the Chicago Board Options Exchange was the Chicago style of trading, where bids and offers are made in the pits by open outcry.

Perhaps the most remarkable thing about financial instruments futures and options is their phenomenal growth. While it took centuries for agricultural markets to develop, the financial markets sprang up in less than 15 years and surpassed the agricultural markets in many ways. Since financial instruments were first introduced at the Chicago Board of Trade in 1975, the number of financial contracts traded annually at the exchange soared from a mere 20,125 to more than 78 million in 1986. Share of total volume also increased tremendously. In 1976, for example, the majority of contracts traded were agricultural and metals futures; less than 1 percent of all contracts traded were financial instruments. Just four years later, financial instruments volume increased to 33 percent and, during 1992, reached 75 percent accounting for over 113 million financial contracts traded.

The growth in financial instruments resulted from a substantially different economic environment—an environment characterized by frequent changes in interest rates, sharp increases in the amount of government debt, and greater financial interdependence among nations.

Worldwide Market Coverage and Expanded Trading Hours

Within the last 10 years, the interdependence of the world's economies has become clearly evident. The U.S. futures industry, because of its sensitivity to the marketplace and its function as a risk-management mechanism, has already reacted to the need for internationalization. By linking up with foreign exchanges, expanding trading hours, opening offices overseas, developing contracts with international impact, and implementing global electronic trading systems, U.S. futures exchanges are making their markets more accessible and attractive to investors and businesses worldwide.

The first link with a foreign futures exchange was established between the Chicago Mercantile Exchange (CME) and the Singapore International Monetary Exchange (SIMEX) in 1984. The CME/SIMEX link allows traders to buy (sell) contracts on one exchange and later sell (buy) them back on the other. Such linkages provide comprehensive market coverage and are being considered by other exchanges as well.

In another move toward globalization of futures markets, some U.S. futures exchanges are adding evening trading sessions to span time zones and attract foreign investors. In April 1987, the first evening-hours session in the history of futures trading opened at the Chicago Board of Trade. The expanded trading hours provide increased liquidity, efficiency, and greater access to markets worldwide. By capturing the morning trading hours in Hong Kong, Sydney, Tokyo, and Singapore, U.S. futures exchanges can compete directly with Japanese and Far Eastern markets.

As the world business environment continues to evolve, new products and instruments will, undoubtedly, continue to be introduced by the futures industry. Exchanges are launching more and more innovative futures and options contracts and the medium in which they trade is also changing. A system such as GLOBEX®, a global after-hours electronic trading system, is an example of how the industry is adapting to meet the needs of today's marketplace. (Chapter 18 explores the concepts, products, and terminology of these innovations in greater depth.)

Futures markets make it possible for those who want to manage price risk, hedgers, to transfer that risk to those who are willing to accept it, speculators. Futures markets also provide price information that the world looks to as a benchmark in determining the value of a particular commodity or financial instrument on a given day and time. These important benefits—risk transfer and price discovery—reach every sector of the world where changing market conditions create economic risk, including such diverse areas as agricultural products, foreign exchange, imports and exports, financing, and investments.

Futures markets evolved gradually. In their earlier years, exchanges were essentially cash markets where physical commodities were bought and sold. As the volume of trading increased, buyers and sellers began trading futures contracts—standardized, legal agreements to make or take delivery of a specific commodity at a designated place sometime in the future.

While cash and futures contracts have common elements, they serve different market functions. This chapter briefly explains some of the differences, gives an overview of futures trading, and describes its economic importance to the world.

OVERVIEW OF FUTURES TRADING

*Hedging,
Speculating,
Clearing,
Price Theory*

2

Cash Transactions

Cash contracts in the agricultural markets are sales agreements for either the immediate or future delivery of a commodity. The quality and quantity of the commodity as well as the delivery terms are agreed upon by both the buyer and seller.

Each of these factors affects the sales price. For instance, if a lower or higher quality of grain than the seller agreed to purchase is delivered, a price discount or premium is calculated in the final price. Quantity also affects the price. If a greater quantity is delivered than initially agreed upon, a price discount is sometimes negotiated.

A typical cash transaction can involve a farmer who wants to sell his grain and a grain elevator operator who wants to purchase it. Typically, the grain elevator operator acts as a middleman between farmers and grain buyers, such as flour millers, who eventually purchase the grain to process.

There are a variety of cash sales agreements used by farmers, grain elevator operators, and other marketers. One type of cash transaction involves the immediate delivery of the commodity. Many farmers use this marketing alternative in the fall. After harvest, they haul the grain to the local elevator where it is priced on the spot based on the quantity and quality of the crop.

Another alternative is a cash forward contract—an agreement in which a seller agrees to deliver a specific cash commodity to a buyer sometime in the future. For example, a farmer could enter a cash forward contract with a grain elevator operator in the winter to deliver 10,000 bushels of wheat the following July. At the time the contract is initiated, the farmer and grain elevator operator agree on the quality and quantity of grain, the delivery time and location, as well as the price. When delivery occurs, the wheat is carefully inspected and price adjustments are made according to the quality and quantity.

In many instances, a cash forward contract might be more appropriate than an immediate cash sales transaction because it allows both buyers and sellers to plan ahead. Not only do they know, in advance, the price they will have to pay or the price they will receive for a specific commodity, they can hold off delivery until they have possession of the grain or are ready to process it. This saves the expense of tying up storage facilities.

Similar cash forward transactions are prevalent in all sections of the economy, such as real estate leases, fixed-rate loans, charge cards, rents, mortgages, even magazine and newspaper subscriptions. In all cases, a product or service is agreed to be delivered sometime in the future at a specific price. Without forward contracts, it is impossible for buyers and sellers to agree on anything and price must be constantly renegotiated.

In contrast to futures contracts, forward contracts are not actively traded on exchanges nor standardized. They are privately negotiated. They also carry some risk to both parties in the agreement—the risk that one side is negotiating in bad faith or without sufficient funds. There also is the risk that future events could prevent one or both sides from fulfilling the contract.

Futures contracts are standardized and meet specific requirements of buyers and sellers for a variety of commodities and financial instruments. Quantity, quality, delivery locations—are all established. The only variable is price, which is discovered through an auctionlike process on the trading floor of an organized futures exchange.

Because futures contracts are standardized, sellers and buyers are able to exchange one contract for another and actually offset their obligation to deliver or take delivery of the cash commodity underlying the futures contract. *Offset* in the futures market means taking another futures position opposite and equal to one's initial futures transaction.

As an example, suppose an investor bought two March U.S. Treasury bond futures contracts. To offset this position, he would have to sell two March U.S. T-bond futures contracts before the contracts called for delivery. On the other hand, if the investor first sold two March U.S. T-bond futures contracts, to offset the position, he would have to buy two March U.S. T-bond futures contracts before the contracts called for delivery.

Standardization of contract terms and the ability to offset contracts led to the rapidly increasing use of the futures markets by commercial firms and speculators. Commercial firms began to realize that futures markets could provide financial protection against price volatility without the need to make or take delivery of the cash commodity underlying the futures contract. Speculators found that standardization added trading appeal because contracts could be bought and later sold, or sold and later bought, at a profit if they were correct in their forecasts of price movement.

Futures Contracts

Hedging, a major economic purpose of futures markets, is buying or selling futures contracts to offset the risks of changing prices in the cash markets. This risk-transfer mechanism has made futures contracts virtually indispensable in efforts to control costs and protect profit margins.

Hedging

Agricultural Scenario

Commercial firms, producers, merchandisers, and processors of commodities use the futures market to protect themselves against changing cash prices. They are able to do so because cash and futures prices usually respond to the same economic factors and tend to move together in the same direction. News of bad weather that would likely result in crop losses and tighter supplies is reflected immediately in higher cash prices as buyers seek to buy and store the commodity in anticipation of later shortages. Futures prices also are bid higher when buyers anticipate a commodity shortage, not only at harvest but throughout the marketing year.

Economic news, on the other hand, that signals higher-than-expected supplies is immediately registered in weakening cash prices as buyers lower bids in anticipation of easily available supplies. At the same time, buyers in the futures markets scale down bids with the prospect of increased supplies.

Commercial firms note the strong tendency for cash and futures prices to move in the same direction by roughly equal amounts, reacting to the same economic factors. These firms realize that, although a single set of economic factors might result in a loss on a cash transaction, it could be offset and sometimes turned into a profit in the futures market. This is possible if they initiate a futures position equal and opposite to their cash market position.

As an example, suppose a Midwest wheat miller agrees to ship 500,000 pounds of flour in six months to a cookie manufacturer in Minnesota. Both agree on a price today even though the flour will not be delivered for another six months. However, the miller does not own the wheat he will eventually process and is concerned that prices will rise during the six-month period.

To hedge against the risk of rising cash prices, the miller buys two wheat futures contracts for delivery in six months. When the miller goes to purchase the cash wheat, prices have risen. The miller then sells two futures contracts and makes a profit in the futures market because futures prices also have increased.

Even though the miller has to pay more for the cash wheat than he originally planned, he was able to offset his loss by making a gain in the futures market.

Financial Scenario

The economic principles that apply to traditional commodity futures contracts, such as wheat futures, also apply to nontraditional contracts like currencies, stock indexes, government bonds, and other financial instruments. These futures contracts are invaluable hedging vehicles for all types of investors.

A portfolio manager can hedge against an increase in the purchase price of bonds using Treasury bond futures. A corporate treasurer planning a bond issue can hedge against higher interest rates and lower bond prices with interest rate futures. An institution can hedge to protect the market value of stocks from a possible decline in value with stock index futures.

For instance, a major financial institution wants to sell a portion of its bond portfolio in four months. However, the company expects interest rates to rise over the next four months, which would result in lower bond prices.

To take advantage of the current bond market, the company sells U.S. Treasury bond futures contracts. In four months, the bond market falls. The company then sells its Treasury bonds in the cash market and offsets its futures position by buying Treasury bond futures contracts. Even though the institution receives less than it would have four months ago for the same portfolio of bonds, it has gained in the futures market, minimizing the potential loss.

Other users of financial futures contracts include bankers, corporate treasurers, state and local governments, insurance companies, investment bankers, money managers, mortgage bankers, pension fund managers, portfolio managers, thrifts, trust fund managers, and underwriters. (For a more complete discussion of hedging, see Chapter 8.)

In all hedging strategies, the common denominator is the desire to establish, in advance, an acceptable price or rate of interest. Every business, regardless of whether it performs a service or manufactures a product, faces some type of financial risk. For each individual or institution attempting to minimize risk, there must be another willing to assume it. Futures exchanges act as a magnet, attracting risk-avoiders (hedgers) and risk-takers (speculators).

Speculators

Speculators assume the risk hedgers try to avoid. While profit is the motive of speculators, they provide the marketplace with an essential element, liquidity, which enables hedgers to buy or sell large numbers of contracts without adversely disrupting the price in the marketplace. This is crucial to institutional investors, processors of commodities, and other commercial and financial firms who buy or sell hundreds or thousands of contracts to hedge a cash market position.

Although speculators usually have no commercial interest in commodities, the potential for profit motivates them to gather market information regarding supply and demand and to anticipate its effect on prices. By buying and selling futures contracts, speculators also help provide information about the impact of current events on expected future demands. In essence, speculators make the market more fluid, bridging the gap between the prices bid and offered by other commodity traders. (For more information on speculating, see Chapter 9.)

Clearinghouses

Essential to the marketplace is an exchange's clearing mechanism. Without it, hedgers and speculators run the risk that some market participants would not fulfill their contract commitments. This would hamper the risk-transfer mechanism of futures markets, making it difficult for traders to offset open positions.

Clearinghouses are responsible for settling trading accounts, clearing trades, collecting and maintaining margin monies, regulating delivery, and reporting trading data.

Clearinghouses act as third parties to all futures and options contracts—acting as a buyer to every clearing member seller and a seller to every clearing member buyer. Buyers and sellers of futures and options contracts do not create financial obligations to one another, but, rather, to the clearinghouses through their clearing member firms.

A clearinghouse severs the direct relationship between buyer and seller, so that each is free to buy and sell independently of the other. As a party to every trade, the clearinghouse assumes the responsibility of guarantor of every trade.

Performance Bond Margins

Exchange clearinghouses are able to guarantee all trades because they require their members to deposit performance bond margins.

Performance bond margins are financial guarantees required of both buyers and sellers of futures contracts to ensure fulfillment of the contract obligations. That is, buyers and sellers are required to take or make delivery of the commodity or financial instrument represented by the contract unless the position is offset before contract expiration.

Margins are determined on the basis of market risk. Because margins are adjusted to risk, they help assure the financial soundness of futures exchanges and provide valuable price protection for hedgers with a minimum tie-up of capital. Margins are normally set at 2 to 5 percent of the value of the commodity represented by the contract.

Price Theory and the Futures Markets

Futures markets are successful because they rely on the economics of price theory.

Supply

The price of a product is discovered by changes in its supply and demand. Supply is the quantity of a product that sellers are willing to provide to the market at a given price. Supply can be graphed as a curve with quantity shown on the horizontal axis and price shown on the vertical axis. It slants upward from left to right, as shown on the next page, and indicates the quantity supplied at a given price. When prices are high, sellers are willing to provide larger quantities of their products to the market; at lower prices, sellers are willing to furnish smaller quantities to the market. This relationship between product supply and its price is known as the *law of supply.*

There are a variety of economic factors that can cause supply to increase or decrease, thus shifting the supply curve. These include changes in production costs, prices of related goods, and number of sellers in the market.

Demand

Demand, on the other hand, is the quantity of a product buyers are willing to purchase from the market at a given price. Demand can be graphed as a curve with quantity shown on the horizontal axis and price shown on the vertical axis. It slants downward from left to right, as shown on the next page, and indicates the quantity demanded at a given price. When prices are low, buyers are willing to purchase greater quantities of a product; at higher prices, buyers are willing to purchase lesser quantities of a product. This relationship between product demand and its price is known as the *law of demand.*

Supply Curve

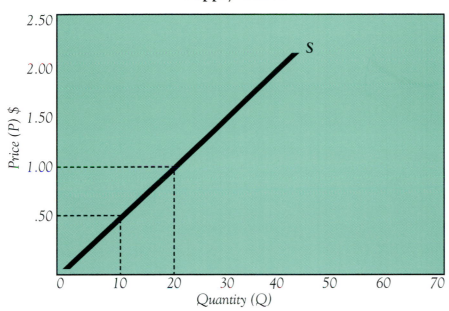

Demand Curve

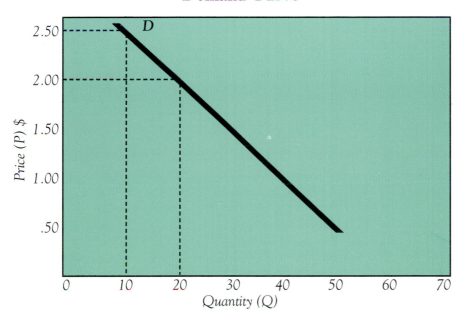

There are a variety of economic factors that can cause demand to increase or decrease, thus shifting the demand curve. These include changes in personal income, prices of related goods, and the number of buyers in the marketplace.

The price of a product or commodity depends on the relationship between supply and demand. If the supply and demand curves of a product are placed on the same graph, the point where they intersect is a product's market price, also known as the *equilibrium price*. At the market price, the quantity supplied equals the quantity demanded.

Equilibrium Price

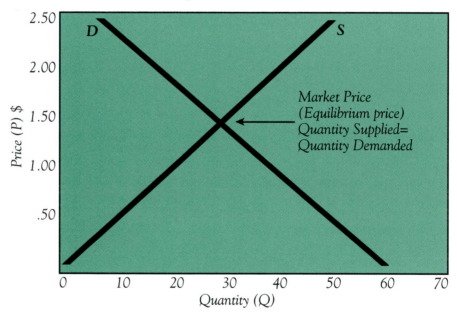

A change in the supply and/or demand for a commodity will cause a shift in the respective supply and/or demand curves. As a curve shifts, the market price may increase, decrease, or remain the same.

Price Information

Hedgers and speculators continually evaluate supply and demand factors as well as other market indicators. Based on their analysis and expectations of future price movements, trades are made and prices are discovered.

Traders constantly adjust their bids and offers to buy and sell futures contracts in relation to a continuous flow of worldwide market information.

News of Brazilian soybean crop conditions is sought, analyzed, and then reflected almost instantaneously in the prices of soybean, soybean meal, and soybean oil futures. The impact of nationalization of foreign-owned copper mines is registered in the price of copper, silver, and other related futures in New York, London, and Chicago. The release of a government report announcing that the Federal Reserve Board is putting more money into the economy is absorbed by the market and noted in the price of U.S. Treasury bond futures.

Futures prices are the most widely used pricing reference in domestic and international financial, metals, and agricultural markets. Once prices are discovered, the futures exchanges are responsible for disseminating these prices to the public on a daily basis through market report systems and newspapers.

While all U.S. futures exchanges share some general characteristics, no two are exactly alike. Many of the differences have to do with their historical development. This chapter not only discusses their similarities, but gives a brief history of each U.S. futures exchange and describes its organizational structure.

Most exchanges are not-for-profit membership associations, incorporated in the states in which they are located. Membership in each exchange is limited to a specific number of individuals, although some exchanges permit the holding of multiple memberships by members. Every membership is owned by an individual; however, companies, corporations, partnerships, and cooperatives may be registered for certain membership privileges.

The exchange conducts a thorough investigation of each member applicant. It focuses on the applicant's credit standing, financial responsibility, character, and integrity.

In recent years, special memberships or trading privileges have been offered by some exchanges. For example, an associate membership at the Chicago Board of Trade allows an individual to trade the financial instrument futures and other designated markets.

Other special memberships at the Chicago Board of Trade include a variety of membership interest holders. Of these, GIM membership interest holders may trade all futures contracts listed in the government instruments

U.S. FUTURES EXCHANGES

Their History & Organization

3

market category (financial instrument futures); IDEMs may trade all futures contracts in the index, debt, and energy market category (gold, municipal bond index, 30-day fed funds, and stock index futures); and COMs may trade all options contracts listed in the commodity options market category (all options listed for trading by the exchange).

The government of each exchange is vested in a board (called the *board of directors, board of governors,* or *board of managers)* and its officers. The board is elected by the exchange membership.

Committees

Committees are composed of exchange members either appointed by the board or elected by the exchange membership; they advise and assist the board and perform specific duties related to exchange operations.

Most exchanges have committees for the following purposes: nominations of board candidates, officers, and those committees elected by the exchange membership; management of the exchange; supervision of finances; supervision and investigation of the business conduct of members; arbitration of disputes; appeal of decisions of disciplinary committees; examination of member applicants; supervision of trading floor activity; supervision of market price reporting; management of the physical facilities of the exchange; amendments to rules and regulations; public relations; marketing and education; supervision of trading and changes in the contracts for commodities traded; and supervision of weighing, warehousing, and inspection of commodities for delivery against the futures contract.

Staff

The administrative staff of an exchange carries out the policies and decisions of the board and the committees. Departmental organization of the staff frequently parallels the functions of the various committees, and each department is responsible to an executive officer of the exchange. The titles, responsibilities, and numbers of these executive officers and staff vary among the exchanges. Following are the histories, committees, and staffs of today's U.S. futures exchanges.

Chicago Board of Trade

The Chicago Board of Trade, founded in 1848, is the world's oldest and largest futures exchange. In addition to futures trading in grains, soybeans, and soybean products, the exchange offers futures markets in U.S. Treasury bonds and notes, municipal bond index, gold, and silver. Options on financial, agricultural, and metals futures also are traded.

Change and growth are a tradition of the Chicago Board of Trade. In recent years, the exchange has taken several steps to make its markets more appealing to an international audience. In addition to expanding trading hours to coincide with business hours in Far Eastern markets during

1987, the Chicago Board of Trade opened a London office in 1986 and a Tokyo office in 1988. Then in 1992, the exchange launched GLOBEX®, a global after-hours electronic trading system.

Membership	3,663 (1,402 full members, 756 associate members, 220 GIM interests, 642 IDEM interests, 643 COM interests)
Governing Body	board of directors—27 (chairman, first and second vice chairmen, 15 full member directors, 3 associate member directors, 5 nonmember public directors, and president)
Officers	chairman, first and second vice chairmen, president and chief executive officer*
Committees	Agricultural Executive; Compensation; Executive; Finance; Financial Executive; Market Development; Member Relations; Membership; Nominating; Operations; Product Development; Regulatory Oversight; Rules; Strategic Planning; Technology
Staff*	728
Executive Officers	president and chief executive officer, vice president/secretary, vice president/treasurer, vice presidents—(administration and planning, administration/Office of Investigations and Audits, communications, computer operations, director/economic analysis, market development, managing director/international relations, government relations, information systems, personnel, real estate, special counsel), general counsel, associate general counsel

The Chicago Mercantile Exchange (CME) traces its origins to a group of agricultural dealers who formed the Chicago Produce Exchange in 1874. This exchange was a market for butter, eggs, poultry, and other perishable agricultural products. In 1898, the butter and egg dealers withdrew from this group to form their own market, the Chicago Butter and Egg Board.

The Chicago Butter and Egg Board was reorganized for futures trading in additional commodities and was renamed the Chicago Mercantile

Chicago Mercantile Exchange

*Not exchange members

Exchange in 1919. Since that time, the exchange has provided a futures market for many commodities, including pork bellies, live cattle, live hogs, and feeder cattle.

The International Monetary Market (IMM), a division of the exchange, was established in 1972 for foreign currency futures trading. Since then, other financial futures have been added, including futures contracts based on 90-day U.S. Treasury bills and three-month Eurodollar time deposits. Another division of the exchange, the Index and Option Market (IOM), was opened for trading stock index futures and options on futures in 1982. Among the contracts traded on the Index and Option Market at the Chicago Mercantile Exchange are S&P 500 Stock Index futures and various options contracts.

In 1984, the Chicago Mercantile Exchange and the Singapore International Monetary Exchange initiated the world's first interexchange futures trading link. The two exchanges trade Eurodollar, Japanese yen, British pound, and Deutsche mark futures, making trading in Singapore equivalent to that in Chicago. And in 1992, the exchange launched GLOBEX, a worldwide electronic trading system listing several of its financial contracts on the system.

Membership	2,724 (625 CME, 812 IMM, and 1,287 IOM)
Governing Body	board of governors—25
Officers	chairman, first vice chairman, second vice chairman, secretary, treasurer, special counsel and chairman of executive committee
Public and Industry Governors	6
Committees	Approved Delivery Facility; Arbitration; Audit; Broilers; Broker Association; Building Improvement and Real Estate; Business Conduct; Butter; Clearing House; Commodity Representative/ Customer Complaint; Common Clearing; Computerized Trade Reconstruction; Contributions; CPO/CTA; CUBS/TOPS; Currency Price Limits; Dual Trading; Education; Equity Indices; Ethics; Facility Coordination; FCM; Feeder and Live Cattle; Finance and Budget; Floor Broker Qualification; Floor Communications; Floor GLOBEX Issues; Floor Orientation; Floor Practices; Floor Services; Foreign Currency; Forest Products; GLOBEX Negotiating; GLOBEX Technical; GLOBEX Terminal Location; Governance;

Gratuity Fund; Interest Rate Futures; Leasing; Live Hogs; Member Booth Space Allocation; Member Services; Membership; New Commodity Products; Options; Pit Committees; Planning; Pork Products; Probable Cause; Rates and Qualification; Restaurant and Club; Strategic Planning; Trade Procedures; Upper Trading Floor
Oversight Committees: Agricultural; Common Goals; Financial Instruments; GLOBEX; Member Activities; Membership and Education; Physical Facilities; Pit Supervision; Public Affairs; Regulatory Oversight; Technological Oversight

Staff*   939

Officers   president and chief executive officer; executive vice president and chief operating officer; executive vice president; senior vice presidents—(clearing house, administration and finance, chief economist/research, marketing, general counsel/legal, operations), vice presidents—(computer operations, product marketing, administration, government relations, commodity marketing and education, trading floor operations, accounting, New York office, management information systems, human resources, systems development, business development (clearing house), clearing house, compliance, advertising and marketing services, audit, public affairs, regulatory, communications, telecommunications, Tokyo office, London office)

The Coffee, Sugar & Cocoa Exchange, Inc., known initially as the Coffee Exchange of the City of New York, was founded in 1882. The exchange was formed by a group of coffee merchants who wished to avoid the risk of a cash market collapse by organizing a market for trading in coffee futures. In 1914, the Coffee Exchange expanded to include futures in sugar, and, in 1916, it became the New York Coffee and Sugar Exchange, Inc. On September 28, 1979, the New York Cocoa Exchange, Inc., which had been in existence since 1925, was officially merged into the Coffee and Sugar Exchange, and the name Coffee, Sugar & Cocoa Exchange, Inc. was adopted.

| **Coffee, Sugar & Cocoa Exchange, Inc.** |

*Not exchange members

Membership	777 (527 full, 250 associate)
Governing Body	board of managers—15 plus president
Officers	chairman, vice chairman, treasurer
Committees	Adjudication; Appeals; Arbitration; Audit; Board of Brazilian Classifiers; Board of Cocoa Graders; Board of Coffee Graders; Building Advisory; Building Project; Business Conduct; Cocoa; Coffee; Compensation; Control; Deliveries and Warehouse Procedures; Executive; Executive Floor; Finance; Floor; Floor Facilities; Margin; Member Space Allocation; Membership; New Product Development; Nominating; Operations & Technology; Option Quotation; Options; Sugar; Sugar Delivery; Sugar Spot Price Roster; Warehouse and License; Warehouse Inspectors
Staff*	106
Officers	president, four senior vice presidents, six vice presidents, three assistant vice presidents, secretary, assistant secretary, assistant treasurer

Commodity Exchange, Inc. (COMEX)

The Commodity Exchange, Inc., (COMEX) of New York was formed in 1933 by the merger of four exchanges that had been trading in hides, raw silk, rubber, and metals. Today, COMEX trades a variety of metals contracts, including silver, gold, copper, platinum, and palladium futures; options on gold, silver, copper, and platinum futures; and Eurotop 100 Index futures and options.

Membership	772[†]
Governing Body	board of governors—25
Officers	chairman, treasurer, vice chairman
Committees	Admissions; Arbitration; Audit; Business Conduct; Clearing Liaison; Control; Development & Communication; Education; Executive; Finance; Floor; Floor Facilities; Long-Range Planning;

*Not exchange members
[†]Multiple memberships available

Margins; Marketing; Membership; Metal Trade; Nominating; Operations; Public Relations; Quotations; Supervisory

Staff*   165

Officers   president, three senior vice presidents

For more than 100 years, the Kansas City Board of Trade has been the world's predominant marketplace for Hard Red Winter wheat, the major ingredient in bread. In 1982, the Kansas City Board of Trade broadened its product base into the financial arena by introducing the first U.S. stock index futures contract, based on the Value Line Index. In 1984, the exchange began trading options on Hard Red Winter wheat futures, providing still another risk-management tool.

Kansas City Board of Trade

Membership   237 (Class A—192; Class B—45)

Governing Body   board of directors—16 directors and 3 officers

Officers   chairman, first vice chairman, second vice chairman, president and secretary, senior vice president, vice presidents—(compliance, marketing, operations), treasurer, assistant treasurer, assistant secretary, assistant vice presidents—(floor operations, Grain Market Review, transportation)

Committees   Ag Options; Ag Options Pit; Appeals; Arbitration (Cash and Futures); Budget; Business Conduct; Complaint; Compliance Advisory; Elevator Warehouse; Finance; Floor; Legislation; Marketing; Market Reports; Mini Value Line Options Contract; Membership; Nominating; Pension; Planning/Project; Rules; Transportation; Value Line Contract; Value Line Pit; Wheat Contract; Wheat Pit

Staff*   30

Officers   president

*Not exchange members

MidAmerica Commodity Exchange

The MidAmerica Commodity Exchange was founded in 1868 and incorporated as the Chicago Open Board of Trade in 1880. The exchange acquired its present name in late 1972. In 1986, the MidAm became an affiliate of the Chicago Board of Trade, and the MidAm trading floor is located in the Chicago Board of Trade building. Most recently, the Chicago Rice & Cotton Exchange was merged into the MidAm. As a result of the merger in 1991, rough rice futures and options are MidAm contracts. The MidAmerica Commodity Exchange is known for a wide variety of agricultural, financial, metals, and foreign currencies contracts that trade in smaller units.

Membership	1,205
Governing Body	board of directors—31
Officers	chairman, first and second vice chairmen, president and chief executive officer*
Committees	Arbitration; Business Conduct; Executive; Floor Conduct; Floor Governors; Market Report and Quotations; Members Advisory; Membership; Pit

Minneapolis Grain Exchange

The Minneapolis Grain Exchange, founded in 1881, is the largest cash grain market in the world. In addition, the Minneapolis Grain Exchange trades spring wheat, White wheat, and oat futures as well as spring wheat and White wheat options.

Membership	402[†]
Governing Body	board of directors—17
Officers	chairman, two vice chairmen
Public Members[‡]	1–4
Committees	Arbitration Pool; Building; Business Conduct; Cash Markets; Changes in Rules; Clearing House; Exchange Room; Finance; Futures Contracts; Futures Trading Conduct; International Markets; Membership; Nominations; Oats; Oats Pit; Options

*Not an exchange member
[†]Multiple memberships available
[‡]Not exchange members (nonmember directors are elected by the board of directors)

Pit; Personnel and Compensation; Public Affairs; Public Relations; Sampling; Weighing; Wheat Classification; Wheat Pit; White Wheat

Staff*   70

Officers   president and chief executive officer, vice president of operations and secretary, treasurer, assistant secretary

New York Cotton Exchange

Founded in 1870 by a group of cotton brokers and merchants, the New York Cotton Exchange (NYCE®) is the oldest commodity exchange in New York. Since its inception, the exchange has been an integral part of the cotton industry and today trades cotton futures and options as well as Cotlook World Cotton™ futures and options.

NYCE® expanded its product line in 1966 forming the Citrus Associates of the New York Cotton Exchange, Inc., an affiliate of the exchange, where frozen concentrated orange juice futures and options are traded. Then in 1985, the exchange entered the arena of financial futures and options through the creation of the FINEX® division. U.S. Dollar Index® (USDX®) futures and options, Treasury Auction Five- and Two-Year U.S. Treasury note futures, and European Currency Unit (ECU) futures and options are among the financial contracts trading on FINEX®. Since March 1, 1992, USDX® and ECU futures and options contracts have traded around the clock.

In 1988, the New York Futures Exchange (NYFE), a subsidiary of the New York Stock Exchange, became an affiliate of the NYCE® and moved its trading operations to the NYCE® quadrant in Four World Trade Center.

Membership   450

Governing Body   board of managers—21–27

Officers   chairman, vice chairman, treasurer

Committees   Adjudication; Arbitration; Business Conduct; Bylaws and Rules; Committee Supervising Simultaneous Purchases and Sales of Cotton and Options Contracts; Committee of Three; Control—Cotton and Options; Cotton Futures and

*Not exchange members

Options Contracts; Distribution of Quotations; Executive; Finance; Floor—Cotton and Options; Futures and Options—Financial Contracts; Information and Statistics; Margin—Cotton and Options; Membership; National Advisory; Nominating; Real Estate; Reception; Special Committee for New Trading Floor Design; Supervisory; Trade Warehouse and Delivery Committee—Cotton; special committees appointed from time to time

Staff*   92

Officers   president, vice president, vice president and counsel, vice president compliance department, assistant vice presidents, secretary, assistant officers

Citrus Associates
Affiliate
of the NYCE®

Membership   200 authorized, 157 outstanding

Governing Body   board of directors—15

Officers   president, two vice presidents, treasurer

Committees   Arbitration; Business Conduct; Bylaws and Rules; Control; Executive; Floor; Finance; Frozen Concentrated Orange Juice; Futures; Information and Statistics; Margins; Membership; Nominating; Options Floor; Supervising Simultaneous Purchases and Sales; Supervisory; Warehouse; special committees appointed from time to time

Staff*   served by the New York Cotton Exchange staff

Officers   executive director, secretary, assistant secretary

FINEX®
Division
of the NYCE®

Membership   New York Cotton Exchange membership

Governing Body   subject generally to board of managers of the New York Cotton Exchange

Officers   chairman, two vice chairmen, treasurer of the division

*Not exchange members

Committees	Delivery; Executive; Finance; Floor; Futures and Options; Margins; Nominating; Offset; Oversight; special committees appointed from time to time
Staff*	served by the New York Cotton Exchange staff

New York Futures Exchange

On April 15, 1979, the New York Stock Exchange entered the financial futures industry by incorporating the New York Futures Exchange as its wholly owned subsidiary. This marked the culmination of an intensive two-year study of the opportunities and potential for financial futures markets, and the service and facilities requirements of the international financial community. In 1988, the New York Futures Exchange became an affiliate of the New York Cotton Exchange. NYFE's financial products include futures and options on the NYSE Composite Index and the CRB Futures Price Index.

Membership	562
Governing Body	board of directors
Officers	chairman, senior vice president—(regulation, operations, and administration), general counsel, secretary
Committees	Appeals; Arbitration Board; Audit/Compliance and Surveillance Oversight; Finance; Floor; Hearing Board; Margin and New Products; Market Emergency; Personnel; Quality of Markets

New York Mercantile Exchange

The New York Mercantile Exchange was founded in 1872 as a market for cheese, butter, and eggs. In 1882, it acquired its present name and, in 1884, it took up occupancy in its own building in the former New York produce market area. In 1977, the exchange moved into joint facilities with other New York exchanges in the World Trade Center.

Membership	816
Governing Body	board of directors—15
Officers	at large
Public Members*	3

*Not exchange members

Committees	Adjudication; Administrative; Arbitration; Business Conduct; Bylaws; Clearing House; Control; Crude Oil; Delivery; Finance; Floor; Marketing; Membership; Metals; Natural Gas; Options; Petroleum Products
Staff*	350
Officers	president, senior vice presidents—(floor operations, general counsel, regulator affairs and operations, strategic planning and information services), vice presidents—(clearing, compliance, finance, government affairs, information services, marketing, operations, research)

Philadelphia Board of Trade, Inc.

The Philadelphia Board of Trade, Inc., a wholly owned subsidiary of the Philadelphia Stock Exchange, Inc., was approved as a designated contract market by the Commodity Futures Trading Commission on May 10, 1985. Futures contracts traded on the Philadelphia Board of Trade include British pound, French franc, Swiss franc, Deutsche mark, Australian dollar, Japanese yen, Canadian dollar, and European Currency Unit.

Membership	320
Governing Body	board of directors—18
Committees	Admissions; Business Conduct; Finance; Floor Procedure; Margin Allocation; Marketing; Nominating
Officers*	president, executive vice president, secretary, treasurer, vice presidents—(general counsel, operations)

Foreign Exchanges

In addition to the U.S. exchanges, there are more than 50 other commodity exchanges around the world that trade a variety of futures contracts. These exchanges include the London International Financial Futures Exchange, London Metals Exchange, Marche a Terme International de France, Singapore International Monetary Exchange, Sydney Futures Exchange, Tokyo Stock Exchange, and Winnipeg Commodity Exchange.

*Not exchange members

Futures exchanges provide a location for buyers and sellers to meet and, through an open outcry auction process, discover a price for specific futures and options contracts. While this chapter focuses on the exchange floor, futures trading also takes place via electronic trading systems, such as GLOBEX®. Electronic trading systems are covered in more depth in Chapter 18. Exchanges also are responsible for disseminating these prices and guaranteeing fulfillment of traded contracts.

This activity is centralized on the trading floor of each futures exchange. While all market participants have indirect access to the floor through their brokers, only exchange members have the privilege of actually trading on the floor.

The size, arrangement, and facilities of the trading floor vary among the exchanges, but many features are common to all. Futures trading is conducted in octagonal and polygonal pits or rings, with steps descending to the center of each pit. Traders stand in groups on the steps, in the center of the pit, or around the waist-high ring according to the contract month of the commodity that they are trading. Buyers and sellers stand throughout the pit, as any trader can buy or sell at any given moment. Generally, one pit or ring is devoted to each futures or options contract traded on the exchange.

Adjacent to the pit or ring (or sometimes in its center) are market reporters, employed by the exchange to record price changes as they occur.

EXCHANGE FLOOR OPERATIONS

Floor Trading, Price Discovery, Market Information

4

The recorded prices are then displayed on computer-operated electronic display boards. Futures prices of commodities traded on other exchanges also are displayed so traders are aware of the most current price movements.

The financial trading floor at the Chicago Board of Trade

Electronic displays and video monitors on the exchange floor provide a constant stream of the latest financial, business, and commodity news from major wire services, and futures and securities exchanges. Large maps and video displays show weather development in relevant agricultural areas. Cash prices, receipts, and shipments of various commodities also are available.

To handle the thousands of calls coming from commercial traders and brokerage firms, batteries of telephone stations and sophisticated electronic equipment are strategically located near the pits. At the Chicago Board of Trade, orders received by phone clerks from various member firms are time-stamped, then rushed by messengers (called *runners*) or flashed (signaled by hand) to brokers in the pit for execution.

The price at which a trade is made and other pertinent information are jotted down by the broker on an order blank and returned by a runner to the firm's phone desk. The order is time-stamped again. Information that the trade is completed is then relayed to the office where the order originated so that the customer may be informed. (For more information on order routing, see Chapter 5.)

The result of this trade, along with the results of hundreds of thousands of other trades, is immediately displayed on quotation boards around the trading floor. At the same time, the price quotes are sent outside the exchange to more than 30 vendors of financial information who, in turn, retransmit the information in a variety of formats to hundreds of thousands of subscribers.

Price boards at the Chicago Board of Trade

Types of Floor Traders

The men and women who trade on the floor of futures exchanges perform a variety of different functions. Some traders known as *floor brokers* fill outside orders for different firms such as commission houses, commercial interests, financial institutions, portfolio managers, processors and exporters, and the general public interested in speculating. Others trade hedging or speculative accounts for the company they work for.

Another group, known as *locals*, trade for their own accounts and speculate on future price movements, adding liquidity to the markets. These speculators fall into one of three categories based on the length of time they hold a position. Position traders hold positions the longest, usually days or weeks. Day traders, on the other hand, initiate and offset their positions in the course of a day's trading session. And, scalpers hold their positions for the shortest time period of all. Generally five minutes is considered a long time.

All the floor traders compete in the auction for sales and purchases of futures and options contracts. The day traders and scalpers, especially, help make the market more fluid by placing incremental prices between the wide bid and offer spreads made by other traders. This creates market liquidity and minimizes price fluctuations.

The Auction

Offers to buy or sell are made by shouting out prices in an auction style so that each trader in the pit has an opportunity to take the opposite side of a trade. This method of vocal trading is so important that it is specifically detailed in the Chicago Board of Trade Rules and Regulations.

In addition to making verbal bids and offers, pit traders also use a simple but highly efficient set of hand and finger signals. In active markets, these signals are indispensable in clarifying bids and offers.

Hand signals vary from exchange to exchange. At the Chicago Board of Trade, the position of the hands tells whether a trader is buying or selling. If a trader has the palm of his hand facing himself, he is buying; if his palm faces outward, he is selling. By holding his arm and the fingers of his hand in a horizontal position, a trader shows with finger signals the fraction above or below the most recent price at which he is making his bid or offer. Vertical finger signals are used to indicate the number of contracts the trader wishes to buy or sell at the price indicated. Traders and brokers use combinations of the signals for price and quantity to indicate a bid or offer.

An important verbal distinction also shows if a trader wants to buy or sell. Buyers call out (bid) price first and then quantity; sellers call out (offer) quantity first, then price.

When a trade is made, each trader writes the completed transaction on a trading card or multipart order form. For instance, any trade that has been carded for T-bond futures includes the contract month, the quantity, the price, the trader's initials, the identity of the other trader, the name of the clearing firm on the opposite side of the transaction, and a code indicating the time.

These trading cards constitute original records, and from them the essential data are transferred to the buyer's and seller's clearing firms. Each trader is financially responsible to his clearing firm, which is a member of an exchange clearinghouse. Each clearinghouse guarantees contract performance of all contracts traded and cleared at that futures exchange. (For details on clearing, see Chapter 6.)

Price Discovery

Futures exchanges are free markets where the many factors that influence supply and demand converge on the trading floor and through

CBOT Hand Signals Indicating Quantities and Prices

Quantity

Buy four contracts

Sell twenty financial futures

Price

Grain futures: ¼ cent
Grain options: ²⁄8 or ¼ cent
Treasury bond & note futures:
7, 17, & ²⁷/₃₂ of a point

Grain futures: ½ cent
Grain options: ⁴⁄8 or ½ cent
Treasury bond & note futures:
9, 19, & ²⁹/₃₂ of a point

Hand signals adjust to the tick size which varies for each contract.

open outcry auction are translated into a single figure—a price. Exchanges, such as the Chicago Board of Trade, act as barometers for price, registering the impact of the many worldwide forces on specific commodities and financial instruments being traded.

Because these economic forces influence cash and futures markets similarly, futures prices usually parallel the actual cash values of commodities and financial instruments. This characteristic of futures prices allows hedgers and speculators to gauge the value of the underlying instrument in the near or distant future.

Millions of people all over the world use the price information generated by futures exchanges to make marketing decisions—whether or not they actually trade futures contracts. The development of new futures exchanges and special futures divisions in older commodity and financial markets in Europe and the Far East underscores the importance of this exchange function.

The rapid developments in telecommunications have created a global marketplace. Recognizing the importance of providing timely, reliable price information to the public, exchanges, like the Chicago Board of Trade, have made a commitment to use only state-of-the-art technology to transmit this vital price information. Space-age electronics and the time-honored use of the open outcry auction have combined to produce one of the most efficient methods of price discovery in the world.

Price Reporting

Transactions made on the trading floor must be reported to the membership and the general public. This is accomplished by futures exchanges through a variety of communications systems. The Chicago Board of Trade's advanced computer system, considered one of the most sophisticated available, is called the *Market Price Reporting and Information System* (MPRIS). Several other exchanges also have computerized price-reporting systems. Although the Chicago Board of Trade system differs in some ways from those used by other exchanges, it will be used here to illustrate modern futures price reporting.

The MPRIS, in a typical market situation, accepts price change information from the many price-reporting terminals on the Chicago Board of Trade floor. This information is reformatted in less than one second and sent to the trading floor's electronic wallboards, to the exchange's price-reporting network, and to a private closed-circuit television network inside the exchange building. Additionally, this price information is available at specific computer terminals within the Chicago Board of Trade building.

At each trading pit, exchange-employed market reporters enter prices into the MPRIS through a cathode-ray (visual display) computer terminal. The terminal on the floor transmits the coded transaction to a large computer system that performs editing functions to ensure that the trade adheres to exchange regulations, such as those governing minimum price fluctuations and trading limits. If the quote is valid, the computer sends a message back to the terminal operator in the pulpit (usually a raised desk area located in each pit) indicating the time the quote entered the system. Simultaneously, the information is displayed throughout the MPRIS network. Master terminal operators communicate with the system to revise, insert, or cancel quotations if an error occurs during trading.

The MPRIS system involves multiple computers; if one fails, another automatically takes over. Also, multiple controllers for the electronic board and television systems provide ready backup to keep the board running normally in emergencies.

Electronic wallboards on the trading floor, designed to be visible from any spot on the floor, display the most current MPRIS price information. In addition, the wallboards provide price information from other actively trading contracts, including those from other exchanges.

Electronic Price Wallboards

The closed-circuit television system disseminates MPRIS price information to monitors within the Chicago Board of Trade building. Televised price information can appear on any of over 1,600 channels in several formats and carries the following information:

Closed-Circuit Television

♦ The three most recent trades for all contracts of each commodity; opening, high, low, and settlement prices; opening and closing ranges, if applicable; suspension and resumption ranges for the extended trading session, if applicable; net price change from the previous trading day.

♦ Current high and low trading limits, if applicable.

♦ The most recent quotations in all commodities combined with simulated ticker tape output.

♦ Specialized display of cash grain information, spread data, margin information, membership prices, and Market Profile® and Liquidity Data Bank® information. Market Profile and LDB® are exclusive to the Chicago Board of Trade and offer daily volume data and time distribution of prices for every commodity traded on the exchange.

As part of the MPRIS system, commodity quotations are released by the Chicago Board of Trade to the press and to its own price-reporting networks. Most subscribers to the exchange quotations service receive their information over computer terminals, although many of the larger offices of some commission houses have electronic wall displays. Price-reporting networks from most futures exchanges also carry other information relevant to trading. Following is a review of the kinds of information provided by the Chicago Board of Trade system.

Commodity Quotations

Presession Data

Line transmission begins daily at about 6:45 a.m. with a test series. Interspersed during the test and at minute intervals throughout the trading session, the correct Chicago time is given as a permanent record of when bids, offers, and trades were made. In addition, each quote transmitted contains the official Chicago Board of Trade time stamp.

Notices

Before trading begins each day, important notices are flashed across the MPRIS system. These include announcements of the last trading day for expiring futures and options contracts, new contract introductions, changes in contract specifications, and new strike prices when applicable. These notices are repeated following the close of the day trading session.

Deliveries

Each day at approximately 6:50 a.m. during a contract's delivery period, the system lists the deliveries that will be made that day. Delivery notices made the previous day are given, and the first notices of delivery that will be made the following day also are listed.

Receipts and Shipments

The next report is the Chicago Daily Receipts and Shipments of grain. The first section of the report gives the estimated number of railcars of grain in Chicago for that day. This is followed by the estimated number of Commodity Credit Corporation (CCC) railcars of grain in Chicago for that day.

Following the estimates are the previous day's receipts and shipments records, including the number of grain railcars loaded out, and the receipts and shipments of grain made by truck and barge.

Options Volume and Open Interest

About 6:55 a.m. each day, the previous day's volume and open interest figures for put and call options are listed.

Previous Day's Volume

At approximately 7 a.m. daily, the previous day's estimated volume figures for all futures contracts are transmitted, based on the clearinghouse's latest run. (During the last run, the clearinghouse makes a final check to match all trades from the previous day.) This report is released before the first trade-checking session during which exchange members reconcile unmatched trades from the previous day.

Data During the Day Session

The current day's trading session rarely opens precisely on the previous session's closing prices. Opening prices are usually a little higher or lower, reflecting changes in available supplies, news events, and a host of other factors that affect buying and selling decisions.

Open

Trading in all futures contracts does not always begin immediately after the opening bell. This is particularly true in distant contract months where trading is generally less active. The first trade made during the trading day carries the opening symbol OPG or resumption, if the trade was made during a previous trading session (evening trading or GLOBEX) of the same trading day, on MPRIS.

Bids and Offers

Prices that appear on the price-reporting system may be the result of a trade, but they also could be indications of bids or offers in which no trades were made. When a price appears on the system, it means that a trade, a bid, or an offer was made at that level.

Errors

Errors in transmission usually are corrected by a notation on the system. A quote might be revised or canceled; a missed quote is inserted.

Spreads

A spread refers to the simultaneous purchase and sale of at least two futures contracts. It also can refer to a sale and purchase of different options or a combination of options and futures contracts.

The Rules and Regulations of the Chicago Board of Trade and most other futures exchanges require that spreads be reported as such on the price-reporting system. It is the responsibility of the floor broker or trader who places a spread to inform the market reporters of the prices at which the spread was executed.

Price Ranges

Trading ranges are reported once after the session, reflecting the highest and lowest prices on all transactions. The commodity and contract-month symbols for the nearby contract are the first to appear, followed by the highest and lowest prices. More distant contract months of the same commodity follow in sequence with the highest and lowest prices.

Close

Five minutes before trading closes, a warning bell is sounded on the trading floor. The tempo of trading increases as traders close out positions and outside customers place orders for execution at or near the close. Another warning bell is sounded one minute before the end of trading. The last 60 seconds is likely to be one of the most active periods in the session. Messengers race back and forth between phones and pit brokers. As soon as the traders confirm execution of their closing orders, the closing, high, and low prices for the day are transmitted through the system. Inactive contracts are shown as having a nominal price, a bid price, or an asked price. (A nominal price is used when no trade has taken place.)

Exchanges also may have modified closing calls (MCC) so brokers have an additional opportunity to complete existing customer orders. The rules of the individual exchanges dictate the procedures to be followed. In the case of the Chicago Board of Trade, the modified closing call is a two-minute trading period for all futures contracts beginning eight minutes after the regular trading session closes and three minutes after the evening trading session ends. Unfilled orders in the brokers' possession at the close may be executed during MCC within the smaller of the closing range or the range a tick above or below settlement for financial contracts and two ticks above or below settlement for agricultural contracts.

Postsession Data

The settlement prices are released by the clearinghouse and reported on MPRIS 15 to 30 minutes after trading ends. The price fluctuation limits for the following day's trading are transmitted after the settlement prices are sent through the system.

Settlement

The first settlement prices to appear are for the agricultural contracts. They are followed by the price limits for each agricultural contract for the next day. Settlement prices for the nonagricultural commodities traded on the Chicago Board of Trade follow, along with the price limits for the next day's trading in these commodities. Any errors in previous transmission, especially in closing prices and high and low prices, are then corrected and reported.

Volume and Open Interest

The final volume of trading and the open interest for the previous day's trading are carried on the system at about 2:15 p.m. Volume figures for each futures and options contract month are reported, as well as total trading volume and open interest for each commodity.

Evening Session

The trading day has been adjusted to accommodate futures contracts that trade during the evening session at the Chicago Board of Trade. The board of directors determined that each extended trading day has a single official "opening time," i.e., 5:20 p.m., and a single official "close," i.e., 2 p.m. the following day.* The end of the evening session is not referred to as a *close* but as a *suspension,* and the reopening of trading at 7:20 a.m. is officially known as *resumption.*

Wallboards and the closed-circuit television system show a suspension price or range following the conclusion of trading each evening, and show a resumption price or range each morning following the continuation of trading.

*During the summer months, the times of the extended trading day are adjusted to allow for daylight saving time.

Master Reports are compiled by the Chicago Board of Trade's Market Information Department based on information received from various sources, including the U.S. Department of Agriculture, private and terminal markets, and storage facilities.

Visible Supply

On Monday of each week, figures on the U.S. visible supply of agricultural commodities compiled by the Chicago Board of Trade are released. The visible supply is the total stock of agricultural commodities in storage in public elevators and some private elevators in the terminal markets plus certain stocks afloat. This information is carried on the system at approximately 2:30 p.m. The figures are reported in thousands of bushels with the last three digits omitted. The first information reported is the total U.S. visible supplies of each agricultural commodity. Increases or decreases in visible supplies from the previous week also are given. Figures representing stocks on hand at the various principal markets are given with corresponding figures for one week ago and one year ago.

Crop Reports

The U.S. Department of Agriculture Crop Reports also are disseminated over MPRIS. Crop reports are compiled by the Crop Reporting Board and are released at 3 p.m. eastern standard time, and reported over the Chicago Board of Trade system at approximately 2:30 p.m. Chicago time on specific days selected by the USDA.

Planting intention reports for the various ag commodities are released from December through March. Following the planting season, production reports are released. Current figures represent estimates in planted acreage, yield per acre, and expected production as of the first of the month in which the report appears. Each crop report also includes a production comparison with the previous month and the previous year. Significant increases or decreases in the anticipated crop size can have a profound influence on grain prices as well as the prices of related commodities. As a consequence, producers, commercial firms, and speculators eagerly await the release of monthly government crop reports.

Newspapers vary in how they publish futures and options prices. As an example, the pages at the end of the chapter list how *The Wall Street Journal* reports futures and options on futures prices. The paper includes open, high, low, and closing prices, as well as the net change from the previous day's close and the high-low price range. These prices are quoted in units specific to each futures and options contract and are listed with the quotes. For instance, grains are quoted in cents per bushel, silver in cents per troy ounce, and cattle in cents per pound.

Master Reports

Newspaper Quotations

MIDIS-System

Historical price, volume, open interest, and other market data also are available through a unique Chicago Board of Trade electronic-information system called MIDIS (Market Information Data Inquiry System). This information system is accessible by computers within the Chicago Board of Trade building.

The price discovery function of futures markets is vitally important to the economy. Futures exchanges, recognizing this role, work to disseminate timely and accurate price information and are constantly improving their price-reporting systems.

FUTURES OPTIONS PRICES

Friday, October 16, 1992.

AGRICULTURAL

CORN (CBT)
SOYBEANS (CBT)
SOYBEAN MEAL (CBT)
SOYBEAN OIL (CBT)
WHEAT (CBT)
WHEAT (KC)
COTTON (CTN)
ORANGE JUICE (CTN)
COFFEE (CSCE)
SUGAR – WORLD (CSCE)
COCOA (CSCE)

OIL

CRUDE OIL (NYM)
HEATING OIL No.2 (NYM)
GASOLINE – Unlead (NYM)

LIVESTOCK

CATTLE-FEEDER (CME)
CATTLE-LIVE (CME)
HOGS-LIVE (CME)

METALS

COPPER (CMX)
GOLD (CMX)
SILVER (CMX)

OTHER OPTIONS

Final or settlement prices of selected contracts. Volume and open interest are totals in all contract months.

CORN (MCE)
GSCI (CME) 1258 X PREMIUM
LUMBER (CME)
MAJOR MKT (INDEX) (CBT)
NYSE COMPOSITE INDEX (NYFE)
NIKKEI 225 STOCK AVG. (CME)
OATS (CBT)
PLATINUM (NYM)
PORK BELLIES (CME)
RICE-ROUGH (MCE)
SILVER (CBT)
SOYBEANS (MCE)
2 YR. TREAS. NOTES (CBT)
WHEAT (MCE)
WHEAT (MPLS)

CURRENCY

JAPANESE YEN (IMM)
DEUTSCHEMARK (IMM)
CANADIAN DOLLAR (IMM)
BRITISH POUND (IMM)
SWISS FRANC (IMM)
MARK/YEN CROSS RATE (CME)
U.S. DOLLAR INDEX (FINEX)

INTEREST RATE

T-BONDS (CBT)
T-NOTES (CBT)
MUNICIPAL BOND INDEX (CBT)
5 YR TREAS NOTES (CBT)
EURODOLLAR (IMM)
LIBOR – 1 Mo. (IMM)
TREASURY BILLS (IMM)
EURODOLLAR (LIFFE)
LONG GILT (LIFFE)

INDEX

S&P 500 STOCK INDEX (CME)

FUTURES PRICES

Friday, October 16, 1992.

Open Interest Reflects Previous Trading Day.

GRAINS AND OILSEEDS
LIVESTOCK AND MEAT
FOOD AND FIBER
METALS AND PETROLEUM
OTHER FUTURES
CURRENCY
INTEREST RATE
S&P 500 INDEX (CME) 500 times index

EXCHANGE ABBREVIATIONS
(for commodity futures and futures options)

CBT-Chicago Board of Trade; CME-Chicago Mercantile Exchange; CMX-Commodity Exchange, New York; CRCE-Chicago Rice & Cotton Exchange; CTN-New York Cotton Exchange; CSCE-Coffee, Sugar & Cocoa Exchange, New York; FOX-London Futures and Options Exchange; IPE-International Petroleum Exchange; KC-Kansas City Board of Trade; MCE-MidAmerica Commodity Exchange; MPLS-Minneapolis Grain Exchange; NYM-New York Mercantile Exchange; PBOT-Philadelphia Board of Trade; WPG-Winnipeg Commodity Exchange.

Futures prices as reported in **The Wall Street Journal.** *Reprinted by permission of* **The Wall Street Journal,** ©1992 Dow Jones & Company, Inc. All Rights Reserved Worldwide.

A Futures Commission Merchant (FCM)* is a firm that transacts futures and options on futures business on behalf of financial and commercial institutions as well as the general public. A number of terms are used to describe FCMs, including *wire houses*, *brokerage houses*, and *commission houses*. FCMs are a highly diversified segment of the financial world. Some conduct business in all types of financial investments; others confine their operations to futures and options markets. There are firms that specialize in hedging accounts, others that concentrate on public speculative trading, and those that do a combination of hedging and speculative business.

FCMs become registered member firms of futures exchanges in order to trade or handle accounts in the markets conducted by those exchanges. Under the rules of most exchanges, however, memberships can be held only by individuals. Usually, officers of partnerships and corporations holding exchange memberships register their memberships for the benefit of the partnership or corporation. The individual member retains full control over the membership and full responsibility for the acts of the firm and its employees under the rules and regulations of the exchange.

The basic function of the FCM—regardless of the name, size, and scope of the firm—is to represent the interests of those in the market who

*According to the National Futures Association, an FCM can be an individual or an organization.

THE
CUSTOMER
AND THE
FUTURES
COMMISSION
MERCHANT

*Registration,
Accounts,
Orders*

5

do not hold seats on futures exchanges. Some of the many services provided by FCMs include placing orders, collecting and segregating margin monies; providing basic accounting records, disseminating market information and research, and counseling and training customers in futures and options trading practices and strategies.

Customer Operations

Most customer operations are handled by Associated Persons (APs),[†] who are employed or associated with a Futures Commission Merchant, an Introducing Broker (IB), Commodity Trading Advisor (CTA), or Commodity Pool Operator (CPO). (IBs, CTAs, and CPOs perform different market services from the FCM. For a description of each, see the following pages.)

Because these individuals or organizations are responsible for a variety of services—determining the financial stability of prospective customers, opening new accounts, placing orders, and accepting money—they must be registered with the Commodity Futures Trading Commission (CFTC) and become members of the National Futures Association (NFA).

The CFTC, the NFA, and the exchanges have strict rules regarding registration as an Associated Person. For example, as early as the mid-1960s, the Chicago Board of Trade required any individual who was not an exchange member but traded for customer accounts to pass a futures examination. Later, the Chicago Mercantile Exchange, Coffee, Sugar & Cocoa Exchange, New York Cotton Exchange, and Commodity Exchange, Inc. adopted similar measures.

By the mid-1980s, the CFTC required everyone who handles customer accounts pass the Series 3 National Commodity Futures Examination and register with the NFA. Exchange members who execute customer orders must register with the NFA as floor brokers and pass exchange exams in lieu of the Series 3 exam. As of 1993, as part of the Futures Trading Practices Act of 1992, floor traders, those who purchase and sell futures and options for their own accounts, also are required to register with the NFA and pass written exams measuring their knowledge of the industry. A complete listing of CFTC registration requirements is on the next two pages.

Typically, a prospective customer will discuss his financial goals with an Associated Person, who explains the risks associated with trading futures and options on futures. Customer financial requirements may vary from one FCM to another, but are usually strictly enforced to protect the customer, the integrity of the firm, the exchanges, and the CFTC.

Once it has been established that trading in futures contracts is appropriate to the financial goals of a prospective customer and that he meets the financial requirements, opening a futures account is quite simple.

[†]Floor brokers, individuals who execute orders for the purchase and sale of futures or options contracts for another person, also are responsible for handling customer accounts. The NFA and CFTC have specific rules regarding registration of floor brokers. For more information, see the following pages or contact the association.

Who Is Required to Register	The information that follows should help you determine whether, by law, you are required to seek CFTC registration. If you have any question as to whether you qualify for a particular exemption from registration, you should seek guidance by referring to the appropriate section of the Act or by consulting NFA personnel.*	
Category	**Description of Business Activity Requiring Registration**	**Exemptions**
Futures Commission Merchant (FCM)	Generally, an FCM is an individual or organization which does both of the following: (1) solicits or accepts orders to buy or sell futures contracts or commodity options, and (2) accepts money or other assets from customers to support such orders.	Registration is required. There are no exemptions.
Introducing Broker (IB)	An IB is an individual or organization that solicits or accepts orders to buy or sell futures contracts or commodity options but does not accept money or other assets from customers to support such orders.	Registration is required unless: (a) You are registered as and acting in the capacity of an AP. *or* (b) You are registered as an FCM. *or* (c) You are registered as a CPO and only operate pools. *or* (d) You are registered as a CTA and either solely manage accounts under powers of attorney or don't receive per trade compensation.
Commodity Pool Operator (CPO)	A CPO is an individual or organization which operates or solicits funds for a commodity pool, that is, an enterprise in which funds contributed by a number of persons are combined for the purpose of trading futures contracts or commodity options.	In general, registration is required unless: (a) The total gross capital contributions to all pools are less than $200,000. *and* (b) There are no more than 15 participants in any one pool. (Cont'd on next page)
	*Requests for exemption or for "no action" opinions with respect to the applicable registration requirements should be submitted to the CFTC and a copy of any such request should be provided to NFA.	

Information from the National Futures Association.

Category	Description of Business Activity Requiring Registration	Exemptions
Commodity Trading Advisor (CTA)	A CTA is an individual or organization who, for compensation or profit, directly or indirectly advises others as to the value of or the advisability of buying or selling futures contracts or commodity options. Providing advice indirectly includes exercising trading authority over a customer's account as well as giving advice through written publications or other media.	Registration is required unless: (a) You have provided advice to 15 or fewer persons during the past 12 months and do not hold yourself out generally to the public as a CTA. *or* (b) You are in one of a number of businesses or professions listed in the Act or are registered in another capacity and your advice is solely incidental to your principal business or profession. *or* (c) Your advice is given through written publication or other mass media and is limited to futures contracts and commodity options traded on foreign exchanges.
Associated Person (AP)	An AP is an individual who solicits orders, customers, or customer funds (or who supervises persons so engaged) on behalf of an FCM, IB, CTA, or CPO. An AP is, in effect, anyone who is a salesperson or who supervises salespersons for any of these categories of individuals or firms. The registration requirements apply to any person in the supervisory chain of command and not only to persons who directly supervise the solicitation of orders, customers, or funds.	Registration is generally required unless: (a) You are already registered as an FCM, IB, or Floor Broker. *or* (b) You are already registered as a CPO if you are to be associated with a CPO. *or* (c) You are already registered as a CTA if you are to be associated with a CTA. *or* (d) You are already registered with the National Association of Securities Dealers and only act in the capacity of an AP associated with a CPO. *or* (e) In certain instances where a firm's commodity interest activity accounts for no more than 10 percent of its annual revenue, the chief operating officer, general partner, or other principal in the supervisory chain of command may be eligible for exception from AP registration. Contact NFA for additional information.
Floor Broker (FB) Floor Trader (FT)	An FB is an individual who executes any orders for the purchase or sale of any commodity futures or options contract on any contract market for any other person. A registered FB need not also register as a FT in order to engage in activity as a FT. An FT is an individual who executes trades for the purchase or sale of any commodity futures or options contract on any contract market for such individual's own account.	

To open an account, the customer must supply his name, address, phone number, social security or tax I.D. number, and business, personal, and banking references.

CFTC regulations require that the Associated Person provide the prospective customer with a risk disclosure statement. Before an account can be opened, the customer must read the statement and sign a document stating that he has read and fully understands it. A separate risk disclosure statement is required for those who wish to trade options.

An example of a futures risk disclosure statement and two other basic commodity account documents—commodity account agreement form and hedge account certificate—are included in the chapter. The commodity account agreement form outlines how the account will be handled by the FCM and the obligations of the account holder. The hedge account certificate lists the cash commodities owned or expected to be owned, or sold or expected to be sold, by the customer.

Other documents not shown include a new account fact sheet, an options risk disclosure statement, a disclosure statement for noncash margin deposits, and a bankruptcy disclosure statement for hedge accounts. These documents can be obtained from an FCM.

While the amount of paperwork may seem excessive at first, it is designed to ensure that customers understand their financial commitment and the risks associated with a futures and options account.

Types of Accounts

Futures and options accounts may be opened on an individual or joint basis. In individual accounts, trading decisions are made by the individual. In joint accounts, all parties have input on trading decisions. Either type of account may be opened for hedging or speculating purposes.

A third type of account—a discretionary account (also known as a controlled or managed account)—can be set up, in which the customer authorizes another person to make all trading decisions. Each exchange and FCM, especially if an Associated Person will be exercising discretion, has specific rules for handling discretionary accounts. One of the most essential is the customer's written power of attorney to exercise discretion.

Exchange regulations also govern those individuals who handle discretionary accounts. On the Chicago Board of Trade, for example, only those APs who have been registered for at least two continuous years may handle such accounts. All discretionary accounts must be supervised by an officer or partner of the FCM. The AP must record, in writing, every transaction for the account, with subsequent confirmation sent to the customer. The customer receives a detailed monthly statement showing the number, size, and terms of the transactions with net and open positions.

The only way to terminate the trading authority established in a discretionary account is by written revocation of the power of attorney either on the part of the customer or the person controlling the account.

Margins

Futures market participants are required to post performance bond margins. Performance bond margins are financial guarantees in the form of cash or T-bills required of both buyers and sellers to ensure they fulfill the obligation of the futures contract. That is, they are required to make or take delivery of the commodity represented unless the position is offset before expiration of the contract.

The main purpose of a performance bond margin is to provide contract integrity. It is not at all like margin in the securities industry, which involves a down payment and a loan by the broker/dealer for the purchase of equities.

Margin requirements for futures contracts usually range between 2 and 5 percent of a contract's face value and are set by the exchanges where the contracts are traded. However, brokerage firms can, and often do, require a larger margin than the exchange minimum; they cannot require less.

Futures margins are determined on the basis of risk and can be changed any time as volatility increases or decreases. In a volatile (or risky) market, a higher margin is usually required; and in a less volatile (or less risky) market, a lower margin is usually required. Margin levels also vary for hedging and speculating accounts. For example, exchanges and brokerage firms generally require lower margins for hedging accounts because they carry less risk than speculating accounts.

Original margin is the amount a market participant must deposit into his margin account at the time he places an order to buy or sell a futures contract. Then, on a daily basis, the margin account is debited or credited based on the close of that day's trading session. This debiting and crediting is referred to as *marking-to-market*. In this way, buyers and sellers are protected against the possibility of contract default.

A customer must maintain a set minimum margin known as *maintenance margin* (per outstanding futures contract) in his account. On any day that debits resulting from a market loss reduce the funds in the account below the maintenance margin, the broker calls on his customer for an additional deposit to restore the account to the initial margin level. Requests for additional money are known as *margin calls*.

FCMs are responsible to see that their customers deposit the required margin promptly. The CFTC requires customer margin monies to be held in segregated accounts from commission house assets, margins on house accounts, and other customer margin funds for commodities not subject to U.S. federal regulations such as London cocoa or sugar.

To ensure the margin system performs efficiently, each exchange has a clearing organization, which not only reconciles the day's trading activity but makes sure brokerage firms have sufficient margin in their accounts to cover their customers' open positions. Just as every buyer or seller of a futures contract must maintain adequate funds in his margin account with the brokerage firm, so must each brokerage firm maintain adequate funds in its margin account with the exchange clearinghouse. (Smaller brokerage houses that are not members of the clearinghouse accomplish this through a firm that is a member.) (For more detailed information on clearing margins and practices, see Chapter 6.)

Handling margins is an important function of the FCM. Responsibility for placing orders, collecting margin deposits, overseeing the account, making margin calls, and notifying the customer when he has surplus margin usually falls on the shoulders of the AP.

Orders

Understanding the customer's objectives and properly relaying orders are vital functions of the AP. He must write and enter orders without vagueness or ambiguity to ensure that they are properly handled on the trading floor. A mistake in this process can be very costly, therefore, both the customer and the AP must accurately communicate the order.

Some of the more common orders follow:

Market

Perhaps the most common type of order is the market order. In a market order, the customer states the number of contracts of a given delivery month he wishes to buy or sell. He does not specify the price at which he wants to initiate the transaction, but simply wants it placed as soon as possible at the best possible price.

Price Limit

The price limit order specifies a price limit at which the customer's order must be executed. It can be executed only at that price or better.

Fill-or-Kill

A fill-or-kill order is a price limit order that must be filled immediately or canceled.

Stop

A stop order is not executed until the market reaches a given price level. For instance, a stop order to buy becomes a market order when the futures contract trades (or is bid) at or above the stop price. A stop order to sell becomes a market order when the futures contract trades (or is offered) at or below the stop price.

Stop orders normally are used to liquidate earlier transactions, to cut losses, or to protect profits. Let's assume a customer bought a U.S. Treasury bond futures contract for $100,000. To prevent a large loss in the event bond prices fall, the customer could place a stop order (also known as a *stop-loss* or *sell-stop order*) at $96,000. His position is liquidated if and when the market price declines to $96,000. Once the market reaches $96,000, the stop-loss order becomes a market order and could be filled at a lower price, say $95,500, rather than the price designated in the order.

Stop orders also can be used to enter the market. Suppose a trader expected a bull market only if it passed a specific price level. In this case, he could use a stop-buy order when and if the market reached this point.

Stop-Limit Order

One variation of a stop order is a stop-limit order. With a stop-limit order, the trade must be executed at the exact price or held until the stated price is reached again. If the market fails to return to the stop-limit level, the order is not executed.

Market-if-Touched

A board or market-if-touched (MIT) order may be executed only if the market reaches a particular price. An MIT to buy becomes a market order if and when a futures contract trades at or below the order price. An MIT order to sell becomes a market order if and when a futures contract trades at or above the order price. (**Note:** This type of order may not be accepted by some brokers.)

Time Limit

Several types of orders specify the time an order must be executed. For instance, a day order must be placed at a given price sometime during that day's trading session. At the Chicago Board of Trade, all orders are assumed to be day orders unless otherwise specified.

A time limit order is good until a designated time during the trading session. If the order has not been filled by that time, it is automatically canceled. An open or good-till-canceled (GTC) order can be executed any time up until the customer cancels the order or the contract expires.

Orders also may be limited to purchases or sales at the open or close of a trading session. These transactions do not have to be the first or last of the session, but must be executed within the opening or closing ranges of a trading session as defined by the rules of the exchange. It is also possible to specify a certain portion of the day or time that an order must be executed.

Opening and Closing Orders, Cancellations

On the Chicago Board of Trade, all orders that reach the trading floor 15 minutes or less before the open or close of trading are accepted solely at the risk of the customer on a "not held" basis. This is because they could involve extraordinary problems if floor brokers don't have enough time to prioritize and organize their orders for execution in the pit.

Canceling

A straight cancel order deletes a customer's previous order.

A cancel-former-order (CFO) eliminates a previous order but replaces it with new instructions. It is most often used to change the price level in a price limit order.

Combination

Combination orders are used to enter two orders at the same time. One example of a combination order is a one-cancels-other (OCO) order. It is a two-sided order in which the execution of one side cancels the other. For instance, a trader, who is long January U.S. Treasury bonds at $98,000 with a price objective of $103,000 and a desired stop point at $96,000, might enter the following OCO order: Sell one January U.S. Treasury bond contract $103,000 limit/$96,000 stop. (**Note:** This type of order may not be accepted on all exchanges.)

Spread orders also are considered combination orders and refer to the simultaneous purchase and sale of at least two different futures contracts. There are a variety of spread orders that can involve the sale and purchase of futures contracts of different delivery months (intramarket or interdelivery spread), the same commodity on different exchanges (intermarket spread), or different but related futures contracts (intercommodity spread).

With respect to options on futures, spread trading takes many forms. Among the most commonly used are vertical spreads (buying and selling options of the same expiration month at different strike prices), conversions (buying a futures contract, buying a put option, and selling a call option), and reversals (selling a futures contract, selling a put option, and buying a call option).

Order Routing

Orders received from customers are sent immediately by an AP by direct transmission to the exchange on which the order is to be executed. A sufficient number of telephone stations are located on the periphery of the trading floor to handle the many orders coming to the exchange from companies and individuals. At the Chicago Board of Trade, for example, there are several steps taken once an order is received on the exchange floor that are described on the next page.

Accounting Services

Written confirmation of all commodity futures and options on futures orders on a same-day basis is the objective of most FCMs even though the confirmation may have been made by telephone.

Confirmation is just the first step in a series of important accounting services that FCMs provide their customers. In addition, firms provide purchase and sales (P&S) statements that show the number of contracts purchased and/or sold in specific futures markets at specific prices and current cash balances.

A customer may obtain full information on the net status of his account by asking his AP. The customer normally receives a regular monthly statement that shows all trading activity, net position, and margin balance less commission and fees.

Route of an Order

The order is time-stamped.

A member firm employee, known as a runner, rushes the order to a broker in the trading pit. (Some orders are flashed by hand signals to brokers in the trading pit and fills are flashed back to the order station. This is generally the practice in many of the financial futures markets.)

The broker fills the order using open outcry and hand signals to communicate price and quantity.

Once the order is filled, the broker reports the price to exchange price reporters in raised pulpits looking down onto each pit. The pit reporters relay price changes as they occur to central quotation computers.

The computer then transmits the price information to electronic price boards facing the trading floor and around the world via information services.

The completed order is picked up by a runner and returned to the telephone desk. The order is time-stamped again. The customer is notified that his order has been filled.

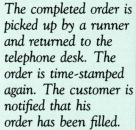

One of the most important FCM services is disseminating market information to its customers. This service can take the form of daily or weekly market letters, prepared by futures specialists, that outline the fundamental supply/demand factors and price outlook.

Some FCMs also provide technical advisory and price-charting services that track historical patterns of price movement, volume, and open interest data as indicators of future price movement.

Market Information and Research

Several exchanges have strict standards for advertising and promotional materials distributed by their member firms and aimed at prospective customers. In general, ads have to be truthful and in good taste. Advertising and sales promotion appeals should avoid misrepresentations about profit potential. Periodically, exchanges will review advertising done by their member firms to make certain it meets generally high standards. In the case of options on futures, all promotional material must be submitted to the exchanges for review. The exchanges' rules on advertising are meant to protect the customer, member firms and their employees, and the exchanges themselves.

Advertising and Promotion

FCMs, futures exchanges, the NFA, and the CFTC share important responsibilities for protecting public customers in futures and options on futures markets. The FCMs, together with the exchanges, are responsible for informing the public not only of the investment potential, but also of the possibility of losses in futures and options on futures trading. They must communicate that gains in futures trading are the product of attentive observation of price movement and a thorough understanding of the economic factors underlying the market, and that there is no guarantee of profit.

By their regulations, auditing procedures, and financial requirements, FCMs and exchanges make certain that customers are prepared to fulfill their financial commitments in futures and options on futures trading. Regulation of the business conduct and financial soundness of member firms, margin requirements, standards of performance for APs, and the segregation of customer margins are not guarantees against customer losses due to adverse price movements, but they do ensure against customer losses due to financial failure or improper handling of customer funds.

Customer Protection

NAME OF FIRM

RISK DISCLOSURE STATEMENT

This statement is furnished to you because rule 1.55 of the Commodity Futures Trading Commission requires it.

The risk of loss in trading commodity futures contracts can be substantial. You should therefore carefully consider whether such trading is suitable for you in light of your financial condition. In considering whether to trade, you should be aware of the following:

1)   You may sustain a total loss of the initial margin funds and any additional funds that you deposit with your broker to establish or maintain a position in the commodity futures market. If the market moves against your position, you may be called upon by your broker to deposit a substantial amount of additional margin funds, on short notice, in order to maintain your position. If you do not provide the required funds within the prescribed time, your position may be liquidated at a loss, and you will be liable for any resulting deficit in your account.

2)   Under certain market conditions, you may find it difficult or impossible to liquidate a position. This can occur, for example, when the market makes a "limit move."

3)   Placing contingent orders, such as a "stop-loss" or "stop-limit" order, will not necessarily limit your losses to the intended amounts, since market conditions may make it impossible to execute such orders.

4)   A "spread" position may not be less risky than a simple "long" or "short" position.

5)   The high degree of leverage that is often obtainable in futures trading because of the small margin requirements can work against you as well as for you. The use of leverage can lead to large losses as well as gains.

This brief statement cannot, of course, disclose all the risks and other significant aspects of the commodity markets. You should therefore carefully study futures trading before you trade.

I have read and understand the above risk disclosure statement furnished to me by Name of Firm.

_____	_____	_____
Date	Signature	Print Name
Date	Signature	Print Name
Date	Signature	Print Name

This form along with the forms on the following pages are taken from sources believed to be reliable, but they are not guaranteed by the Chicago Board of Trade as to accuracy or completeness.

HEDGE ACCOUNT CERTIFICATION

The undersigned certifies that trades in futures and/or options on futures contracts in his/her account with Name of Firm are bona fide hedging transactions and that the positions maintained are bona fide hedge positions.

The undersigned further certifies that provided below is a true and accurate list of the cash commodities owned or expected to be owned, or sold or expected to be sold by the customer; and that checked below are futures therefore eligible as bona fide hedge positions.

		COMMODITY FUTURES	CASH COMMODITY
_____	A.	Grains-wheat, corn, oats, soybeans-meal, oil, etc.	_____
_____	B.	Meats-cattle, hogs, broilers and products, etc.	_____
_____	C.	Metals-gold, silver, copper	_____
_____	D.	Financials-T-bills, T-bonds, GNMA, Eurodollars, CDs, etc.	_____
_____	E.	Currencies-Brit. Pounds, Mex. Pesos, Swiss Francs, Jap. Yen, etc.	_____
_____	F.	Sugar, Coffee, Cocoa	_____
_____	G.	Cotton, Frozen O.J.	_____
_____	H.	Petroleum Products-unleaded gas, heating oil, etc.	_____
_____	I.	Forest Products-lumber	_____
_____	J.	Indexes-NYSE Index, S&P, Value Line, MMI, etc.	_____

CFTC regulations require that all commodity brokers notify their hedge customers of the following: You have the opportunity to state at this time whether in the unlikely event of this company's bankruptcy you prefer that open contracts held in your hedging account be liquidated by the trustee without seeking your instructions.

_____   I would not prefer such liquidation.   _____
                                                          Customer's Signature

_____   I would prefer such liquidation.   _____
                                                          Customer's Signature

COMMODITY ACCOUNT AGREEMENT

| Name | Account No. |

1)   In consideration of the agreement of Name of Firm to act as broker for the undersigned in the purchase or sale of commodities (which term shall include contracts relating to immediate or future delivery of commodities and options thereon) the undersigned agrees, in respect to all commodity accounts which the undersigned now has or may at any future time have with the firm, or its successors including accounts from time to time closed and then reopened, as follows:

2)   Orders for the purchase or sale of commodities shall be received and executed with the express intent that actual delivery is contemplated. All transactions shall be subject to the constitution, by-laws, rules, regulations, customs and usages of the exchange or market where executed (and of its clearing house if any) and to any law, rule and regulation applicable thereto, including but not limited to, the provisions of the Commodity Exchange Act, as amended, and the rules and regulations thereunder. The firm reserves the right to refuse to accept any order.

3)   If the undersigned should die or become incompetent, any pending order shall be validly executed by the firm, up to the time it receives written notice of the death or incompetence of the undersigned, and the firm is hereby indemnified against loss arising therefrom.

4)   To secure any indebtedness or other obligation owed by the undersigned to the firm, the firm is hereby granted a lien on all of the undersigned's property at any time held by the firm. The firm may without notice transfer any money or other property interchangeably between any accounts of the undersigned except that any transfer from a commodity account which is subject to regulations under the Commodity Exchange Act to a nonregulated account shall have such other authorization by the undersigned as is required by such regulations.

5)   The undersigned recognizes that margin deposits are due and must be paid immediately upon entering into positions on commodity exchanges and from time to time as market conditions dictate and agrees to make such deposits immediately on demand. The firm shall have absolute discretion to set and revise margin requirements. Customer acknowledges the firm's right to limit, without notice to customer, the number of open positions which customer may maintain or acquire through the firm.

6)   The undersigned agrees to pay promptly on demand any and all sums due to the firm for monies advanced, with interest thereon at 1% over the prime rate. The undersigned agrees to pay when due the firm's charges for commissions at rates established between us and to pay interest at 1% over the prime rate on past due commission charges.

7)   The firm shall have the right, whenever in its discretion it considers it necessary for its protection, or in the event that a petition in bankruptcy or for the appointment of a receiver is filed by or against the undersigned, or in the event of the death of the undersigned, or in the event the undersigned is adjudged incompetent, to sell any or all commodities, or other property in any account of the undersigned and to buy any or all commodities which may be short in any account of the undersigned, and to close out

and liquidate any and all outstanding contracts of the undersigned, all without demand for margin or additional margin, notice of sale or purchase, notice of advertisement of any kind whatsoever, and any such sales or purchases may be made at the firm's discretion on any exchange or other market where such business is then usually transacted, and on any such sale the firm may be the purchaser for its own account; it being understood that a prior demand, or call, or prior notice of the time and place of such sale or purchase, if any be given, shall not be considered a waiver of the firm's right to sell or to buy without demand or notice as herein provided; and the undersigned shall at all times be liable to the firm for the payment of any debit balance owing in the accounts of the undersigned with the firm, and shall be liable for any deficiency remaining in any such account in the event of the liquidation thereof in whole or in part, and shall be liable for any reasonable costs of collection including attorneys' fees.

8)   Any notices and other communications may be transmitted to the undersigned at the address, or telephone number given herein, or at such other address or telephone number as the undersigned hereafter shall notify the firm in writing, and all notices or communications shall be deemed transmitted when telephoned or deposited in the mail or telexed or telegraphed by the firm or the firm's representative, whether actually received by the undersigned or not. Confirmations, purchase and sale statements and account statements shall be deemed accurate unless objected to in writing within 5 business days from the date of such notice and delivered to the firm.

9)   The firm will not be responsible for delays or failure in the transmission of orders caused by a breakdown of communication facilities or by any other cause beyond the firm's reasonable control.

10)   The undersigned represents that he or she is 18 years of age or over and that he or she is not an employee of any exchange nor of any corporation of which any exchange owns a majority of the capital stock. The undersigned further represents that he or she is not an employee of a member of any exchange nor of a firm registered on any exchange or if he or she is so employed then a written consent of his or her employer is attached herewith.

11)   This agreement is made under and shall be governed by the laws of the State of Illinois in all respects, including construction and performance.

12)   The undersigned acknowledges that the firm is a wholly owned subsidiary of Company A and that the market recommendations of the firm may or may not be consistent with the market position or intentions of Company A, its subsidiaries and affiliates. The market recommendations of the firm are based upon information believed to be reliable, but the firm cannot and does not guarantee the accuracy or completeness thereof or represent that following such recommendations will eliminate or reduce the risks inherent in trading commodities futures.

13)   The firm is hereby granted permission to record telephone conversations between its employees and the undersigned.

14)   This agreement shall be irrevocable as long as the undersigned shall have any account with the firm; it shall be binding upon the undersigned and upon the undersigned's executors, administrators, heirs and assigns; it can be amended only in writing duly signed by the undersigned and an officer of the firm.

Clearinghouses exist to ensure the financial integrity of all futures and options contracts traded on U.S. futures exchanges. Clearinghouses ensure the integrity of the markets by not only committing substantial capital as third party guarantors to every futures and options transaction, but they also are an integral part of trading operations. Their role in trading operations is comprehensive and includes the daily matching of trades (each long position is matched with a short), collecting and maintaining performance-bond margin monies, monitoring open position risk of clearing firm members and large traders, settling accounts daily, and reporting trade data. The exacting nature of these operations is underscored by the cash flow associated with the daily settlement of accounts, also known as *marking-to-market*. At the Chicago Board of Trade, for example, marking-to-market typically results in a daily cash flow averaging $200 million.

In short, the third-party guarantee of clearinghouses draws great strength from the comprehensive and exacting clearing system that has evolved since the late-1800s. This chapter gives an overview of the clearing process and covers some of the responsibilities entrusted to the clearinghouses of U.S. futures exchanges.

CLEARING OPERATIONS

*Preserving
the Integrity
of the
Markets*

6

Formal Clearing Organizations

Clearinghouses are either a department within a futures exchange or a separate corporation. In either case, their memberships are usually held by international commission houses, commercial processors, independent trading companies, and financial institutions. This is different from memberships on futures exchanges, which are held by individuals only. On some exchanges, however, an individual may apply for clearing privileges but is only permitted to clear trades for his own account and not for customers or third parties.

The level of capitalization required for clearing member firms varies depending upon the type and size of their business. Financial requirements also vary among exchanges but are uniformly rigid to help ensure the financial soundness of the clearinghouses. Some clearing firms even require members to purchase and hold shares in the clearing organization.

Third-Party Guarantors

Clearinghouses act as third parties to all futures and options contracts—acting as a buyer to every clearing member seller and a seller to every clearing member buyer. Buyers and sellers of futures and options contracts do not create financial obligations to one another, but, rather, to the clearinghouse through their clearing member firms.

A transaction in which Smith sells futures to Adams means that Smith's clearing firm would be obligated to the clearinghouse to offset before the contract expires or to make delivery. Adams's clearing firm also would be obligated to the clearinghouse to offset or take delivery. The clearinghouse would act as the buyer to Smith's clearing firm and the seller to Adams's clearing firm.

- Adams buys and Smith sells one T-bond futures (US) at 95-00.
- Clearinghouse matches buy and sell orders.
- Adams's clearing firm guarantees Adams's trade and Smith's clearing firm guarantees Smith's trade.
- After trade is matched, Adams and Smith have commitments only to their clearing firms. They have no direct commitment to each other.

Because the direct relationship between buyer and seller is severed, each is free to buy and sell independently of the other. As a party to every trade, the clearinghouse assumes the responsibility of guarantor of every trade. (See diagram on the next page.)

Clearing Process

A *Typical Order Process*

1. Customer places order through a brokerage firm.

2. Brokerage firm fills order.

3. Order is cleared through a clearing member firm. (If the brokerage firm is not a member of a clearinghouse, it clears through another firm that is a clearinghouse member.)

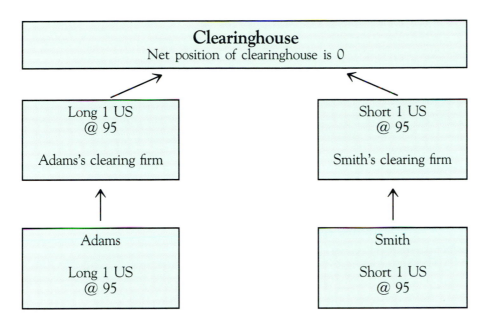

Source: David Mirza, Loyola University, Chicago.

4. Clearing member firm transmits order to clearinghouse.

5. Clearinghouse confirms order, guarantees trade, and adjusts clearing firm's account based on the gain or loss from the transaction.

Collecting Trade Data

Trading information is transmitted to an exchange's clearinghouse either from clearing member firms or exchange staff. This information is usually sent to the clearinghouse via computer transmission from a firm's back-office system or direct input from a trade-entry system within an hour after a trade has occurred. Some exchanges are working together to standardize the method used to relay trading data. In particular, the Chicago Board of Trade and Chicago Mercantile Exchange are developing a hand-held electronic trading card called AUDIT™, which will transmit data directly from the trading floor to the clearinghouse immediately following a trade. (AUDIT stands for Automated Data Input Terminal.)

Trade Matching and Registration

Once the clearinghouse receives completed trade data, computer systems at the clearinghouses compare both sides of a trade, making sure the price, contract(s), and other important trade data match. Unmatched trades are displayed on-line throughout the trading day so clearing members can make corrections.

Trades remaining unmatched after the close of the trading day are reconciled at a trade-check session. This usually takes place in the morning on the trading floor before the markets reopen.

Because a majority of clearinghouse guarantees become effective at the time a trade is matched, successful and timely comparison of trades is important. AUDIT promises to improve the timing as clearinghouses develop on-line matching systems to instantly compare trade data following transmission from the AUDIT device.

Clearinghouse computer systems provide all clearing member firms printed verification of all reconciled (matched) trades. Clearinghouses then calculate original margin requirements for each clearing firm's open positions. This registration process is crucial to clearing firms because it is the official record of a day's trading activity.

Daily Settlement of Accounts

The single most distinguishing feature of futures markets and the most vital procedure for maintaining the financial integrity of the markets is the daily settlement of gains and losses. Daily settlement prior to the market's opening the next day confirms that each clearing member firm is solvent and can continue to conduct business with clearinghouses.

Clearing Margins

Clearinghouses require members to deposit margin monies based upon their customers' positions. Clearing margins act as financial safeguards to ensure that clearing member firms perform on their customers' open futures and options contracts. These margins are recommended by the clearinghouse margin committee and set by the board of directors. Clearing margins are distinct from the brokerage margins that individual buyers and sellers of futures and options contracts are required to deposit with their brokers. (Refer to Chapter 5 for more information on these margins.)

The original clearing margin is the amount a clearing member firm must have on account at the time an order is placed to buy or sell a futures contract. On the Chicago Board of Trade and most other exchanges, a clearing member's original clearing margin deposits are based on the net long (buy) or net short (sell) futures position. As an example, a clearing member firm with a short position of 10 corn futures contracts and a long position of 4 corn futures contracts would be required to deposit margin money on the net short position of 6 corn contracts.

The clearinghouses of the Chicago Mercantile Exchange and the New York Mercantile Exchange require margin deposits on both the long and short futures positions in each commodity rather than on the net position.

(For options contracts, however, margin is required only from the short position. Options on futures are explained more fully in Chapter 12.)

Margin levels are set consistent with market risks. Naturally, market participants assuming greater price risks are required to post more margin.

Clearing margins may be posted in three forms or in combinations of the following: cash, interest-bearing obligations of the federal government, and letters of credit issued by approved banks. The member firm does not have access to this money until it is released by the clearinghouse.

As a member's position changes from day to day, so does the required margin. After each trading session, the clearinghouse recomputes the margin requirement for each clearing member. Every evening, the clearinghouse provides a margin statement to the clearing firm. If a net position increases, additional margin must be deposited before the market opens the next day. If a net position declines, excess margin money may be returned to the clearing member firm. Some firms prefer to keep their surplus margin in reserve rather than to draw it back on a daily basis.

In most cases, original margins are sufficient to cover daily maximum price fluctuations. At the Chicago Board of Trade, original margin deposits are collected within 24 hours of the time a trade is executed (in some instances, within 10 hours).

In periods of great market volatility or in the case of high-risk accounts, the clearinghouse can call on a member firm to deposit additional margin money at anytime during a trading session to cover adverse price changes. This call for additional money is known as a *variation margin call,* and, within one hour, the member firm must pay the amount called for by wire transfer of funds. Variation margin is called twice per day and more if volatile markets exist. For example, the Board of Trade Clearing Corporation collected variation margin three or four times on October 19, 1987—the day the U.S. stock market fell 508 points. Once again, these payments had to be made within one hour of the margin call, even if the clearing member firm's customer had not deposited additional funds. This amount is applied to the settlement for the day and does not go into the standing or original margin account.

In this way, the clearinghouse maintains very tight control over margins as prices fluctuate. It ensures that sufficient margin money is on deposit at all times—another means of ensuring the financial integrity of futures contracts.

Monitoring the Markets

Clearinghouses monitor the markets as well as the members' positions. The Board of Trade Clearing Corporation, for example, uses a sophisticated computer risk-analysis program known as *Simulation Analysis of Financial Exposure* (SAFE). SAFE monitors the risk of clearing members and large-volume traders. It evaluates the risk of open positions by calculating the risk a firm is carrying if there is a change in market prices or volatility.

Guaranteeing Funds

In the unlikely event that a clearing member firm cannot meet its margin call and to prevent contract default, clearinghouses guarantee funds. These funds are pools of money deposited or stock purchases in the clearinghouse. The size of funds ranges from a few million dollars at some futures exchanges to over $100 million at the Board of Trade Clearing Corporation (BOTCC). At the BOTCC, there are additional funds available, making it possible to draw funds in excess of $375 million—the largest in the futures industry. The two Chicago clearing organizations, the Board of Trade Clearing Corporation and Chicago Mercantile Exchange Clearing House, have never experienced a default on a futures contract.

Every day, the clearinghouse settles each account on its books. All futures accounts, long or short, whether traded during the most recent session or not, are adjusted daily as to gain or loss. This debiting and crediting on the basis of price changes, known as *marking-to-market*, takes place following the close of each trading day. Those accounts short of funds are required to deposit additional margin.

Accounts are adjusted by calculating the difference between the day's settlement price and the price at which the position was initiated. In the case of options on futures, the full premium is received from the buyer and passed on to the seller.

Although the method of determining the settlement price varies among exchanges, the following methods are the most common. When there is a single price at the close of trading, that price becomes the settlement price. However, in the flurry of last-minute trading, it is common for several separate transactions to be made at different but closely related prices. In this circumstance, averaging the closing range is the most common way to determine the settlement price.

Delivery

Another responsibility of clearinghouses is overseeing the delivery process. While all futures positions are either offset before a contract expires or delivered against the contract, the vast majority are settled by offsetting trades, and only 1 to 3 percent result in delivery of the actual commodity.* Yet, the fact that buyers and sellers can take or make delivery helps assure that futures prices reflect the actual cash value of the commodity.

Clearinghouses generally do not make or take delivery of the actual commodity.† Rather, they provide the mechanism that enables sellers to make delivery to qualified buyers. The delivery process varies somewhat from exchange to exchange but, in all cases, delivery is possible by

---

*The advent of index-based futures contracts, such as stock index and municipal bond index futures, has seen the development of cash-settled contracts. Rather than specifying delivery of a commodity or financial instrument, transactions are settled in cash based on the actual value of the index on the last trading day.
†For some contracts, the clearinghouse does make or take delivery. For example, the Chicago Mercantile Exchange and MidAmerica Commodity Exchange will make or take delivery on currencies and cattle futures.

completing a series of steps. As an example, the following three-day delivery process is required by the rules of the Chicago Board of Trade.

Day 1 (Position Day)

The clearing firm representing the seller notifies the Board of Trade Clearing Corporation that its customer wants to deliver on a futures contract.

Day 2 (Notice Day)

Prior to the market opening on Day 2, the clearing corporation matches the buyer with the oldest reported long position to the delivering seller. The clearing corporation then notifies both parties.

The clearing firm representing the seller prepares and sends an invoice to the Board of Trade Clearing Corporation for distribution to the clearing firm representing the buyer. The seller's clearing firm also must prepare a copy of the invoice for the clearing corporation. The buyer's clearing firm receives the seller's invoice from the clearing corporation.

Day 3 (Delivery Day)

The buyer's clearing firm presents the delivery notice with a certified check for the amount due at the office of the seller's clearing firm. Upon receiving a check from the buyer's clearing firm, the seller's clearing firm gives the warehouse receipt[‡] to the buyer's clearing firm.

Market Information

Daily recording of trading volume and open interest is a service provided by all clearing organizations. (Trading volume is the number of contracts traded each delivery month of every futures and options contract, and open interest is the number of open futures and options positions.)

Exchanges are required to make this information available to the general public, on a daily basis, according to the Commodity Exchange Act, as amended in 1974. Open interest and trading volume are used by the Commodity Futures Trading Commission to compile monthly reports that analyze traders' positions based upon the size of accounts and whether trades are used for speculative or hedging purposes. Both daily and monthly open interest and volume information are reported in the newspaper.

Conclusion

The clearing process is a vital function of all futures exchanges. The financial requirements of clearing member firms as well as the policies enforced by clearinghouses preserve the financial integrity of the markets.

[‡]Only certain commodities require a transfer of a warehouse receipt.

U.S. futures markets have a long history of self-regulation that dates from the mid-1800s, predating both state and federal regulation.

The rules and regulations of the exchanges are extensive and are designed to support competitive, efficient, liquid markets. Most state and federal regulation, which began shortly after futures trading developed in the United States, has been designed to enforce self-regulation by the exchanges.

This chapter reviews some of the principal rules and trading practices followed on most U.S. exchanges, as well as federal and industry regulation of futures trading. Keep in mind that rules may vary among exchanges due in part to their highly diverse histories and patterns of development, but those described here are based on the Rules and Regulations of the Chicago Board of Trade.

Note that the rules and regulations are scrutinized continuously by the exchanges, and are periodically amended to reflect the needs of market users. The adoption of many new rules and regulations, as well as the amendment of existing ones, requires the approval of the Commodity Futures Trading Commission (CFTC), the U.S. federal regulatory agency for futures and options on futures trading.

REGULATION OF FUTURES TRADING

Exchange,
Industry,
Federal
Regulation

7

EXCHANGE REGULATION

Exchange rules and regulations cover many areas of futures trading—from contract specifications to trading practices to arbitration procedures. Following are some of the more important rules, which should serve as a useful guide to exchange self-regulation.

Open Market

Transactions must be made in the open market. This means all bids and offers are made in an exchange-approved trading arena—either in the trading pit by open outcry or on an electronic trading system—and available to all members present.

Nonclearing and Clearing Members

Nonclearing members must follow certain clearing procedures when trading futures and options on futures contracts. Most importantly, nonclearing members are required to clear all trades through a clearing member firm; the clearing member is liable for those trades until the clearing arrangement is officially terminated through procedures specified by the exchange. Immediately following a trade, a nonclearing trader or broker must report the name of his clearing firm to the trader on the other side of the transaction. (Clearing operations are described in Chapter 6.)

At the Chicago Board of Trade, buyers and sellers must check a trade not longer than 15 minutes after the time it is executed and provide the name of their clearing member. The Chicago Mercantile Exchange and most others also require that this information be exchanged within a reasonable amount of time following a trade.

Nonmembers: Floor Personnel

Nonmember employees on the trading floor have very specific job descriptions as defined in the rules and regulations of most futures exchanges. For example, floor clerks are authorized to deliver and receive messages, write broker cards from endorsed orders, operate order-processing terminals, and perform other routine clerical and telephone functions. Trade checkers may only check trades.

Position Limits

Position and daily trading limits are designed to ensure the market's financial integrity and reduce price volatility. A position limit is the maximum number of futures and/or options on futures contracts that may be held by a market participant and is determined by the CFTC and/or the exchange where the contract is traded. The daily trading limit refers to the maximum price range allowed each day for a contract and is set by the exchange.

Limits on the long or short positions of a given commodity are usually listed in the contract specifications. Positions at or above specific levels must be reported daily to the CFTC and/or the exchange where the contract is traded.

Position limits apply to speculative as well as hedging accounts; however, there are certain procedures a hedger can take to expand his position limits.

Daily trading limits are listed in the contract specifications. Trading is prohibited outside of an established price range, which is based on the settlement price of the previous business day plus or minus an amount set for each futures contract.* For example, if soybeans close at $6.64 per bushel and the normal daily trading limit is 30 cents per bushel, beans may be traded within a range of $6.34 and $6.94 on the following business day.

During periods of extreme price volatility, the Chicago Board of Trade has a variable limits provision under which the price limit of a futures contract is automatically expanded by 50 percent of the daily price limit. The provision applies when three or more delivery months of a given commodity in a particular contract year experience limit bid or limit sellers moves† on a single day. For instance, the daily trading limit for soybeans is 30 cents per bushel. Under the variable limits provision, the daily trading limit in soybeans for the following business day would be increased by 50 percent of the normal daily limit, or 15 cents. The variable price limit would then be 45 cents.

Variable limits stay in effect for a minimum of three days. If the markets move limit bid or limit sellers on the third day, the expanded position limits continue for another three days. If the markets do not move limit bid or limit sellers on the third day, price limits drop back to their original level.

Other exchanges, including the Chicago Mercantile Exchange, also have provisions for expanded daily trading limits in periods of unusual price volatility. These regulations are complex, and the rule books of the individual exchanges should be consulted.

Types of orders that are permitted vary among the exchanges. The following are acceptable for execution on the Chicago Board of Trade:

Types of Orders

- ◆ Market orders to buy or sell
- ◆ Closing orders to buy or sell
- ◆ Limit orders to buy or sell
- ◆ Stop orders to buy or sell

---

*For some futures contracts, the price limit does not apply on or after two business days preceding the first business day of the current month.
†Limit bid: The market closes at an upward price limit on an unfilled bid.
Limit sellers: The market closes at a downward price limit on an unfilled offer.

♦ Stop-limit orders to buy or sell
♦ Limit or market spread orders

On several exchanges, various time and contingent orders are generally prohibited on the last day of trading,‡ but are otherwise accepted. (Various orders and their purposes are discussed in more detail in Chapter 5. Consult the rule books of the individual exchanges to determine the kinds of orders that each exchange accepts.)

Price Reporting

Both traders in a transaction are generally responsible for ensuring that the market reporter has accurately recorded the price of the trade. In those market situations when a price is not recorded by a market reporter, exchange pit committees are authorized to insert prices. However, each exchange has specific rules governing price insertion.

On the Chicago Board of Trade, pit committees are authorized to change an opening range only within 30 minutes after an opening and to change a closing range only within 15 minutes of the close of that day's market. Only the board of directors has the authority to insert prices that affect an open, high, low, or closing price after that time, though it is not a common practice. The Chicago Mercantile Exchange has a 15-minute limit on inserting prices after the opening and a 5-minute limit on the close. Most other exchanges follow similar practices.

Offenses

The following acts are considered offenses on most exchanges, and will likely result in suspension, expulsion, or fines for the members or member firms:

♦ Violating any rule or regulation of the exchange regarding the conduct or business of members, or violating any agreement made with the exchange
♦ Fraud, dishonorable conduct, behavior inconsistent with equitable principles of trade, and default
♦ Making a fictitious transaction or giving an order for the purchase or sale of a futures contract that, when executed, would involve no change in ownership
♦ Purchases or sales, or offers to buy or sell, that are made to upset market equilibrium and result in prices that do not reflect fair market values
♦ A false statement made to the board of directors, a standing or special committee, or on a membership application

‡The business day prior to the last seven business days of the delivery month.

- Any act detrimental to the interest or welfare of the exchange such as reckless and unbusinesslike conduct
- Circulating rumors to manipulate the market and affect prices
- Failing or refusing to submit books or papers to the board of directors or to a standing or special committee when requested
- Attempted extortion; trading systematically against orders or positions of one's customers; manipulation of prices or attempts to corner the market; giving out false market information; trading or accepting margins after insolvency; trading for the account of a clearing member, or giving up the name of any clearing member without authority; failing to comply with an order of the Arbitration Committee

Most exchanges also have rules dealing with trading behavior. The following practices are prohibited:

Trading Behavior Rules

- Disclosing an order at any time, or divulging, trading against, or taking the other side of any order revealed to a member through his relationship with a customer
- Trading with yourself
- For a member to withhold from the open market any order or part of any order for the convenience of another member
- Buying or selling as an accommodation to another trader (such as prearranged trading) at any time; using one order to fill another order or part of an order; buying or selling simultaneously at a prearranged price
- For a broker to trade for his own account (at the market price or customer's requested price) before filling customer orders
- For traders to fail to make sure that the market reporter has accurately recorded the price of a trade

FCM Responsibility

Futures Commission Merchants (FCMs) and floor brokers are liable for losses that occur due to error or mishandling of a customer order.

Responsibility for the customer account is assumed immediately after accepting an order. If an error occurs, the floor broker, FCM, or both are held responsible for the loss, depending on who made the error.

Grievances

Defaulting on Contracts

Chicago Board of Trade members who default on exchange contracts may be suspended until the contract is performed or the debt is satisfied. If the default is denied, then the member is entitled to arbitration of the claim.

Arbitration

The rules and regulations of most exchanges have long defined procedures for arbitration of disputes between members, and between members and customers. As early as 1859, the Chicago Board of Trade had arbitration committees to settle disputes that were voluntarily submitted.

Information regarding arbitration procedures can be obtained from the current rule books of the individual exchanges and current CFTC regulations.

Committees

Floor Governors

On most exchanges, floor trading practices are governed by one or more committees called the Floor Governors Committee, the Floor Practices Committee, or the Exchange Room Committee. These committees oversee the practices and conduct of members on the trading floor to ensure compliance with exchange rules and regulations.

When charged by the Floor Governors Committee with a violation, a member is entitled to a hearing before the Hearing Committee and faces possible disciplinary action. The Hearing Committee may reprimand, fine, and/or suspend a member from the trading floor. For serious violations, the Appellate Committee or board of directors may fine or suspend a member and the board of directors may expel the member from the exchange.

Business Conduct, Financial Compliance

Each of the exchanges has a committee governing the business conduct of its members and member firms. On the Chicago Board of Trade, the Business Conduct Committee is responsible for preventing manipulation of prices, the cornering of any futures contract, and overseeing the "back-office" activity of member firms.

The committee reviews staff investigations of transactions by members and member firms. The committee may examine members' books and papers and refer relevant cases to the Hearing Committee. Members are required to stop any activity or business conduct that the Hearing Committee finds unfair, in violation of exchange rules, or damaging to the exchange's reputation. Any member or member firm may appeal a disciplinary decision of the Hearing Committee by filing a written notice of appeal to the Appellate Committee within 10 business days.

Another important Chicago Board of Trade committee is Financial Compliance, which is responsible for monitoring and ensuring the capital and financial integrity of exchange members and member firms. The committee has authority over the financial organization of member firms and the financial interrelationship between member firms and their wholly owned affiliates.

Exchanges have various methods to enforce rules and monitor their markets. At the Chicago Board of Trade, for example, the Office of Investigations and Audits conducts surveillance programs, such as the Computerized Trade Reconstruction (CTR) system. Developed by the Chicago Board of Trade in 1986, CTR is able to pinpoint in any trade, the traders, the contract, the quantity, the price, and time of execution to the nearest minute. A program within the system—CTR PLUS®—is able to reconstruct the trading activities of members and member firms to detect patterns of conduct that might indicate rule violations.

In addition, since the 1980s, futures, stock, and options exchanges have been pursuing different ways to enhance market efficiency and regulatory compliance through cooperative efforts. This includes sharing financial information of common member firms as to their overall risk exposure in related markets. Also, registered firms of several different futures, stock, and options exchanges generally have been able to undergo a single financial audit by one exchange, which is then shared with the other exchanges.

Ensuring Compliance

FEDERAL AND INDUSTRY REGULATION

U.S. futures exchanges are required by state and federal laws to regulate the conduct of exchange members, member firms, and their employees. The obligations of the exchanges to enforce their own rules and regulations were enhanced in the 1900s with the passing of several federal acts, including the Grain Futures Act of 1922, the Commodity Exchange Act of 1936, the Commodity Futures Trading Commission Act of 1974, and various Futures Trading Acts.

The farm depression following World War I generated intense speculation in grain futures. The Futures Trading Act, the first federal law regulating futures trading, was passed in 1921. Shortly thereafter, it was declared unconstitutional by the Supreme Court. In 1922, Congress passed the Grain Futures Act, based on the interstate commerce clause of the Constitution.

Under the Grain Futures Act, futures trading in specific commodities could take place only on federally licensed exchanges. This legislation focused on exchange responsibility for preventing market manipulation by their members, member firms, and employees. If an exchange failed to adequately supervise market activity, its license could be revoked.

Grain Futures Act of 1922 and Amendments

Commodity Exchange Act of 1936

U.S. Department of Agriculture (USDA) studies over a period of several years led to the introduction of a number of amendments designed to strengthen the government's regulatory powers. In 1936, these revisions and additions to the law were consolidated in new legislation, the Commodity Exchange Act, which extended regulation from the grains and flaxseed to cotton and other agricultural commodities.

The new act created the Commodity Exchange Commission, which was comprised of the Secretary of Agriculture, the Secretary of Commerce, and the Attorney General, or their designated representatives. The commission was responsible for: (1) licensing futures exchanges, (2) determining procedures for registering Futures Commission Merchants and floor brokers, (3) protecting customer funds, (4) setting position and trading limits for speculative trading, (5) prohibiting price manipulations, false market information, and illegal trading, and (6) enforcing the Commodity Exchange Act and dealing with violations.

The Commodity Exchange Act was administered by the Commodity Exchange Commission until 1947 when the Commodity Exchange Authority was established. In addition to administering the act, the Commodity Exchange Authority provided information on futures trading to the general public.

Changing Needs for Regulation

During the early 1970s, rising affluence in many of the world's industrially developed countries was coupled with declines in crop production in several major producing nations. During the same period, two devaluations of the U.S. dollar made imports of U.S. agricultural goods less expensive and stimulated foreign sales. The result was heavy new demand on reduced supplies of feed grains and vegetable protein. In less than three years, previously ample USDA Commodity Credit Corporation holdings of surplus grain shrunk significantly. By late 1974, it was widely estimated that world feed-grain supplies had dwindled to the level of a month's supply.

As supplies continued to shrink and demand and grain prices rose, the public and members of Congress began to question the existing regulation of the futures markets. There also were new pressures to extend regulation to other futures markets not covered by the Commodity Exchange Act, such as metals, lumber, and currencies.

In response, the government began a series of hearings in September 1973 on proposed regulatory changes. The result was the Commodity Futures Trading Commission Act of 1974.

CFTC Act of 1974

The new act amended the Commodity Exchange Act and created an independent Commodity Futures Trading Commission (CFTC) to replace the Commodity Exchange Authority of the USDA. Existing Commodity Exchange Authority and Commodity Exchange Commission personnel, records, and appropriations were transferred to the new commission. And, on April 21, 1975, the CFTC assumed federal regulatory authority over all commodity futures markets.

The agency's five full-time commissioners are appointed by the President with Senate confirmation. They serve staggered, five-year terms with one designated to serve as chairman. There are three staff divisions—Economic and Analysis, Trading and Markets, and Enforcement. Each division director reports to the commission chairman, who performs the daily administrative duties.

The legislation creating the CFTC contained a sunset provision under which the commission would have ceased to exist on September 30, 1978, unless it was reauthorized. Extensive hearings were conducted early in 1978, resulting in the Futures Trading Act of 1978, which extended the life of the agency for another four years. CFTC reauthorization continues on a regular basis. The most recent reauthorization occurred in 1992, and is subject to renewal in 1994. (See Chapter 18 for details.)

The Futures Trading Act of 1978 also expanded the jurisdiction of the CFTC, clarifying some earlier provisions of the Commodity Exchange Act.

Futures Trading Act of 1978

The amended Commodity Exchange Act gave the CFTC the authority to regulate trading in all futures contracts—those currently trading as well as those that will be traded in the future. Prior to 1974, several futures contracts—such as currencies, financial instruments, and metals—were not regulated by the federal government.

CFTC regulation of options on financial futures began in 1981 with the initiation of a pilot program. The success of this program led to the approval of nonagricultural options in 1982. Then, in 1984, the CFTC extended trading in options to agricultural futures.

Requirements of the CFTC Act

During the 1982 reauthorization of the CFTC, Congress adopted the Shad/Johnson Accord Index Act, developed by CFTC Chairman Johnson and SEC Chairman Shad, to define the jurisdiction of the CFTC and the Securities and Exchange Commission (SEC) over stock indexes.

The amendments gave the CFTC exclusive jurisdiction over stock index futures and options on stock index futures contracts. The SEC, on the other hand, is responsible for the trading of options on any security or index of securities or options on foreign currencies traded on a U.S. securities exchange.

Shad/Johnson Accord

The CFTC's regulatory powers extend to exchange actions and to the review and approval of futures contracts proposed by an exchange. Before a new contract is approved for trading, the CFTC must determine that a

CFTC Regulation of Exchange Actions

futures contract is in the public interest. In making that assessment, the commission examines how contracts are used commercially for pricing and hedging to ensure that they serve an economic purpose.

One of the first actions taken by the commission in 1975 was to redefine the term *hedge*. The definition was broadened to permit anticipatory hedging and cross-hedging within certain limits. Anticipatory hedging allows market users to buy or sell a futures contract before they actually own the cash commodity. Cross-hedging enables market users to hedge a cash commodity using a different but related futures contract when there is no futures contract for the cash commodity being hedged and the two markets follow similar price trends. For example, a hedger could use corn futures to hedge barley, or soybean meal futures to hedge fish meal.

Exchanges must submit all proposed trading rules and contract terms to the CFTC for approval. When reviewing trading rules, the commission tries to assure that the rule will not restrict competition, and may require the exchange to amend its proposal. Exchange regulations of major economic significance must be made available to the public, and are published in the Federal Register.

Delivery points for commodities that underlie futures contracts also are governed by the CFTC. The commission has the right to require an exchange to add or change delivery locations when necessary.

Review of Exchange Actions

Review of exchange actions—denying membership, access privileges, or disciplining members—is another responsibility of the CFTC. In reviewing actions, the commission may affirm, modify, or set aside an exchange's decision. The commission also will take emergency action in the markets under certain conditions, such as actual or threatened market manipulation, or some other event that prevents the market from reflecting true supply/demand factors.

Regulation of Market Participants

The CFTC has broad regulatory powers over floor brokers and floor traders, Futures Commission Merchants (FCMs), Associated Persons (APs), Commodity Pool Operators (CPOs), Commodity Trading Advisors (CTAs), Introducing Brokers (IBs), and other market participants. For example, the commission is authorized to register Associated Persons and office managers, and to establish eligibility requirements that may include proficiency tests.

Federal authority to establish minimum financial requirements for Futures Commission Merchants was established in the Commodity Exchange Act of 1936. This same legislation required Futures Commission Merchants to segregate customers' margin deposits from company funds, and prohibited the use of one customer's funds to meet the margin requirements of another customer's account. These requirements are enforced today by the CFTC.

Arbitration

Exchanges are required to have arbitration or claims settlement procedures to handle customer claims against members or their employees. The act stipulates that the CFTC establish procedures that can be used as an alternative to exchange arbitration or civil court actions.

Reparations

The CFTC provides a reparation procedure for investors to assert claims based on violations of federal commodities law. Claims are heard by an administrative law judge whose decision can be reviewed by the CFTC. The procedure is flexible depending on the amount of money involved and the consent of the parties.

Powers of Injunction

The former Commodity Exchange Authority did not have the power to prohibit an exchange or exchange member from violating the Commodity Exchange Act. However, the Commodity Futures Trading Commission has that power and, in addition, may require an exchange or exchange member to perform a specific act. In the case of a violation that is also a criminal offense, criminal penalties may be imposed.

Daily Trading Record Requirements

Exchanges and their clearinghouses are required by the CFTC to maintain daily trading records. Also, exchanges must publish daily trading volume before the next day's opening, if practical.

National Futures Association

Under the CFTC Act of 1974, the futures industry was authorized to create registered futures associations. One such organization is the National Futures Association (NFA)—an industrywide, industry-supported, self-regulatory organization for the futures industry.

NFA was formally designated a registered futures association by the CFTC on September 22, 1981, and became operational on October 1, 1982. The primary responsibilities of NFA are to: (1) enforce ethical standards and customer protection rules, (2) screen futures professionals for membership, (3) audit and monitor futures professionals for financial and general compliance rules, (4) provide for arbitration of futures-related disputes, and (5) promote consumer and member education concerning NFA's role in the futures industry.

Customer Protection

To protect customers, NFA's ethical standards prohibit fraud, manipulative and deceptive acts and practices, and unfair business dealings. In addition, employees who handle discretionary accounts must follow procedures similar to CFTC requirements.

Membership Screening

Membership in NFA and CFTC registration are mandatory for Futures Commission Merchants, Commodity Trading Advisors, Commodity Pool Operators, floor brokers, and Introducing Brokers working with customer accounts as well as floor traders.

The CFTC requires associate membership in NFA and CFTC registration for most Associated Persons. Associated Persons solicit orders, customers, or customer funds for FCMs, IBs, CTAs, or CPOs. Membership is voluntary for futures exchanges, commercial banks, and commodity-related commercial firms.

Regulation of futures professionals begins with applicant screening. In addition to approving applicants for NFA membership, NFA is authorized by the CFTC to screen and approve applications for federal registration. Eligibility requirements are strict and specific, and are designed to ensure high standards of professional conduct and financial responsibility.

NFA staff handle the initial screening process. If an applicant is denied membership or registration, then the final decision is made by the NFA membership committee.

Proficiency testing is another NFA activity and required for CFTC registration. FCMs, IBs, CTAs, CPOs, and APs applying for registration must pass the National Commodity Futures Exam (Series 3), which tests their knowledge of trading futures and options and understanding of regulations. Floor brokers and traders also must pass written exams measuring their knowledge of the industry.

Financial and General Compliance

One of NFA's major functions is to establish, audit, and enforce minimum financial requirements for its FCM and IB members. No such requirements are currently established under NFA rules for other NFA members, such as CPOs and CTAs.

NFA conducts unannounced audits of all its members except those that are members of an exchange. In those cases, the audits are conducted by the exchange.

NFA audits are all-inclusive and cover every facet of the firm's futures-related business activities. Rule violations may be referred to Regional Business Conduct committees for appropriate disciplinary action.

General compliance rules require members to maintain complete and timely records, and segregate customer funds and accounts. Advertising and sales practices must be clear and honest, and customer orders equitably handled.

NFA financial requirements are patterned after existing financial standards of futures exchanges, as approved by the CFTC. NFA's computerized Financial Analysis Auditing Compliance Tracking System (FACTS) maintains financial records of NFA member firms and assists in monitoring their financial conditions.

Certain financial matters, such as the setting of margin levels, remain exclusively with the exchanges.

NFA has an Office of Compliance responsible for financial auditing and ethical surveillance. If an audit or investigation reveals a possible NFA rule violation, the infraction is reported to one of three regional Business Conduct committees. Each committee is made up of NFA members in the region where the member under investigation lives. The committee either closes the matter or serves a formal complaint against the member accused of violating a rule. In the latter case, the member must answer the complaint and is entitled to a hearing before the committee. If the committee decides against the member, he may appeal the decision to the Appeals Committee (a subcommittee of the NFA Board of Directors). The decision of the Appeals Committee is final, following a review by the CFTC.

NFA has authority to discipline any member (other than floor brokers or traders). NFA may expel, suspend, prohibit contact with members, censure, reprimand, or impose fines of up to $250,000 per violation. In emergency cases, when there is imminent danger to the markets, customers, or other members, NFA's president with the agreement of the Executive Committee or board can require the firm to stop doing business immediately. This action may be issued with or without a hearing. If a hearing is not held before the action is taken, a hearing will be scheduled as soon as possible before the appropriate Business Conduct Committee.

Arbitration

Another important function of NFA is to provide a centralized, uniform arbitration system. In most cases, when requested by a customer, arbitration is mandatory for all NFA member firms and their employees including FCMs, IBs, CPOs, CTAs, and APs. Counterclaims made by members and disputes between NFA members also may be heard by NFA arbitrators. Decisions of the arbitrators are generally final and may not be appealed to NFA. Alternatives to NFA arbitration include the CFTC's reparation procedure, exchange arbitration, or any other arbitration system mutually agreed to by the member and customer. After a particular method is chosen, no other may be used unless both parties agree.

Under NFA compliance rules, any NFA member or employee of a member is subject to disciplinary action for failure to comply with an arbitration decision.

Education

NFA educational efforts are directed to both members and the investing public. Members are assisted in complying with NFA rules and CFTC regulations. For the investing public, NFA produces materials concerning such topics as the fundamentals of futures trading and recognizing and avoiding investment fraud.

Structure

NFA is governed by a 42-member board of directors. This board makes decisions concerning priorities, policies, plans, funding, budget, and bylaws. It represents all sectors of NFA membership as follows: 14 directors represent Futures Commission Merchants; 3 directors represent Commodity Trading Advisors; 2 represent Commodity Pool Operators; 2 directors represent Introducing Brokers; 3 represent commodity-related commercial firms; 2 represent commercial banks; and 13 represent futures exchanges. The remaining 3 are public directors, that is, individuals with no present direct affiliation with the futures industry. All, except for the public directors, are selected by NFA members during the annual election held in January. Public directors are chosen by the board; all directors serve three-year terms.

Executive Committee

Although the full NFA board makes all major decisions, the direction and supervision of day-to-day operations are provided by an Executive Committee. The Executive Committee is comprised of 10 members including the NFA president, the chairman of the board of directors, plus 8 other members of the board. Of the 8 directors, 3 represent FCMs or IBs, 2 represent exchanges, 2 represent industry participants (CTAs, CPOs, commercial firms and banks), and there is 1 public director.

Both the board and Executive Committee are designed to provide balanced representation by membership category and geographic location. Thus, the number of directors allowed from the same NFA geographic region (Eastern, Central, or Western) is limited for each category.

A primary economic function of futures markets is price-risk management, the most common method of which is hedging. Hedging, in its simplest form, is the practice of offsetting the price risk inherent in any cash market position by taking an equal but opposite position in the futures market. Hedgers use the futures markets to protect their businesses from adverse price changes.

Price risk exists throughout all business, commerce, and finance. In agriculture, for instance, a prolonged drought affects a farmer's crop supply as well as the income he receives. But the drought also affects the price paid by grain companies for corn, wheat, soybeans, and oats. Those prices, in turn, directly impact consumer prices for cereals, cooking oils, salad dressings, bread, meat, poultry, and countless other items purchased at the local supermarket.

For manufacturers, an extended labor strike or the embargo of a raw material could result in a diminished supply and eventually a sharp price increase of a specific manufactured product. These economic factors directly affect the price manufacturers and consumers pay for an array of commodities ranging from gasoline and home heating oil to jewelry. For a bank, savings and loan, or other financial institution, an increase in interest rates affects the rate the institution pays on certificates of deposit as well as the cost of an automobile or home loan.

HEDGING IN THE FUTURES MARKETS

Economic Justification for the Futures Markets

8

There's no escaping the varying degrees of price fluctuation, i.e., risk, in every sector of today's economy: agriculture, manufacturing, business, and finance. Hedging in the futures markets minimizes the impact of these unwanted price changes.

PROTECTION AGAINST PRICE CHANGES

Although we may not give it much thought, hedging is a dominant feature of our daily lives. The buyer of an automobile acquires insurance to protect against collision damage and the possibility of total loss of that vehicle. A homeowner takes out an insurance policy to protect against possible fire or storm damage. Because the insurance can be purchased for a fraction of the home's value, the local bank or savings and loan is more willing to lend funds for the purchase of the home. Likewise, to guard against the cost of replacing an appliance, one may choose to purchase, for a minimal cost, an extended warranty covering part replacement and labor charges. Or, a family—contemplating the cost of college for a newborn son or daughter—may begin a savings program to help meet the rising cost of a higher education.

These everyday examples illustrate hedging by consumers—a defensive strategy to protect against unwanted price change and the possibility of total loss. Hedging functions the same in the futures markets. It is a conscious effort to reduce the price risk inherent in buying, selling, or even holding a cash market commodity.

Who Hedges with Futures

Hedgers are individuals or companies that own or are planning to own a cash commodity—corn, soybeans, wheat, U.S. Treasury bonds, notes, bills, etc.—and are concerned that the cost of the commodity may change before they either buy or sell it. Virtually anyone who seeks to protect cash market commodities from unwanted price changes can use the futures markets for hedging—farmers, grain elevator operators, merchandisers, producers, exporters, bankers, bond dealers, insurance companies, money managers, pension funds, portfolio managers, thrifts, manufacturers, and others.

For example, suppose a soybean processor agrees to sell soybean oil to a food manufacturer six months from now. Both agree on a price today even though the oil will not be delivered for six months. The soybean processor does not yet own the soybeans he will eventually process into oil, but he is concerned that soybean prices may rise during the next six months, causing him to lose money.

To hedge against the risk of rising prices, the soybean processor buys soybean futures contracts calling for the delivery of the soybeans in six months. When five and a half months have passed, the soybean processor purchases the soybeans in the cash market and, as feared, prices have risen. However, because he hedged in the futures market, the soybean processor can now sell his futures contracts at a profit, since futures prices also have increased. He uses the gain on the futures contracts to offset the higher cost of soybeans, protecting his profit on the sale of the soybean oil.

Hedging works the same way in the financial markets. Suppose a major financial institution holds a significant amount of long-term U.S. Treasury bonds. The firm's financial officers are concerned that interest rates may rise in the near term, causing a decline in the value of the bonds. Knowing there is a substantial risk in holding this unhedged cash position, they elect to sell U.S. Treasury bond futures.

A month later, as expected, interest rates rise and bond prices decline. In offsetting its futures position by purchasing U.S. T-bond futures, the firm succeeds in protecting the value of the cash bonds, because the profits from closing out the futures position offset the decline in the cash market value of the Treasury bonds.

Of course, the market does not always move as expected. But a hedger accepts that possibility even though he may forfeit the opportunity to make a gain in the market. To an experienced hedger, it is more important to establish a market objective that protects his investment rather than worry about the possibility of a missed profit opportunity.

Cash-Futures Relationship

Cash market transactions involve the purchase and sale of actual commodities at current prices. For instance, the term *cash corn* refers to the actual physical product—kernels of corn that are either fed to livestock or processed into various animal feeds, human food, or industrial products. Delivery of the commodity can be immediate or within a specific number of days of the transaction.

In the futures market, however, buyers and sellers agree to take or make delivery of a specific commodity at a predetermined place and time in the future. The date of the purchase or sale may be weeks or months away—hence the term *futures*.

What Is Basis?

The difference between the cash price of a commodity at a specific location and the price of a specific futures contract for the same commodity is defined as the *basis*. To calculate the basis, subtract the futures price from the cash price: cash price − futures price = basis. It is assumed, when speaking of basis, that one is referring to the nearby futures month (the contract month closest to delivery), unless otherwise specified.

For instance, if a country elevator operator in central Illinois buys soybeans from a farmer at $7.80 a bushel on October 3, and the November soybean futures contract is $7.90 on the same day, the basis at the local grain elevator would be 10 cents under (−10 cents) the November contract. If a Nebraska farmer is selling wheat, and the local cash price on June 10 is $4.10 a bushel and the July wheat futures contract is $3.60, the basis at the Nebraska location is 50 cents over (+50 cents) the July futures contract.

Calculating the basis for financial instruments is essentially the same. If the cash market price of a U.S. Treasury bond is 88-16,* and the June adjusted futures price is 90-22, the basis is 2-06 under the June contract.

Given the variety of U.S. Treasury bonds and notes that are eligible for delivery against the Chicago Board of Trade's U.S. Treasury bond and note futures contracts, a modification in calculating the basis occurs. This is done by adjusting the bond or note futures price to a futures-cash equivalent. The change to a cash equivalent is made using a conversion factor to compare the cash market Treasury bond or note with the 8 percent coupon standard of the T-bond or note futures contract. The conversion factor is multiplied by the futures price to obtain the cash equivalent.

Suppose in late February the March T-bond futures contract, which calls for a nominal 8 percent coupon, is priced at 67-02. The cash market price of a U.S. Treasury bond carrying a 12 percent coupon and maturing August 15, 2013, is 97-00.

Although there is a specific equation to calculate the conversion factors for T-bonds and T-notes, a booklet is available from the Chicago Board of Trade that lists the different conversion factors for cash market notes and bonds of varying maturities and coupon rates. In this case, assume the conversion factor of the 12 percent T-bond is 1.4251. Because cash and futures prices are quoted in 32nds, the first step in calculating the cash equivalent is converting the quoted futures price to a decimal ($67\frac{2}{32} = 67.0625$). The futures-cash equivalent is obtained then by multiplying the conversion factor by the futures price:

$$\text{Futures-cash equivalent} = 67.0625 \times 1.4251$$
$$= 95.57 \text{ or } 95^{18}\!/_{32}$$

Once the futures-cash equivalent is calculated, the basis is the difference between the cash price and the futures-cash equivalent:

Basis = (bond cash price) − (futures price × bond conversion factor)
Basis = 97-00 − 95-18 = $1^{14}\!/_{32}$

As these examples illustrate, the basis can be either positive or negative, depending upon whether the cash price is higher or lower than the futures price. If the basis moves from 10 to 1, it has become more negative (less positive). On the other hand, if the basis moves from −5 to 2, the basis has become more positive (less negative). If the cash and futures prices are the same, the basis is expressed as zero.

*T-bond futures contracts are quoted in 32nds but the prices generally are written as follows: $88^{16}\!/_{32} = 88\text{-}16$.

Factors Affecting Basis

There are a variety of factors that can cause the basis to change. If the demand for cash grain is strong and/or the available supply is small, cash market prices could rise relative to futures prices. However, if there is a large supply of grain and little demand, cash prices could fall relative to futures prices.

Other factors that affect the basis of ag commodities include:

♦ Carryover stocks from the previous year
♦ Expectations of the current year's production
♦ Supply and demand of comparable substitutes
♦ Foreign production
♦ Foreign demand
♦ Storage costs
♦ Availability of sufficient storage facilities
♦ Transportation costs
♦ Transportation problems
♦ Insurance costs
♦ Federal policies
♦ Seasonal price fluctuations

Similarly, several factors affect the basis for financial instruments. These factors include:

♦ The cost of credit, i.e., interest rates
♦ Federal Reserve Board monetary policies
♦ Fiscal policies reflected in the deficit (government spending less tax receipts)
♦ Time until expiration of the futures contract
♦ Cost of funding margin requirements
♦ Coupon of the cash market instrument being hedged against the 8 percent futures contract coupon standard
♦ Supply of deliverable cash market instruments
♦ Domestic and foreign demand for cash market instruments
♦ Inflationary expectations
♦ General level of business activity
♦ Seasonal factors (such as estimated quarterly tax payments by corporations and self-employed individuals)
♦ Liquidity of nearby versus distant month contracts

The basis cannot be predicted precisely, but it is generally less volatile than either the futures or cash price. By knowing the basis, the hedger replaces the risk of price fluctuation with the lesser risk of a change in the relationship between the cash and the futures price of the commodity. Even so, a change in the basis during the time of the hedge can influence the results of a transaction. Hedgers must pay close attention to this relationship. Without knowledge of the usual basis and basis patterns for a given commodity, it is impossible for a hedger to make a fully informed decision about whether to accept or reject a given price (cash or futures); whether, when, and in what delivery month to hedge; when to close a hedge; or when and how to turn an unusual basis situation into a possible profit opportunity.

Price Relationships: Grains

Grain generally is harvested within a span of a few months each year, but only a small portion is actually used at harvest. The rest is stored until needed for feeding, processing, exporting, and so forth. The expenses of storage—known as *carrying charges*—normally are reflected in futures prices for different delivery months. They include not only the cost of using storage facilities for the grain, but also such costs as insurance on the grain and interest on the invested capital.

Buyers usually are willing to pay a higher price for grain as the marketing year progresses to cover the carrying charges. Consequently, these carrying charges tend to be reflected in the price of futures contracts. More distant or deferred futures contracts tend to trade at higher prices than do nearby futures contracts. For example, futures prices for delivery within the same marketing year[†] are normally stair-stepped upward from one delivery month to the next. If the total cost of storing corn were, say, 4 cents per bushel a month, and if futures prices reflected the full carrying charge, the prices for the different delivery months might look something like this:

Dec	Mar	May	Jul	Sep
$2.00	$2.12	$2.20	$2.28	$2.36

This example illustrates normal market conditions. In reality, the market usually reflects less than full carrying charges or even negative carrying charges, which is referred to as an *inverted market*. An inverted market can occur for a variety of reasons, including a strong immediate

[†]The crop marketing year varies slightly with each ag commodity, but it tends to begin following harvest and end before the next year's harvest, e.g., the marketing year for soybeans begins September 1 and ends August 31. The futures contract month of November represents the first major new-crop marketing month and the contract month of July represents the last major old-crop marketing month for soybeans. At the beginning of the soybean marketing year, November is considered the nearby month, and subsequent contract months are referred to as *deferred months*.

demand for cash grain or the willingness of elevator owners to store grain for their own accounts at less than the full storage rate.

Price Relationships: Financial Instruments

The basis for debt instruments is almost totally dependent upon interest rates, so the historical basis behavior does not carry the same emphasis as it does for the grains. There are repetitive tendencies, however, within the financial markets. For example, those individuals and companies in the financial cash and futures markets know estimated quarterly tax payments due from corporations and self-employed individuals may have a tendency to unduly affect short-term (usually overnight) interest rates on the 15th of April, June, September, and December. These abrupt changes in short-term rates may impact long-term prices in both the cash and futures markets a day or two before and after the 15th.

In another case, the equity markets during the 7- to 10-day period marking the end of each calendar quarter (March, June, September, and December) are closely watched for changes in equity cash and futures prices. Because a portfolio manager's performance is sometimes measured against the Standard & Poor's 500 Index, managers often adjust their market positions (that is, sell losing positions and/or buy winning positions) before the end of the quarter and the subsequent release of reports to clients.

In the case of interest rate futures, deferred futures months (those that expire later in the year) are generally priced lower than the nearby futures month (the next contract month that will stop trading) in a normal market. On September 13, 1988, for example, U.S. Treasury bond futures prices closed at 88-22 (Dec '88); 88-03 (Mar '89); 87-16 (Jun '89); 86-30 (Sep '89); 86-13 (Dec '89); 85-29 (Mar '90); and 85-14 (Jun '90).

Furthermore, for interest rate futures, futures-cash equivalent prices are normally lower than cash prices, reflecting what is referred to as the *positive cost of carry*. The cost of carry reflects the actual costs of financing an investment. It includes any interest payments received, less any short-term borrowing costs, if any, and transaction costs.

The cost of carry can be either positive or negative. If it is positive, as illustrated in the example below, it can be profitable to hold the instrument until delivery. Suppose the cost to finance a 12 percent $100,000 U.S. Treasury bond selling at par for one month is 10 percent. Under these circumstances, the investor earns $167 a month by holding the T-bond.

Annual coupon payment	$100,000 × 12%	= $12,000
Annual finance cost	$100,000 × 10%	= $10,000
Annual cost of carry	$ 12,000 − $10,000	= $ 2,000
Monthly cost of carry	$ 2,000 / 12	= $ 167

Under this "normal" market environment, the cash instrument is priced at a premium to the futures contract. Since these gains increase as the holding period increases, the nearby futures contract trades at a premium to the deferred futures month, as noted in the September 13, 1988, example of T-bond futures prices. On the other hand, if the cost of carry is negative, the investor loses money holding the investment until delivery. Suppose the cost of financing the same security rises to 14 percent. In this instance, the cost of carry is negative and the investor loses $167 a month carrying the bond until delivery.

Annual coupon payment	$100,000 × 12%	= $12,000
Annual finance cost	$100,000 × 14%	= $14,000
Annual cost of carry	$ 12,000 − $14,000	= ($ 2,000)
Monthly cost of carry	($ 2,000) / 12	= ($ 167)

To compensate for his negative carry, the investor trades the cash instrument at a discount to the futures contract. Since carrying costs rise as the holding period increases, the futures price of the nearby contract month trades at a discount to the deferred contract month.

Yield Curve

The cost of carry—the relationship between long-term and short-term interest rates—is reflected in the yield curve. The yield curve is a chart or graph visually depicting yield to maturity[‡] for debt instruments of different maturities but with the same rating. U.S. government debt instruments (Treasury bills, notes, and bonds) are most often used because

Positive Yield Curve

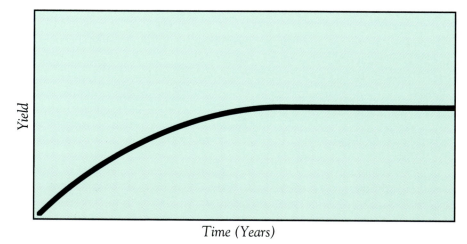

Time (Years)

[‡]Yield to maturity is the rate of return an investor receives if an interest-bearing instrument is held until its maturity date.

all government debt carries the same credit rating and offers investors maturities ranging from days up to 30 years.

The yield curve is positive when long-term rates are higher than short-term rates. In such an environment, investors are willing to accept a lower yield on short-term investments and are compensated for lending their money for an extended time period.

However, when short-term rates are higher than rates on long-term investments, the yield curve is negative or inverted. A negative yield curve typically occurs during inflationary periods, when heavy credit demand pushes short-term rates higher than long-term rates.

Negative Yield Curve

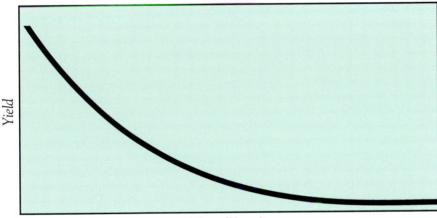

Time (Years)

A crucial relationship exists between interest rates and prices in both the cash and the futures markets: when interest rates rise, the prices of interest rate futures and cash market instruments decline; when interest rates decline, prices of interest rate futures and cash market instruments rise. (This inverse relationship is discussed in Chapter 17.)

DELIVERY: CASH AND FUTURES LINK

The fundamental reason why hedging works is that changes in futures prices generally track changes in cash prices. The link between futures and cash prices is the delivery/settlement process, which is unique to the futures market. As a matter of fact, delivery links cash and futures so closely that the futures price equals the cash price at expiration at the futures delivery location.

Delivery

Futures contracts for traditional commodities, such as grains, require all market participants holding contracts at expiration to either take or make delivery of the underlying commodity. This responsibility to make or take delivery of the actual commodity forces futures prices to reflect the actual cash value of the commodity.

Like other contractual obligations, predetermined delivery steps must be completed within a specific time period to comply with the terms of the agreement. For example, the Chicago Board of Trade specifies that in the case of corn, the deliverable grade is No. 2 Yellow or permitted substitutions at differentials established by the exchange. Delivery of financial instruments also must satisfy established criteria. A particular U.S. Treasury bond is eligible for delivery against the T-bond futures contract if it has a remaining time to maturity, or time to call if callable, of at least 15 years as of the first day of the delivery month.

Cheapest Deliverable Bond or Note

The pricing of futures contracts on government debt instruments (e.g., 5-year notes, 10-year notes, and bonds) remains highly correlated to the value of the deliverable instrument at expiration. Both bond and note contracts are designed to accept a range of issues for delivery, and, at any given time, one of these issues will be more economical than the others to acquire in the cash market and deliver against the futures contract. Because anyone trading bond futures can assume that a seller will deliver the most economical instrument, these contracts tend to trade to the price of that issue. Therefore, in addition to following the credit markets in general, it is important to track the price of whichever bond or note is least expensive to deliver at any point in time.

One technique for identifying the cheapest bond or note to deliver against a particular contract is to identify which bond has the smallest basis. But it is important to remember that price relationships between cash market instruments change daily. Therefore, reconfirming the cheapest deliverable bond or note at the close of each trading session is essential. This method, however, is only a quick rule-of-thumb procedure.

Cash Settlement

Futures contracts that track indexes (e.g., stock or bond index futures contracts) are cash settled. Cash-settled futures contracts are specifically designed to converge with the value of the underlying index at expiration, ensuring that delivery month pricing remains correlated to the underlying index.

While delivery acts as a link between cash and futures prices, only about 3 percent of all futures contracts are actually delivered. Instead, most are offset before they expire. To offset a futures position, a hedger takes a second futures position opposite his initial transaction. For instance, if an open position is established with the sale of five July wheat contracts, that position can be closed with an offsetting transaction—the purchase of five July wheat contracts. In other words, most futures traders use the futures market as a pricing mechanism; few actually deliver or take delivery of the cash commodity.

Arbitrage

When cash prices are higher than the futures prices, or vice versa, traders generally buy the lower-priced, or "cheaper," instrument and sell in the higher-priced, or "dearer," instrument, thereby quickly minimizing any price disparities. If cash prices are well below futures prices (after carrying costs are netted out), then a trader can sell the futures contract, buy the cash instrument, and make a profit. Because many traders attempt to capitalize on these price distortions, their actions have the net effect of forcing prices back into line.

This trading practice is known as *arbitrage*. Arbitrage is crucial to preserving the relationship between the cash and futures markets and helps ensure that the basis approaches zero by the time the contract expires. Without this equilibrium, it would be impossible for hedgers to transfer their unwanted risk because the futures contract might have little, if any, price correlation to the cash market.

Exchange for Physicals

In addition to making or taking delivery of a commodity, hedgers can enter into an exchange for physicals (EFP) transaction. Also known as *against actuals* or *versus cash*, EFPs generally are used by two hedgers who want to "exchange" futures for cash positions. EFPs are the only type of futures transaction allowed to take place outside the trading pit and are permitted according to specific exchange and Commodity Futures Trading Commission rules.

For instance, assume a grain exporter commits to a forward sale of grain and simultaneously hedges with a futures purchase. On the day he must acquire the grain for shipment, he makes a cash bid to an elevator operator expressed in basis. The elevator operator also has hedged, but with a short futures position to protect against a possible decline in value of the stored grain. Both the exporter and elevator operator agree to the basis.

The elevator operator (short hedger) delivers the actual cash grain to the exporter (long hedger) in exchange for a long futures position. That long position offsets the elevator's initial short futures position, thus ending the hedge. The grain exporter, in turn, acquires the actual grain needed for shipment and assumes a short position, which automatically offsets his initial long futures position.

The price of the cash grain contracted between the elevator operator and grain exporter is determined by the agreed-upon basis plus the agreed-upon price at which the futures contracts were exchanged. For example, if December corn futures were exchanged at $2.50 and the basis is 10 cents under (−10 cents), then the cash price agreed to in the EFP would be $2.40.

EFPs involving financial instruments, usually fixed-income instruments, frequently occur. Institutions with opposite cash-futures positions find it profitable and convenient to use U.S. Treasury bonds, notes, or bills in EFP transactions.

Exchange for physicals are important to commercial users because if both the long and short hedger were required to liquidate their futures positions by open outcry auction in the pit, they might have to do so at different prices. This would mean that the effectiveness of the agreed-upon basis for both buyer and seller would be lost. Consequently, many cash commodity dealers who trade the basis often specify when trading the cash market commodity that they will do so only against an exchange of futures.

BASIC HEDGING STRATEGIES

Hedging in the futures market is a two-step process. Depending upon the hedger's cash market situation, he will either buy or sell futures as his first position. The hedger's next step will be to offset his opening position before the futures contract expires by taking a second position opposite the opening transaction. The contract in both the opening and closing positions must be the same commodity, number of contracts, and delivery month.

If a hedger's first position involves the sale of futures contracts, it is referred to as a *selling*, or *short*, *hedge*. On the other hand, if the hedger's first position involves the purchase of futures contracts, it is referred to as a *long*, or *buying*, *hedge*.

Institutions and individuals use selling, or short, hedges as a temporary substitute for a later cash market sale of the underlying commodity, and the purpose of the short hedge is to lock in a selling price. With financial instruments, primarily fixed-income assets such as U.S. Treasury bonds, the selling hedge not only locks in a sale price, it also locks in a yield because of the price/yield correlation between interest rates and price.

The purchasing hedge, or long hedge, is used by institutions and individuals planning to buy the actual cash commodity at a later date. The purpose of the long hedge is to establish a fixed purchase price. With financial instruments, the long hedge not only establishes a purchase price, it locks in a yield.

For ease of explanation, basis is not taken into consideration in the following strategies. There is one exception—the short soybean hedge. As shown in that example, a change in basis affects a hedger's ultimate price. Because of this, in any real-life hedge transaction, traders include basis analysis in their hedging programs.

Selling Futures for Protection Against Falling Bond Prices

Consider a primary dealer in government securities who has just bought $1 billion of U.S. Treasury bonds (10¾ percent maturing August 2005) in the recent auction for 99-00.** Before the dealer completes its intermediary role of selling the bonds to the retail market, interest rates could rise forcing bond prices down. To manage its exposure, the dealer initiates a short hedge by selling 10,000 Dec T-bonds at 83-00.

As expected, interest rates rose, causing the cash market value of the T-bonds to fall by $90,000,000 to 90-00. However, the fund manager offset some of the decline with a gain in his T-bond futures position. Remember, the initial futures position was a sale; to close the position, the futures contracts were bought, at a lower price of 75-00.

Cash	Futures
Sep	
Holds $1,000,000,000 T-bonds at 99-00, or $990,000,000 total	Sells 10,000 Dec T-bond contracts at 83-00, or $830,000,000 total
Nov	
Market value falls to 90-00, or $900,000,000	Buys back 10,000 Dec T-bond contracts at 75-00, or $750,000,000 total
Result	
($90,000,000)	$80,000,000

This and other examples in this chapter do not include commission or transaction costs.

Because the futures position produced a profit, the cash market loss was almost entirely offset. And, the results of this hedge could have been

**In this example, the size of the T-bond futures contract equals $100,000 worth of U.S. Treasury bonds, and prices are quoted in ½₂ of a percent of the contract size. A price quote of 99-00 means the contract is worth 99 percent of $100,000 or $99,000. A ½₂ of a percent change of $100,000 equals $31.25 ($100,000 ×.01)/32. So, a price quote of 99-16 (or 99¹⁶⁄₃₂) equals $99,500 (($31.25 × 16) + $99,000).

improved by "adjusting" the number of futures contracts used to hedge the cash market position.

Weighted Hedge

To compensate for the greater decline in the dollar value of a cash bond versus the decline in the futures price, a weighted hedge is used. In a weighted T-bond hedge, one way to determine the number of futures contracts needed to effectively hedge a cash position is by multiplying the conversion factor of the T-bond by the par value of the cash bonds divided by the par value of the futures contract. In this example, the conversion factor for T-bonds maturing August 15, 2005, is 1.2495.

$$\text{Number of futures contracts} = 1.2495 \times (\$1,000,000,000/\$100,000)$$
$$= 1.2495 \times 10,000$$
$$= 12,495$$

In this instance, suppose the portfolio manager rounds 12,495 to the lowest whole thousand, 12,000. Given the same situation in the previous example, the results obtained using the weighted hedge are significantly different.

Cash	Futures
Sep Holds $1,000,000,000 T-bonds at 99-00, or $990,000,000 total	Sells 12,000 Dec T-bond contracts at 83-00, or $996,000,000 total
Nov Market value falls to 90-00, or $900,000,000 total	Buys back 12,000 Dec T-bond contracts at 75-00, or $900,000,000 total
Result ($90,000,000)	$96,000,000

The advantage of using the weighted hedge is clear. The portfolio manager not only offset the $90 million decline in the cash market value of the Treasury bonds, but realized a net profit of $6 million. **Note:** Since hedging is a defensive strategy, it is unlikely to produce net profit results such as those just illustrated. Nonetheless, the example illustrates how futures are used to offset the risk of holding U.S. government securities.

A farmer can use the futures markets to establish a price for his crop long before he sells it. But to do so requires calculating the basis.

Assume in June a farmer expects to harvest at least 10,000 bushels of soybeans during September. By hedging, he can lock in a price for his soybeans in June and protect himself against the possibility of falling prices.

At the time, the cash price for new-crop soybeans is $6 and the futures price of November soybean futures is $6.25. The delivery month of November marks the beginning of the new-crop marketing year for soybeans. The current basis of 25 cents under is weaker than the historical harvest level and the farmer sees the potential to gain if the basis becomes less negative between now and the time he sells cash beans.

With this market information, the farmer short hedges his crop by selling two November 5,000-bu. soybean futures at $6.25. (Typically, farmers do not hedge 100 percent of their expected production, as the exact number of bushels produced is unknown until harvest. In this scenario, the producer expects to produce more than 10,000 bushels of soybeans.)

By the beginning of September, cash and futures prices have fallen and the basis became less negative moving from -25 cents to -23 cents. When the farmer sells his cash beans to the local elevator for $5.72 a bushel, he lifts his hedge by purchasing November soybean futures at $5.95. The 30-cent gain in the futures market offsets the lower price he receives for his soybeans in the cash market, making his net selling price $6.02 per bushel.

Cash	Futures	Basis
Jun		
Price for new-crop soybeans at $6.00/bu	Sells 2 Nov soybean contracts at $6.25/bu	−$0.25
Sep		
Sells 10,000 bu soybeans at $5.72/bu	Buys 2 Nov soybean contracts at $5.95/bu	−$0.23
Result	Sep cash sale price	$5.72/bu
	Futures gain	0.30/bu
	Net selling price	$6.02/bu

Had the farmer not hedged, he only would have received $5.72 a bushel (the September cash price)—30 cents lower than the price he received. Since the basis strengthened from 25 cents under the November contract to 23 cents under, the farmer's selling price was actually 2 cents higher than his initial price objective of $6 a bushel. If the basis had become more negative instead, the farmer's selling price would have been lower than his expected price objective, but he would have been protected from the drop in price, since he was hedged.

Long Hedge to Establish the Price of Silver

Suppose a film manufacturer wants to establish a ceiling price for the 20,000 troy ounces of silver he plans to purchase during December and January. Anticipating a price increase, he would like to take advantage of the current cash price of $5.21 per troy ounce but does not want to buy the silver right now.

On June 15, silver futures for December delivery are trading at $5.71 per troy ounce. The manufacturer decides to purchase 20 December silver futures contracts.

Several months elapse, with silver prices continuing to rise. The manufacturer decides to purchase silver in the cash market at $9 and close his futures position by selling 20 December silver contracts at $9.45.

Cash	Futures
Jun	
Needs 20,000 oz of silver in Dec.; silver at $5.21/troy oz	Buys 20 Dec silver contracts at $5.71/troy oz (contract size: 1,000 troy oz)
Nov	
Acquires 20,000 oz of silver at $9.00/troy oz	Closes long position by selling 20 Dec silver contracts at $9.45/troy oz
Result	
Nov cash sale price	$9.00/troy oz
Futures gain	$3.74/troy oz
Net purchase price	$5.26/troy oz

In this instance, the futures gain of $3.74 per troy ounce cushioned the cash price increase, resulting in an additional cost of only 5 cents per troy ounce from what he initially expected to pay. By hedging, the manufacturer only paid $5.26 per troy ounce versus the $9 per ounce he would have had to pay if he had not hedged in the futures market.

Institutional investors frequently use the futures markets to reduce their exposure to the risk of fluctuating interest rates. For instance, the investment manager of an insurance company wants to take advantage of the high yield offered on U.S. Treasury notes in May but its cash inflows are weak due to unexpected policy payouts and low new policy sales. By September, it expects cash flows to return to normal. At the time, long-term September Treasury note futures are trading at 84-12, while the cash notes are priced at 99-16. Desiring to purchase the 8½ percent T-notes maturing May 15, 1997, he calculates that a weighted hedge requires 103 September T-note futures and buys them at 84-12 in May.

During the next couple of months, interest rates decline, raising the cash market value of the T-notes to 101-04. The price of the T-note futures rises to 86-00.

Long Hedging Using Treasury Note Futures

Cash	Futures
May	
T-notes at 99-16, or $9,950,000 total (for $10,000,000 par value)	Buys 103 Sep T-note contracts at 84-12, or $8,690,625 total
Aug	
T-notes at 101-04, or $10,112,500	Sells 103 Sep T-note contracts at 86-00, or $8,858,000 total
Result	
($162,500)	$167,375

Had the investment manager not established a long hedge, it would have cost him an additional $162,500 to purchase the Treasury notes in the cash market. Using T-note futures to hedge the purchase price, the investment manager not only avoided that additional cost, but generated a modest profit of $4,875, which reduced the effective purchase price.

While the previous example illustrates a hedge in which an investment manager made an additional profit on his futures position, this is not always the case. If T-note futures and cash prices had fallen, to 81-00 and 96-04, respectively, instead of rising, the investment manager would have lost money on his futures position. However, his losses on his futures contracts would be offset by a lower purchase price of T-notes in the cash market. Remember, one of the primary reasons hedging works is that cash and futures prices tend to follow parallel price trends. So if the cash price of a commodity falls, the futures price tends to follow a similar trend.

Cash	Futures
May	
T-notes at 99-16, or $9,950,000 total (for $10,000,000 par value)	Buys 103 Sep T-note contracts at 84-12, or $8,690,625 total
Aug	
T-notes at 96-04, or $9,612,500	Sells 103 Sep T-note contracts at 81-00, or $8,343,000 total
Result	
$337,500	($347,625)

Even though the investment manager may have lost $347,625 on his futures position, the purchase price of the T-notes in the cash market is $337,500 lower than he anticipated. He reminds himself that a few weeks ago when he initiated the hedge, he was satisfied with a purchase price of 99-16 on his cash bonds. In fact, the price hedgers pay for protection is the inability to take advantage of a price move after a hedge has been established. An experienced hedger is willing to forfeit this opportunity so he can have price protection.

Conclusion

Hedging is an indispensable risk-management tool for institutional and individual investors. The futures markets offer a forum for reducing undesired cash market price change. Because there is always some price risk in buying, selling, or holding a commodity for any length of time—grains, metals, even money itself—it is important that financial managers, farmers, grain companies, and other institutional and individual investors take advantage of the opportunities to protect their business profit margins against unwanted and unforeseen price fluctuation. The futures markets perform a critical economic function by offering hedgers an outlet to offset unwanted price risk in an increasingly volatile and globally linked marketplace.

Futures markets facilitate the transfer of price risk. On one side of this transfer is hedgers. Since they are involved in the cash market, hedgers are exposed to adverse price movements, i.e., price risk. This existing risk is assumed by speculators in the futures markets in anticipation of making a profit. This chapter examines various aspects of speculating in the futures markets including its economic contribution to the marketplace, types of speculators, and different trading strategies.

OVERVIEW OF SPECULATING

Most importantly, speculators assume the price risk that already exists for producers, users, or inventory holders of commodities or financial instruments. By taking and holding the other side of a hedger's trade, speculators add capital to the market and alleviate a hedger's exposure to price risk.

Speculators also add liquidity. In the futures market, without risk takers, short hedgers would only be able to trade with long hedgers. This would be a time-consuming and costly process, as finding a hedger with the exact opposite position is difficult. Bridging the gap between long and short hedgers—speculators provide an important market function.

SPECULATING IN THE FUTURES MARKETS

An Essential Ingredient for Liquidity

9

In addition to assuming risk and providing liquidity, speculators stabilize the market by dampening extreme price moves. For example, by purchasing futures when the price is too low, speculators add to demand. Increasing demand raises prices; thus, extreme price swings that might have occurred are softened by speculative activity.

Speculators also enhance the price discovery role of futures markets by bringing additional information to the marketplace. Since speculators are adding to their risk exposure, they gather and analyze data to judge whether a market price is too low or too high as well as to formulate expectations on market direction. This process adds information to the marketplace, which enhances the price-discovery function of futures markets.

There are many external factors speculators study that affect price. The price of grain, for example, changes along with supply and demand. Plentiful supplies at harvesttime usually mean a low price for grain. Higher prices may result from such things as adverse weather conditions during the growing season or an unexpected increase in export demand (both of which decrease grain supplies). Financial instruments fluctuate in price due to changes in interest rates and various economic and political factors.

Buy Low, Sell High

When speculating in futures markets, both profits and losses are possible—just as in owning the actual cash commodity. But speculators rarely have an interest in owning the cash commodity or financial instrument that underlies a futures contract. Speculators buy contracts when they believe prices are too low in order to profit by making an offsetting sale at a higher price. Speculators sell contracts when they believe prices are too high in order to profit by making an offsetting purchase at a lower price. What is unique about futures is that a speculator can enter the market by either purchasing a futures contract or by selling a futures contract. The speculator's decision of whether he should buy or sell first depends on his market expectations.

The profit potential is proportional to the speculator's skill in analyzing data and forecasting price movement. Potential gains and losses are as great for the selling (short) speculator as for the buying (long) speculator. Whether long or short, speculators can offset their positions and never have to make or take delivery of the actual commodity.

Types of Speculators

There are several ways of classifying speculators. The simplest, or most direct, is to refer to speculators as long or short. If a speculator is long futures, then he has purchased one or more futures contracts; if a speculator is short futures, then he has sold one or more futures contracts.

Large or Small

In addition to long or short, speculators may be classified by the size of their positions as designated by the Commodity Futures Trading Commission (CFTC). Speculators' positions must be reported periodically to the CFTC after they reach a specific number of open contracts. These speculators are classified as large position holders and include professional traders who hold memberships on futures exchanges and public speculators who actively trade through commission houses. Public speculators who carry smaller positions are not required to report their positions to the CFTC.

Fundamental or Technical Analysis

Another method of categorizing speculators is by the price forecasting methods they use. Fundamental analysts look at supply and demand factors; technical analysts use charts to plot price, volume, and open interest movements in current and recent years. (Price forecasting methods are discussed in Chapter 10.)

Position Traders, Day Traders, and Scalpers

Still another means of classifying speculators is by their trading methods. One type is the position trader who initiates a futures or options position and then holds it over a period of days, weeks, or months. Position trading is used by both public and professional traders.

A day trader, on the other hand, holds market positions only during the course of a trading session and rarely carries a position overnight. Most day traders are futures exchange members who execute their transactions in the trading pits.

Scalpers are professional traders who trade for themselves in the pits. The technique is to trade in minimum fluctuations, taking small profits and losses on a heavy volume of trades. Scalpers' willingness to buy at the bid price and sell at the asking or offer price creates the largest amount of total speculative liquidity. Like day traders, scalpers rarely hold positions overnight.

Spreaders

Finally, speculators also may be spreaders. Spreaders observe the market and note the shifting price relationships between different delivery months of the same commodity, between the prices of the same commodity traded on different exchanges, between the prices of different but related futures contracts, or between cash and futures prices of the same commodity. In each case, there are normal relationships that exist from month to month reflecting usual market situations. When those price relationships vary from their usual patterns, spreaders sell the overpriced market and buy the underpriced market. Their actions serve an important economic function by pulling prices back to a more normal relationship. (Spreading is discussed in Chapter 11.)

Leverage

Leverage, which is inherent in futures trading, is an important part of futures markets. Leverage is an attractive feature of futures markets for speculators because it enables them to control the full value of a futures contract with relatively little capital.

As an example, if a trader buys one soybean contract (5,000 bushels) at $6.50 per bushel ($32,500 for the contract), the required margin might be $1,400 (approximately 4 percent of the contract value or about 28 cents per bushel). This capital requirement is not a down payment for the futures contract, it is a security deposit to ensure contract performance. If the market moves against the position, the speculator will be required to deposit additional margin. And if the market moves in favor of the position, his account is credited.

Trading Plan

When speculating in futures markets, it is important to develop a trading strategy or plan to guide market activity. Although such a strategy must be geared to the individual speculator, a systematic approach to speculating is helpful.

Know Your Futures Contract

In order to make sound judgments about price movement, it is essential to have adequate knowledge about the contract being traded and to limit the number of contracts that are followed. This is true whether using fundamental analysis, technical analysis, or a combination of both trading techniques. Even experienced traders usually have difficulty following more than three different futures contracts at a time.

Profit Objective/Maximum Loss

Price forecasts must be combined with a realistic and potentially profitable trading strategy. And the profit potential should be large in relation to risk. When deciding whether or not to initiate a futures position, traders should specify profit objectives as well as the maximum losses they are willing to sustain. Personal preferences determine the acceptable minimum levels for profits and maximum levels for losses.

Determine Risk Capital

After the profit objective and loss limit have been set, determine the amount of money to be risked. To maximize returns, experienced speculators often recommend limiting the amount of money risked on a single trade. Also, open positions should be limited to as many as can be adequately followed, and some capital should be reserved for additional opportunities.

Successful speculators often advise that additions to an initial position should be made only after the initial position has proven correct (that is, when it shows a profit). Additional investments should be in amounts less than the initial position. Liquidation of a position should be based on the original trading plan. Market conditions may change, however, so it is essential that speculators maintain some degree of flexibility.

The desirability of a trade (based on potential profits compared to risks) depends on a speculator's experience and preferences. Determining profit objectives and loss limits, additions to the original position, and when to close a position also depend on personal preference and experience. Successful price forecasting and trading are ultimately influenced by individual temperament and objectivity, as well as the analysis and trading plan that were developed.

Guidelines

In addition to a systematic approach, many successful speculators follow a number of useful guidelines. Listed below are a few that they may use:

♦ Before initiating a futures position, they carefully analyze that market. They avoid quick actions based on rumors and tips.

♦ They do not speculate without a trading plan, or if there is doubt about the price forecast.

♦ Speculators rarely are able to buy at the lowest market price or sell at the highest. Orders are generally executed close to the best possible prices.

♦ Speculators give equal priority to forecasts of falling prices and short positions as they do to forecasts of rising prices and long positions.

♦ They speculate when the potential profit is great relative to risk.

♦ Successful speculation requires limiting losses and letting profits run. Traders should be prepared to accept numerous small losses; a limited number of highly profitable trades should offset those losses.

♦ In addition to a careful analysis of futures contracts, successful speculation requires a well-developed trading plan. This includes limiting the amount of money risked on any single trade and maintaining capital in reserve.

BASIC SPECULATING STRATEGIES

The 1975 corn futures market offers a good example of how a variety of fundamental and technical factors affects corn prices. The following example of a long corn position illustrates that speculators need to know the most current market conditions as well as to watch changing events and shifting market attitudes.

On June 30, 1975, the December 75 corn futures contract marked a new seasonal low of $2.32½ per bushel. A seasonal low (or high) is the

Long Position in Corn

lowest (or highest) price a particular futures contract has traded at since it opened. Among the bearish fundamental factors was an excellent outlook for the new crop. This was highlighted in a subsequent U.S. Department of Agriculture (USDA) crop report indicating that farmers had planted 1.8 million more acres in corn than had been estimated in the March 1 planting intentions report. In addition, weather conditions had been ideal for fieldwork, planting, and early corn growth, and export sales had been slow.

Also, domestic demand for corn was down due to lower livestock numbers. Thus, it appeared that the fundamental situation was basically bearish as the supply prospect seemed to be increasing and the demand outlook appeared to be deteriorating. Both situations implied an increased carryover supply at the end of the crop year. However, despite this prevailing bearish sentiment, the technical indicators gradually began to indicate that a change was occurring in the value of corn and its price.

Bullish Market Trend

Within six trading sessions after the market's new seasonal low, the December contract advanced by more than 25 cents per bushel to $2.58 on July 9. In the process, prices exceeded the highs of the previous month. This price rise also occurred with increasing volume, which was a technically positive indicator.

At about the same time, the fundamental supply/demand picture began to change. On July 10, the USDA crop estimate was reported at 6.05 billion bushels, a figure below previous expectations, which had ranged as high as 6.5 billion to 7 billion bushels. Temperatures continued above normal in the second half of June and into July for the Corn Belt and the southeastern United States. These above-normal temperatures during the critical tasseling stage for corn raised concerns that U.S. corn production could be lower than normal.

Furthermore, unconfirmed reports began to filter into the marketplace suggesting that Soviet crop conditions also were deteriorating due to record high temperatures and below-normal precipitation.

Bought December Corn

After carefully reviewing and analyzing these various factors, and considering that the majority opinion was quite bearish just the week before, a speculator decided to initiate a long corn futures position. So, at the market opening on July 11, the speculator bought one December corn futures at $2.55. Although the speculator assumed that prices would continue moving up and planned to sell his position at around $2.85, he entered a protective 10-cent stop-loss order to sell at $2.45 in the event that his timing or market judgment proved to be wrong.

Later that day, corn futures prices advanced sharply, closing at $2.64¼, reflecting reports of Russian ocean-freight bookings, and further reports of hot, dry weather in the United States and abroad. After the market close, the CFTC released the June 30 report on Commitments of Traders, which showed the average speculator had a large net short position. This was due to the generally bearish opinion that had prevailed just 11 days earlier.

On Monday, July 14, there was further buying and short-covering (buying futures to offset short futures positions), and the December contract reached $2.69. At that point, the speculator already had a potential profit of 14 cents per bushel. But since the uptrend was expected to continue, he held on to the position. However, the most aggressive traders that day were sellers on the probable thought that the 36½-cent advance in only two weeks was sufficient to discount the still minor concern over domestic and Russian crop supplies.

On that day, July 14, the market closed at $2.59½. During the balance of the week, prices fluctuated between a high of $2.71 and a low of $2.54¼, and finally closed Friday, July 18, at $2.55¼. This closing price was only a quarter of a cent above the speculator's purchase price. His profit opportunity appeared to have been lost.

Although discouraged at having possibly missed the chance to profit, he reviewed the fundamental situation and the technical indicators and decided to stick with his basic plan.

By the next Friday, the December contract closed at $2.70¼ after an earlier high of $2.74¾. At $2.74¾, he had potential gain of nearly 20 cents per bushel. Once again, the trader reviewed the multitude of technical and fundamental information and decided to stay with his initial trading plan.

More adverse crop news was reported over the weekend. This led to a limit-up move Monday and again Tuesday that pushed the December price to $2.90¼. Although the speculator's initial plan was to sell at around $2.85, the market action, the severity of the crop news, and the weather forecast caused him to revise his basic plan. He raised his profit objective another 30 cents per bushel to $3.15, and placed a new protective stop-loss order to sell at $2.65 to lock in at least an 8- to 10-cent profit should the market reverse itself. Subsequently, the December contract sold down to $2.75½, but still held above his stop.

Based upon news and the basic uptrend, he decided to hold the position. Later, the market advanced and closed August 8 at $3. On the following Friday, August 15, the market closed at $3.18¾ after reaching a high of $3.25. The speculator again revised his profit objective because he was more and more impressed with the market's strength and the substantial uptrend. In addition, there was very bullish news coming from Iowa, Nebraska, and the Soviet Union regarding the deteriorating condition of the crops. Also, the hog and cattle markets were making new highs, which suggested that domestic feed demand would improve as farmers increased livestock production.

Once again, he raised his profit objective by 30 cents per bushel to $3.45 and raised his stop-loss order another 20 cents to sell at $2.85. He felt this stop would probably assure him of at least his original profit objective of 30 cents per bushel.

Position Offset
The following week, prices again advanced, and the December contract reached $3.30¼ on August 21. However, somewhat surprisingly, the market reacted sharply late in the session and closed about 4 cents lower on a day with the heaviest trading volume since the uptrend had begun in early July. Though not conclusive, this negative technical signal suggested that the trader needed to make a critical review of the market's technical and fundamental factors. As a result, the speculator raised his sell stop-loss order to the previous low of that week, $3.10. A penetration of that price level, following the high volume reversal that occurred on August 21, would suggest that the uptrend might be over. The following week, prices did decline as the weather pattern changed, and the speculator's position was stopped out on that Wednesday's market opening at $3.08 per bushel.

Date	Action
Jul 11	Buys 1 Dec corn contract at $2.55/bu
Aug 27	Sell-stop order executed at $3.08/bu
Result	Gains $0.53/bu or $2,650 on 1 contract

In this example, the speculator did not buy at the bottom or sell at the top of the market. That rarely happens. However, considering his risk/reward ratio, he made the decision to buy when he recognized a clearly developing uptrend and took his profit when the market seemed to suggest that his position had reached its potential.

Long Position in Treasury Bonds

This example, based on events surrounding the stock market decline of October 19, 1987, highlights the importance of analyzing the economic factors and conditions that both directly and indirectly affect futures markets.

Before the Stock Market Decline
A speculator has been studying the bond and equities markets since the beginning of 1987. For the first three months, bond prices were relatively stable. By late March, however, bond prices began to fall as

interest rates rose. Several interrelated factors appeared to be affecting the direction of bond prices:

- ◆ Weakness of the U.S. dollar—there was widespread fear among investors that a weak dollar would produce greater inflation and higher interest rates (lower bond prices).
- ◆ U.S. trade deficit seemed to be worsening—this occurred despite efforts to spur U.S. exports and decrease imports through a weaker dollar.
- ◆ Appearance that the Federal Reserve was tightening monetary policy—because of a weakness in the dollar and/or market worries about inflation.

During the summer, bond prices continued to drop and the market sentiment remained primarily bearish. Despite the bearish mentality and expectations of higher interest rates, several noted economists predicted a market turnaround. These economists believed the bond market was in the process of establishing a major bottom. Prices had been falling for nearly two years, and reached a two-year low on Friday, October 2, before closing up for the day. In fact, bond prices actually closed up for that week. It had been a month since bond prices had closed higher for the week (Monday through Friday) and over three months since the bond market had closed higher from one Friday to the next. These technical indicators seemed to be pointing to a bond market rally.

In addition, some economists focused on the state of the stock market—claiming that the market was overbought and stocks were overvalued—forecasting an end to the five-year bull market that had tripled stock prices.

Bought T-bonds

Taking all of these factors into consideration, the speculator believed that the bear market in bonds was about to end or at least take a breather. He was worried about the highly overvalued stock market and felt that a major break was about to occur—a break that would send investors flocking to bonds. On October 12, the speculator decided to take a long futures position in bonds and bought two December T-bond futures contracts at 79-08* or $79,250 per contract.

Events throughout the week led to a drop in bond prices. The huge trade deficit number released October 14 especially impacted bond prices, and the December T-bond contract closed down for the week at 77-30 (a loss of 1-10 or $1,312.50 × 2 on the position). The speculator continued

---

*T-bond futures contracts are quoted in 32nds but the prices generally are written as follows: 70⁸⁄₃₂ = 70-08. The minimum price fluctuation for one Chicago Board of Trade T-bond futures (contract value of $100,000) is ¹⁄₃₂ of a percent. A ¹⁄₃₂ of a percent change on a $100,000 contract equals $31.25 (100,000 × .01)/32.

to hold the opinion that the market was bullish, however, and stayed long bonds.

Over the weekend, investors began to lose confidence in the U.S. stock market. Comments made by then U.S. Treasury Secretary James Baker threatening to let the dollar drop made foreign investors nervous. There was worldwide uncertainty and fear regarding the status of the U.S. economy, and by Sunday night, European and Japanese investors had begun selling stocks heavily.

Events of October 19

When the markets opened Monday, October 19, panic had already set in. There was selling pressure from foreign investors and portfolio insurers as everyone tried to get out of stocks and into other investment vehicles. The Dow Jones Industrial Average plunged a record 508 points on the 19th, and cash bond prices, in response to falling stock prices and selling pressures that had begun on the New York Stock Exchange, rallied 2 points immediately following the futures market close at 2 p.m. The speculator's decision to stay long bonds turned out to be a good one.

After the Decline

The immediate impact of the stock market crash was heightened uncertainty over the future direction of interest rates, the value of the dollar, and the health of the economy. Many economists and market analysts began predicting a recession—and possibly even a depression—for 1988.

To ensure the liquidity of the financial system and avert the collapse of securities firms, the Federal Reserve decided to suspend its tight monetary policy. By acting as the ultimate supplier of funds, the Fed flooded the banking system with dollars by purchasing government securities, thus driving down interest rates.

Bond prices rallied significantly as interest rates fell and investors began pouring money into fixed-income securities.

In what is termed a *flight-to-quality*, investors transferred their dollars from stocks to bonds as they sought a safe harbor for their funds. Within just one week's time, the December T-bond futures contract rose about 11 percent—the closing price of 77-30 on October 16 had increased to 86-18 by the close of trading on October 23.

Profits for the speculator at this point, if he had chosen to offset his position, were $14,625. After reviewing the current market, the speculator decided to stick with his position. It was expected that the Fed would continue its easy monetary policy (lower interest rates) to ensure market liquidity, and predictions of a recession for 1988 were still being made.

Throughout the next few weeks, bond prices continued to climb, reaching a high of 90-15 the week of November 2. During the next two weeks, the December T-bond contract more or less stabilized, fluctuating between 88-00 and 89-00. The speculator kept a close watch on market conditions, especially the dollar, economic growth, and the Fed's monetary policy. By mid-November, fears of a recession for 1988 were beginning to subside. The impact of the crash on the overall economy was not clear and the economy was stronger than expected. Some experts began again to worry about the possibility of inflation and the higher interest rates that would be needed to contain it.

Toward the end of November, bond prices began to fall. On November 27, the December T-bond contract closed down for the week at 87-02; and throughout the following week, prices ranged from a high of 88-13 to a low of 86-15. Considering the mixed economic statistics following the crash, the various predictions of recession or inflation for 1988, and the recent downtrend in prices, the speculator reviewed his position and decided that it was time to close his position. Following the opening of trading on December 7, the speculator offset his position by selling two December T-bond futures contracts at 87-20. The profit on the position was $16,750, or $8,375 per contract.

Date	Action
Oct 12	Buys 2 Dec T-bond contracts at 79-08
Dec 7	Sells 2 Dec T-bond contracts at 87-20
Result	Gains 8-12 ($8,375 per contract or $16,750 on the position)

Note: The time frame and trading opportunities summarized in this example may not be representative of most market conditions due to the unusually wide price swings that occurred following the stock market decline in October 1987.

The following example is based on the price of gold in 1978. (It should be noted that gold has since moved to much higher levels, accompanied by even greater volatility. Although the Chicago Board of Trade currently trades a 100-ounce gold futures contract and a kilo gold futures contract, this example uses 100-ounce gold futures.)

A speculator had been studying the gold market and found that most indicators pointed to a decline in cash and futures prices of gold. Among these indicators were a reported tapering off of a previously heavy demand for gold jewelry and industrial uses, and an improvement in the exchange rate of the U.S. dollar versus foreign currencies. On March 8, gold was trading at $184 per troy ounce on the spot market, and the September gold futures were trading between $197 and $200 per troy ounce.

Short Position in Gold

Sold Gold Futures

The speculator decided the time was right to take a short position and told his broker to sell three September contracts at the market price. (A market order does not specify an exact price, but is to be filled as soon as possible at the best price available in the trading pit.) Later, the broker informed his customer that the order was filled at $198 per troy ounce.

In the following weeks, the speculator's expectations of falling gold prices became a reality. There was, along with improvement of the U.S. dollar exchange rate with foreign currencies, a decline in European demand for gold as an investment and a decline in U.S. and European demand for gold jewelry. By March 30, weak demand pushed the September futures price down to $188 per troy ounce, for a gain on the speculator's position of $10 per troy ounce. This amounted to $1,000 per contract, or $3,000 on his position. After reviewing his position, the speculator saw no sign of a trend reversal. He resisted the temptation to take his profit and let the position stand.

Position Closed—Bought Gold Futures

By April 21, September gold futures prices were about $175. However, when the price moved to $171.80, large buying developed, apparently due to speculative profit-taking on signs of an oversold market. The speculator believed that this was the beginning of a trend reversal. On May 4, he called his broker and told him to buy three September contracts at the market. Later, the broker confirmed that the order was filled at $177.60 per troy ounce. The result of the speculator's position was:

Date	Action
Mar 8	Sells 3 Sep gold contracts at $198/troy oz
May 4	Buys 3 Sep gold contracts at $177.60/troy oz
Result	$20.40/troy oz gain or $2,040 per contract or $6,120 on the position

This and other examples in this chapter do not include commission or transaction costs.

Note: In all three scenarios, the speculators realized a profit. However, if the speculators had been incorrect in their price forecasts or overlooked one or more changing market conditions, any of the positions could have resulted in a loss. This is why it is important to keep a close watch on the market and develop a trading plan before initiating a futures position.

Two basic techniques are used by market analysts to forecast price movement in futures markets: fundamental and technical analysis. While there are purists of both techniques, many traders use a combination of fundamental and technical analysis to forecast price. Forecasting price movement based on the fundamental approach requires the study of supply and demand factors affecting the price of a commodity or financial instrument, whereas the theory behind technical analysis states that prices can be projected based on historical price movement and current market activity. Technical and fundamental factors affect prices and some knowledge of both methods is important to understanding price movements in the futures market.

THE FUNDAMENTAL APPROACH

The trader who uses fundamental analysis watches the economic factors that affect supply and demand in attempting to forecast prices and develop profitable trading strategies. Fundamental analysts operate on the principle that any economic factor that decreases the supply or increases the use of a commodity tends to raise prices. Conversely, any factor that

10

increases the supply or decreases the use of a commodity tends to increase stocks and lower prices. A good example of how price is affected by changes in supply and demand occurred in 1983 when the price of corn fluctuated greatly. The United States had a huge supply of corn in storage following a bumper crop in 1982. Many market participants expected farmers to plant another large corn crop in 1983. The expectation of a potential corn glut drove prices to record lows. To curtail additional surpluses, President Reagan announced the Payment-In-Kind (PIK) acreage-reduction program in January 1983. Later that year, drought and hot weather brought corn production down, lowering potential supplies even more. These factors led farmers and traders to believe that corn prices would skyrocket.

However, potential buyers of corn, anticipating rising prices, chose to reduce the amount of corn they would need by cutting livestock numbers, using other grains as feed, or substituting or decreasing the amount of corn sweetener used in prepared foods and beverages. As demand for corn dropped, so did prices.

The scenario described involved some of the basic fundamental factors that can affect agricultural commodities—weather, yield, other feed grain usage, carryover, and politics.

The supply and demand factors a fundamentalist needs to study depend on the commodity or financial instrument he is interested in trading. (Specific supply and demand information for each commodity is discussed in Chapters 13–17.)

Agricultural Markets

Carryover stocks of agricultural commodities are among the most critically watched factors by fundamentalists. (Carryover is the amount of grain or oilseeds that remains at the end of a marketing year.) The size of the carryover affects the strength or weakness of the price of the commodity in the near or distant future.

Carryover

Carryover indicates the tightness of supply. A tight supply would be reflected in higher prices, while an ample supply would lower prices. The projection of ending stocks rises or falls based on the level of projected demand and production. With the exception of some nonstorable commodities such as livestock, fundamentalists keep a constant watch on stock levels as price indicators. And, even in the case of livestock, the inventory of breeding animals, the livestock on feed, and the number of livestock brought to slaughter help to forecast meat production.

In using carryover figures to forecast price movement, other factors also must be considered. The size of the upcoming crop, for example, may be more important in predicting prices than the current carryover.

Yield

Yield is the amount of grain harvested per acre planted, and it directly affects the attitude and action of buyers in the marketplace. This attitude determines how high or low prices will move. Production of agricultural commodities such as corn is a combination of acreage and yield, with yield per acre dictated by weather and the latest farm technology.

Agricultural Reports

Monitoring the production of agricultural commodities requires the fundamental analyst to watch the regularly scheduled government and private reports on farm production in the United States and abroad.

Numerous U.S. Department of Agriculture (USDA) reports exist for all types of agricultural products from livestock to orange juice. The information for these reports is gathered by each state and compiled in Washington, D.C. Because traders place such importance on these national figures, safeguards are taken to ensure that the statistics are released at precisely the scheduled time.

Corn and wheat reports, for example, are issued monthly. The reports early in the calendar year show the number of bushels produced the previous year. Later reports indicate the number of acres farmers are expected to plant. Information released through the summer months details the size of the crop and, at the end of the year, the harvested crops. (For a list of government crop reports, see Sources of Information under Chapter 13 in the Appendix.)

Weather

The uncertainty of weather can cause more anxiety in the marketplace than all other fundamentals combined.

Traders monitor the amount of moisture, the time of frost, and the temperature during the growing season and its impact on world growing conditions to gauge how crop production is affected around the world. Weather conditions also influence livestock production. During periods of drought, livestock producers are forced to reduce livestock numbers due to the high cost of feed. This presents a glut of meat and lower prices in the short term. But in the long term, meat prices rise due to a shortage of livestock after the drought-related slaughter. During winter months, blizzards can close roads, temporarily delaying livestock shipments to market.

Economic Conditions

Domestic and international economic conditions also affect commodity prices.

There is a direct relationship between the supply and demand of livestock and grains. For instance, the affluent consumer is more likely to eat red meat, which, in turn, influences the demand for livestock. A rise in livestock numbers increases consumption of feed, which contains large amounts of corn. This eventually decreases the supply of corn. On the other hand, the less money available to consumers, the less spent on more expensive foods like red meat.

Livestock feeders make a larger profit when grain prices are low, which encourages the number of livestock to increase. When livestock supply becomes too large, livestock prices drop. Feeders are forced to cut their herds, which leads to lower grain usage and, eventually, lower grain prices.

Another important variable monitored by the fundamentalist is the pattern of consumption for a commodity. Take, as an example, the breakdown of U.S. corn usage: approximately 55 to 60 percent is used for livestock and poultry feed; exports represent 25 to 30 percent; and food, industry, and seed uses account for another 15 to 20 percent.

Other Factors to Watch

Competition with Other Commodities

The ability to substitute one commodity for another in a product can have a great effect on price. For instance, when soybeans are scarce and priced high, livestock producers may substitute cottonseed meal as a feed additive, or vegetable oil manufacturers may use coconut or palm oil as a base rather than soybean oil. Of course, each substitute has specific qualities and one may be more appropriate to use than another.

Politics

Policies made by different governments regarding agricultural production can influence the prices of commodities both domestically and worldwide.

In the United States, for instance, the government offers special acreage-reduction programs to farmers to cut the number of acres planted in specific crops. This lowers production and, eventually, reduces supply; lower supplies can lead to higher prices.

Other U.S. programs of particular importance to the supply of various commodities include feed-grain and loan programs, as well as the management of stocks accumulated from defaulted loans.

Other countries or organizations such as the European Economic Community offer similar programs to farmers in an effort to control production and prices.

Worldwide Competition

The United States is a major producer of several agricultural commodities including soybeans, corn, and wheat. These crops and others also are grown in many other countries throughout the world. As an example, Australia and Canada produce large quantities of wheat for export. The Commonwealth of Independent States also is a major wheat producer but, at times, imports large quantities of wheat. Brazil and Argentina are expanding their export markets, especially for soybeans.

Because these countries as well as several others are either large exporters or importers of agricultural commodities, the growing conditions there are closely monitored by fundamentalists. Both devastating weather conditions and optimum growing environments can greatly affect production and, thus, the supply and price of crops.

Other long-term factors influencing the supply of and demand for agricultural commodities include seasonal usage trends; the number of potential producers of a commodity and their capacity to produce that commodity; international trade; foreign exchange rates; and general economic conditions, such as interest rates, unemployment rates, inflation, and disposable income.

Fundamental price analysis in the financial instrument area involves forecasting the supply of and demand for credit and the price of fixed-income securities. It is the simultaneous evaluation of economic information, political forces, and investor attitudes as they interact.

Financial Instruments

U.S. monetary policy is formed by the Federal Reserve Board and is administered through the Federal Reserve System. Because the Federal Reserve controls the circulation of money, its policies and actions have a great impact on interest rate levels. In a slow economy, the Federal Reserve can lower the discount rate* in an effort to increase spending. And, during inflationary times, the Fed can raise the discount rate to reduce borrowing.

Federal Reserve System

The demand for money is comprised of four major areas of financing: business, consumer and personal, mortgage, and government. Each of these financial areas competes with the others for available capital. In an expanding economy, the combined money needs of these sectors tend to create upward pressure on interest rates. Theoretically, interest rates rise to the level that brings demand for funds into balance with the supply of funds. On the other hand, in periods of sluggish economic activity, interest rates fall, helping to stimulate borrowing.

Private and government issuers of debt instruments compete for available capital by adjusting the interest rates they pay lenders and investors. Among the financial instruments affected by these influences are long-term U.S. Treasury bonds, long- and intermediate-term U.S. Treasury notes, short-term U.S. Treasury bills, foreign currency, precious metals, stocks, corporate and municipal bonds, and prime commercial paper or time deposits of various maturities.

The task of a fundamental analyst is to sort through the volume of financial information, pinpoint the significant factors, and accurately weigh their effect on the supply and demand for credit.

Economic reports released by the U.S. government are excellent sources of financial information. The elements that make up these reports

Government Reports

---

*If a bank is short on reserves relative to its loan demands, it may borrow funds from the Federal Reserve. The bank is required to pay an interest rate, set by the Fed, that is known as the *discount rate*.

can be grouped into three categories: leading, concurrent, and lagging indicators.

Leading Indicators

Leading indicators signal the state of the economy for the coming months. They imply possible changes in the business cycle and, as a result, provide the analyst with an early indication of interest rate trends. The U.S. government has combined a number of these statistical elements into a single index called the *Leading Indicator Index*. Components of the index are:

♦ Average workweek of production workers in manufacturing
♦ Initial claims for unemployment insurance
♦ Orders for consumer goods and materials
♦ Percentage of companies reporting slower deliveries
♦ Change in manufacturers' unfilled orders for durable goods
♦ Plant and equipment orders
♦ New building permits
♦ Materials prices
♦ Index of consumer expectations
♦ Stock market prices
♦ Money supply

A value change in one of the index's components is often an early signal of a production and/or investment change within the economy. An increase in demand for goods requires additional labor, which, more than likely, would be seen first in the lengthening of the manufacturing workweek. Eventually, there would be an increase in the number of manufacturing workers hired. Similarly, when demand for goods falls, a cut in hours worked precedes layoffs.

Traders usually react immediately to these indicators as they are released throughout the month, resulting in short-term volatility in prices.

Concurrent and Lagging Indicators

Concurrent and *lagging* indicators show the general direction of the economy and confirm or deny a trend implied by the leading indicators. The market adjusts quickly as investors react to these economic signals.

Some key concurrent and lagging monthly indicators are:

♦ Unemployment—released at the start of the month, reports the change in employment for the preceding month and shows current economic activity.

♦ Trade balance—reveals the difference between imports and exports of merchandise over a period of time. The balance of trade can indicate the strength of the dollar, which is followed very closely by the market as an indicator of potential foreign purchases of securities. A strong dollar increases private foreign buying but often causes foreign central banks to sell financial securities.

♦ Domestic car sales—lists the number of cars sold during the previous month. This is a good measure of consumer confidence and overall economic activity.

♦ Retail sales—summarizes the value of credit and cash retail purchases, and is a good indicator of consumer confidence and overall economic activity.

♦ Producer Price Index (PPI)—shows the cost of resources needed to produce manufactured goods during the previous month. PPI lists the rate of inflation for raw materials, and is a good indication of future consumer price increases.

♦ Business inventories—reflects the demand for short-term credit by businesses. As inventories build, they are usually financed through bank loans or commercial paper. Therefore, inventory increases or decreases usually signal changes in the demand for short-term credit. Inventory levels also generally indicate the duration and intensity of business slowdowns or speedups. If inventories are high when a slowdown begins, a longer and more severe recession is usually expected because factories then run at reduced levels until inventories are sold off. High inventories also may act as short-term support for interest rates. When inventories are high and the economy is in a business slowdown, demand for credit to finance inventories can keep interest rates higher longer than normal. Low inventories going into an upturn in the business cycle can result in a short inflation spurt and a quick acceleration of business activity. Rebuilding inventories creates jobs and ultimately causes consumer demand to increase. This demand often cannot be met by existing inventories, so prices climb, economic activity increases, and factories are opened.

♦ Housing starts—shows the demand for long-term mortgage money and short-term construction loans. They also are indicators of the number and type of mortgage-backed securities that the market will need in the near future.

♦ Industrial production—gives the level of factory output in the previous month and shows the level of intensity for economic recessions and booms.

♦ Personal income—reflects consumers' buying power and weighs potential demand for goods and services.

♦ Gross Domestic Product (GDP)—reports the value of all final goods and services produced by an economy over a particular time period, normally a year.

♦ Gross National Product—Gross Domestic Product plus the income accruing to domestic residents as a result of investments abroad less income earned in the domestic market accruing to foreigners abroad.

♦ Consumer Price Index—measures inflation and is a key factor in bond prices, as investors usually demand a real rate of return of at least 2 percent for government bonds over the long term. Traders watch these numbers closely, since they usually indicate future changes in long-term bond and money market rates.

These indicators and figures are reported in daily newspapers as information is released. Market experts, however, make forecasts of the data prior to the actual release, because the market often begins to react before the news is actually announced.

No one indicator permanently dominates and "the most important" indicators replace each other as factors in the market. Sometimes the market will concentrate on one or two elements and ignore others for a time. It is the job of the fundamental analyst to identify the factors currently of most concern.

For example, during most of 1982, many market analysts watched the money supply and ignored other indicators. (Money supply is the amount of money in the economy consisting primarily of currency in circulation plus deposits in banks.) The feeling was that the Federal Reserve was going to dominate the market and make policy decisions based on money growth and inflation rates. Later that year and in early 1983, money supply and inflation were downplayed as other economic indicators showed that the economy was in a general slide, and the Fed indicated it was going to pay less attention to money supply in policy-making.

By late 1990 and early 1991, many market analysts watched precious metal and oil prices as everyone was speculating on what effects the Gulf War would have on the markets. A year later, the war was over and analysts had turned their attention to the economy. Traders were keeping close tabs on housing starts, durable goods, nonfarm payroll, and unemployment, as well as the Consumer Price Index (CPI) and Producer Price Index (PPI), as indicators of how the economy was doing. Several others were also looking at money supply.

Information Available from the Federal Reserve

The Federal Reserve system provides information that is helpful in analyzing the economy and predicting Federal Reserve activity. These weekly reports contain information on:

♦ The money supply growth on a one-week lagged basis

♦ Loan demand
♦ The average rates for fed funds
♦ Dealers' positions in Treasury issues
♦ The condition of the accounts at the New York Federal Reserve Bank

The Fed reports the level of reserves the banks must maintain at the central bank, which provides information about transactions that affect the federal funds rate. The fed funds rate is the interest rate charged among banks for reserves borrowed and lent to each other. It is watched as a good indicator of short-term Federal Reserve policy.

The total of commercial paper and industrial loans outstanding at financial and nonfinancial institutions is also reported weekly by the Fed. These statistics show the overall demand for credit and the sectors of the economy demanding it.

The minutes of the Federal Reserve Open Market Committee monthly meeting are another important source of fundamental information.

The information needed by fundamentalists to forecast prices of agricultural, metals, and financial markets is vast and complex. Many fundamentalists collect these figures on their own, but services are also available that gather this information.

According to price theory, the point where the quantity demanded and the quantity supplied are equal is called the *equilibrium* or *market price*. The purpose of fundamental analysis is to pinpoint and recognize the major factors in the market and to predict their effect on the equilibrium price of a commodity. Profit opportunities exist when a fundamentalist can project how these factors will affect both the short-term and long-term equilibrium price.

Using Fundamental Analysis

Using fundamental analysis involves formulating an economic model—a systematic description of the various supply-and-demand factors that interact to determine price. The sophistication of these economic models varies greatly—from complex models with thousands of variables to a simple equation that relates the price of a commodity to a few key demand and supply statistics.

Use of Computers

In the last few years, technological advances in computer hardware and software programs have been applied to fundamental analysis. This has resulted in the development of even more sophisticated and complex fundamental analysis systems. Using computer analysis and modeling techniques to describe in mathematical terms the relationship between economic factors such as interest rates, government policies, and capital is known as *econometrics*.

Treasury Bonds
September 1993
Chicago Board of Trade

Source: Custom Charts Inc., Chicago, Illinois

The use of computers by fundamentalists, however, still requires a measure of judgment since each piece of data fed into the computer must be weighted as to its particular significance. Such evaluation is an inherent part of the use of economic models as price-forecasting tools.

What is important to remember is that, while the indicators of supply and demand may vary greatly from one commodity to another, the process of fundamental analysis is similar for all.

THE TECHNICAL APPROACH

Although fundamental analysis provides some very general indicators of price, many traders believe that even if all the supply and demand information affecting a particular product were known, one still would not be able to forecast price movement. They believe that to know and understand every factor that may affect supply and demand is impossible, and that, at times, a trader may overlook something that could substantially affect the market.

These traders prefer to anticipate market movement by studying price patterns in the past using historical prices, trading volume, open interest, and other trading data. They are called *technicians* and the technique they use to forecast prices is referred to as *technical analysis.*

Probably the oldest method of technical analysis is known as *charting.* There are two basic price charts—bar charts and point-and-figure charts. Both are easy to construct if a trader has price information, however, there are companies that provide ready-made charts for a fee. Examples of bar and point-and-figure charts are shown in this chapter for illustrative purposes only to give the reader a general idea of what traders look for.

Charting

Bar Charts

Bar charts are one of the most common types of price charts. An example of a bar chart is shown to the left that also displays open interest and trading volume.

In a bar chart, the vertical axis represents price and the horizontal axis represents time. For daily bar charts, each trading day is represented by a vertical line that connects the lowest and highest price of the day. The day's closing price is indicated by a horizontal bar that crosses the vertical line.[†] Prices for the following days are plotted to the right of the first bar. Typically, most bar charts illustrate five vertical bars per week, representing

---

[†]Depending on the charting service, some bar charts indicate the opening price by a horizontal bar marked to the left and the closing price by a horizontal bar marked to the right of the vertical axis.

Live Cattle
August 1987
Chicago Mercantile Exchange

Source: Data Lab Corporation, Niles, Illinois

the number of business days in a week. If there is a weekday holiday, the bar for that day is omitted.

Not only can bar charts be graphed on a daily basis, many traders plot this information for a week's activity. This type of bar chart tracks the weekly high, low, and closing prices of the nearby delivery month for a specific commodity throughout the life of the contract. When the contract expires, the weekly prices of the next delivery month are graphed on the same chart.

As price data are plotted, technicians begin to see different chart formations that tend to recur over time. Analysts use this information to predict future price movement. While it is impossible to explain every possible chart, this chapter reviews some of the most prominent bar formations.

Day Formations

Bar Chart Formations

The *inside day* is one in which the high and low prices of a trading day are within the previous day's price range. The close on such a day is not perceived as too significant. What is important to watch is the way prices move out of the narrow range in subsequent trading. The technician will either buy or sell depending on which end of the range prices surpass in the days ahead.

The *outside day* formation—the opposite of the inside day—occurs when the high/low prices exceed the previous day's range. In this case, the closing price is given great weight. The chartist adjusts or adds to his position in the direction of the closing price.

The *closing price reversal* is a formation in which prices initially continue in the same direction as the previous trading day but reverse to close opposite the previous day's close. This type of price action is viewed as a strong warning signal that a minor price trend may have ended.

The *key reversal* combines the outside day and the closing price reversal. The essential pattern difference from the closing price reversal is that both opening and closing prices exceed the extremes of the previous day's range. The key reversal, particularly on a weekly chart, is perceived as the probable forerunner of the end of a trend. Many technicians reverse their position in the market after one occurs.

Weekly Nearby Corn Futures
1976-1985
Chicago Board of Trade

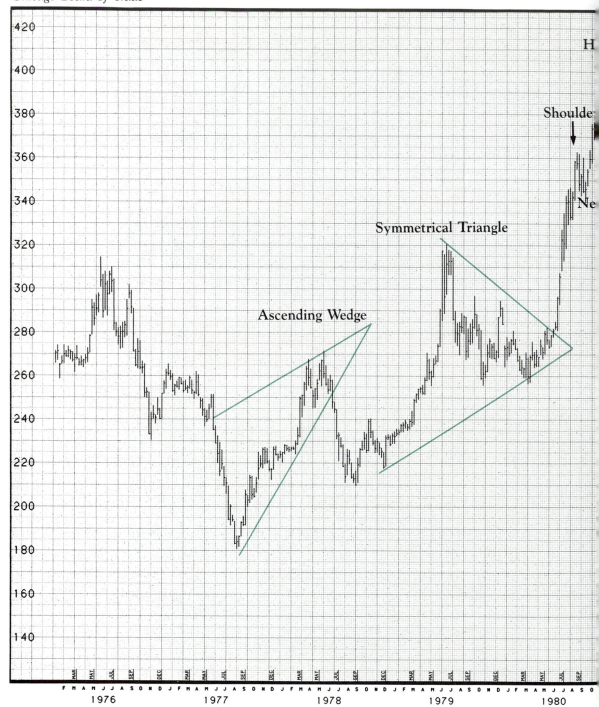

Source: *Commodity Perspective, A Knight-Ridder Business Information Service, Chicago, Illinois*

Oats

March 1988
Chicago Board of Trade

Source: Commodity Trends Service, North Palm Beach, Florida

Support and Resistance

The chartist uses several terms to describe different market conditions. For example, sometimes the market rallies and then falls back to a previous price range or there may be a price decline that is stopped due to buying pressure. Traders use several different terms for these formations. One of the terms is *support*—the place on a chart where the buying of futures contracts is sufficient to halt a price decline.

The opposite of support is *resistance*. The market rallies to a particular price level then falls back to a previous price area. Resistance on a chart indicates a price range where selling pressure is expected to stop a market advance.

After a trading range is established for at least a month or two of sideways price movement, prices tend to meet support at the lower end of the range or resistance at the upper end of the range. If prices break out of a specific support or resistance area, some traders use this information to make buying or selling decisions.

Trends

A standard definition of an uptrend is a sequence of both higher highs and higher lows and is considered to be intact until a previous low point is broken. Conversely, a downtrend is a sequence of lower lows and lower highs and is considered to be intact until a previous rally is surpassed. It is important to realize, however, that a break in a pattern of higher highs and higher lows (or lower highs and lower lows) should be looked at as a clue and not as an indicator of a possible long-term trend reversal.

Uptrends and downtrends also are defined in terms of trend lines. An uptrend line connects a series of higher lows and a downtrend line connects a series of lower highs. Trend lines are considered by some technicians to be more reliable if they are at approximately a 45-degree angle to the horizontal axis representing time. However, it is not uncommon for a trend to start at a much smaller angle and escalate until the angle of ascent or descent becomes too great.

Channels

Sometimes the lines connecting highs and lows run almost parallel to a trend line. This type of price movement creates channels, and if the price breaks a major trend line, it may indicate a substantial market move in the direction of the penetration.

Chart analysts rely on specific chart formations that recur over time to forecast future price movements. After trend lines and channels have been established, one of the most important decisions a trader has to make is determining a major top in a rising market or a major bottom in a declining market.

Corn
December 1988
Chicago Board of Trade

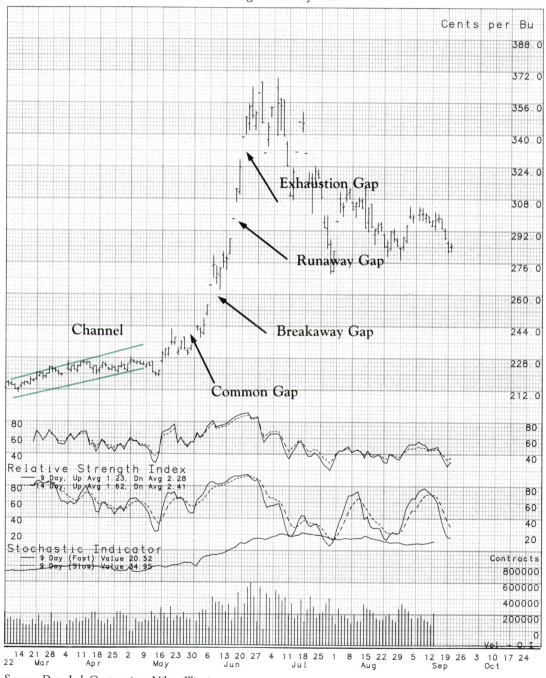

Source: Data Lab Corporation, Niles, Illinois

The most common chart indicators are:

♦ Head-and-shoulders or inverted head-and-shoulders
♦ Double tops and double bottoms
♦ Rounded tops and rounded bottoms
♦ Gaps

Head-and-Shoulders

The *head-and-shoulders* formation is one of the most reliable patterns indicating a major reversal in the market. This formation consists of four phases: the left shoulder, the head, the right shoulder, and a penetration of the neckline. The head-and-shoulders formation is complete only when the neckline penetration occurs. Some theorists believe that once prices break through the neckline, the distance from the top of the head to the neckline signals the extent of the movement away from the neckline. The head-and-shoulders occurs in a rising market; its opposite, the *inverted head-and-shoulders*, occurs in a declining market.

Double Tops and Double Bottoms

Double tops and *double bottoms* are exactly what their names suggest and have a tendency to indicate major market moves. These formations are usually considered complete when prices move past the first reaction point following the first top or bottom.

Rounded Tops and Rounded Bottoms

Rounded tops or *rounded bottoms* (also called *saucers*) are usually reliable indicators of future price movement. The size of the saucer frequently signals the extent of an upcoming price advance or decline. An additional feature of this formation may be the development of the platform that is generally the forerunner of the primary price move.

Gaps

Gaps in price charts also are watched with interest by the chartist. Gaps represent a price area where the market did not trade. There are several types of gaps including the common gap, the breakaway gap, the runaway gap, and the exhaustion gap.

The *common gap* can appear at any time and has no particular significance. Frequently, this gap is filled in during later trading. The *breakaway gap* occurs when prices jump beyond a trading range leaving an area in the chart where no trading took place. A breakaway gap is useful in predicting the end of a consolidation phase of the market, and it can signal a dynamic move. A *runaway gap* appears when a trend accelerates and is quite typical of a strong bull or bear market. The *exhaustion gap* occurs after a relatively long period of steadily higher or lower prices. As the name implies, chartists theorize that the exhaustion gap signals the imminent end of a trend.

Other Bar Chart Formations

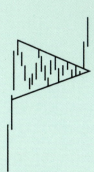

Pennant

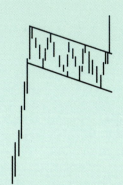

Flag

Rounded Top

Rounded Bottom

Double Bottom

Many of the newer financial futures are based on instruments that trade in "24-hour markets." This has created more gaps on financial instrument charts compared to agricultural futures charts.

Other Patterns

Triangles, in many forms, recur in futures price charts. Their reliability as a means of predicting price behavior, however, is open to some question, and they frequently become part of other chart formations. The three triangle patterns are the ascending triangle, the symmetrical triangle, and the descending triangle.

The *ascending triangle* can point to a breakout on the upside of the triangular area. Conversely, the *descending triangle* can point to a breakout on the downside of the triangular area. The *symmetrical triangle* is the least dependable of the three and merely forecasts that a substantial move out of price congestion may take place. The symmetrical triangle is often a formation in which a breakout favors the continuation of the previous price trend.

Two more important chart patterns are the flag (or *pennant*) and the wedge formations. The *flag* is formed when a substantial upward price move is followed by a modest downward price drift, giving the appearance of a flag on a pole in the absence of wind. After the flag is formed, the upmove is abruptly resumed. An upside objective is calculated by measuring the length of the pole and adding that amount to the low point of the flag.

The *ascending wedge* is a series of price-up days that fail to accelerate. The irony of the wedge is that even though prices are rising, the upscale movement is usually not significant compared to the initial days of the formation. To the trained chartists, this is a negative pattern that will reverse to the downside.

Point-and-figure charts are unique in that they illustrate all trading as one continuous path and ignore time. As with bar charts, the vertical axis of the point-and-figure chart represents prices, however, there is no time reference along the horizontal axis.

The point-and-figure chartist uses an **x** to indicate an uptick and an **o** for a downtick. Generally, point-and-figure chartists set their price objective by counting the **x**s and **o**s of specific chart formations. The point-and-figure chartist theorizes that the amount of price movement at a given level is important in forecasting prices, which is quite similar to the logic of support and resistance used in bar charting.

Point-and-figure charts are used to track intraday price moves or long-term trends. As with bar charts, there are several formations revealed in point-and-figure charts as shown on the next page.

While the methods of charting—bar charts and point-and-figure charts—described here are used to identify trends, traders also try to

Point-and-Figure Charts

Statistical Analysis

Point-and-Figure Chart Formations

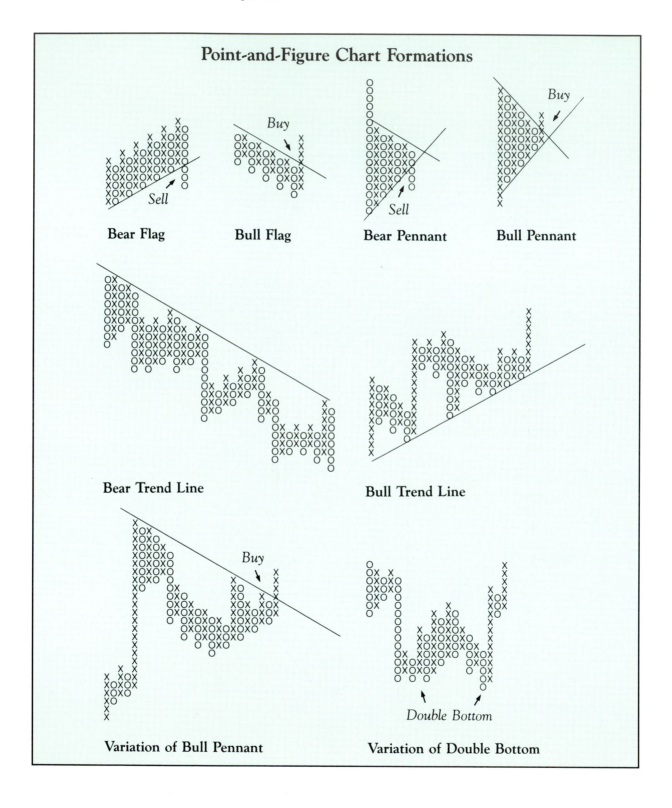

recognize different price trends through statistical methods, which is known as *statistical analysis*.

Moving-Average Charts

Probably one of the simplest and best-known statistical approaches is the moving average—an average of a series of prices. Moving-average changes are calculated for any period of time such as 3 days, 5 days, 10 days, or 30 days. One advantage of the moving average is that it tends to smooth out some of the price irregularities that can occur. However, the moving-average value always lags behind the current market by a day.

Deciding the average to use depends on several elements. The technician has to ask how sensitive he wants the average to be relative to the market. The more sensitive a trader wants the average to reflect turning points in a trend, the fewer the number of days that should be averaged. On the other hand, the more days incorporated in the average, the less the effect short-term market factors will have on the average price.

To calculate a moving average, a trader can use opening, closing, average, high, or low prices for a given day, however, most tend to use closing prices. Each price average—number of days and the price selection—serves a different purpose, so a trader has to look at his market objective and determine the type of moving average most appropriate to his market needs.

While it is beyond the scope of this text to explain how to calculate every type of moving average, there are a variety of books referenced in the Appendix that cover the topic of moving averages. However, one example of a three-day average is described here.

A three-day average is calculated by adding prices from three consecutive days. That total price is then divided by three to determine the first moving-average point. As an example, suppose the closing prices of silver futures for three consecutive days were $6.69, $6.62, and $6.68. Adding these three numbers equals $19.99. If $19.99 is divided by three (since this is the time frame of the moving average in this example), $6.66 is obtained. The $6.66 becomes the first moving-average point.

After the close on the fourth trading day, substitute the fourth closing price for the first and determine a new three-day average. Assume the closing price for silver on the fourth day was $6.81. Averaging the closing prices of the three previous days, $6.62, $6.68, $6.81, equals $6.70—the second point of this particular moving average.

A technician could determine the moving average for a particular contract as long as it traded if he chose to. If the closing prices for the next five trading days were $7.33, $7.36, $7.32, $7.18, and $7.23, the moving average would be calculated as follows:

Corn

September 1988
Chicago Board of Trade

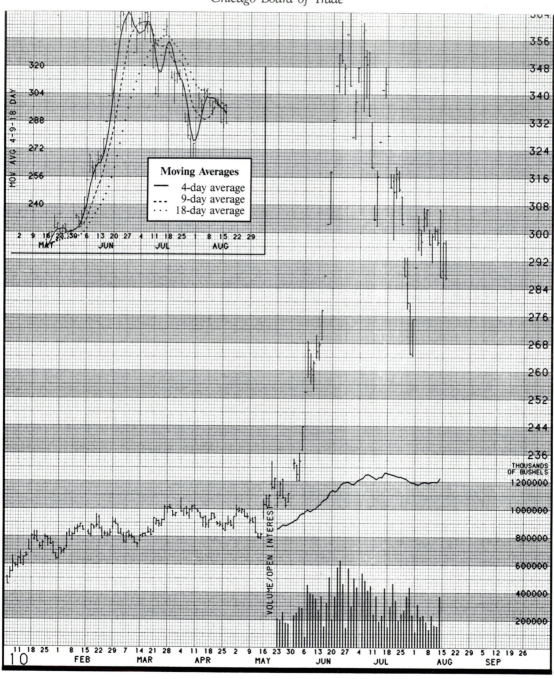

Source: *Commodity Perspective, A Knight-Ridder Business Information Service, Chicago, Illinois*

	Closing Prices Used	Total	Average
Day 5	$6.68 + $6.81 + $7.33 =	$20.82	$6.94
Day 6	$6.81 + $7.33 + $7.36 =	$21.50	$7.17
Day 7	$7.33 + $7.36 + $7.32 =	$22.01	$7.34
Day 8	$7.36 + $7.32 + $7.18 =	$21.86	$7.29
Day 9	$7.32 + $7.18 + $7.23 =	$21.73	$7.24

In a graph of a moving average, the horizontal axis represents the trading day or calendar day and the vertical axis represents price. The average points are plotted and a line can be drawn to connect the points. Examples of a 4-, 9-, and 18-day moving-average graph are illustrated in the upper left-hand corner on the previous page.

The problem many technicians have is distinguishing false signals from the true ones. The trader might find himself buying on the high or selling on the low, with the unfortunate consequence of having to close out these positions at a loss. Therefore, the trader must learn to interpret different signals before taking action.

Some traders adjust their trading rules to accommodate the possibility of false signals by delaying entering or exiting the market a day or two. This allows more time for a trend to develop or for a false signal to reveal itself.

Oscillator

Many analysts use moving averages to forecast prices in trending markets. In sideways markets, technicians use oscillators. An oscillator is a technical indicator that allows a trader to measure overbought or oversold conditions in sideways markets.

The simplest example of an oscillator is the difference between the current closing price and the closing price a specific number of days earlier. As long as prices trend upward, the oscillator will be positive. However, for the oscillator to increase, prices must rise at an accelerated rate. The fact that sharp increases or decreases in the oscillator can occur only in markets that witness accelerated advances or declines suggests that this measure of price movement might be used as an overbought or oversold indicator.

Many moving-average and oscillator programs are computerized so technical analysts have this information at their fingertips. In addition, there are other price-information programs for computers that analysts can either develop or purchase. In fact, several firms write their own computer programs for price analysts and have formed membership organizations. Members subscribe to these services and, thereby, have access to the most up-to-date price analysis programs.

Technical Analysis by Computer

Other Technical Tools

In addition to charting and statistical analysis, a technician may use other techniques to assist him in predicting future price moves. Volume and open interest analyses are important examples.

Trading volume is the total number of contracts traded for a given period of time. Technical traders hypothesize that changes in volume are associated with price movements in the same direction. For example, a gradual increase in volume during a downtrend often indicates a continuation and acceleration of the price decline, while gradually increasing volume during an uptrend suggests a further rise in prices. Rapidly accelerating volume after a substantial price move, however, often signals the approach of a major high or low and an impending price reversal.

Open interest refers to the number of contracts that have been entered into and not yet liquidated by delivery or offset. As with volume figures, each contract represents both a long and a short position. Some technicians use open interest figures to get a handle on future price moves as the following examples illustrate.

♦ A rise in both prices and open interest indicates that new buyers are entering the market. Since there is an increase in open interest, new contracts are being created, and the rise in prices means buyers are more aggressive than sellers.

♦ A rise in open interest and a decline in prices signal that traders are selling contracts. Once again, with open interest rising, new contracts are being established, but since prices are decreasing, sellers are more aggressive than buyers.

♦ A decline in both open interest and prices shows previous selling pressure. An increase in open interest and declining prices indicate new selling pressure.

♦ A decline in open interest accompanied by a rise in prices suggests that traders are covering their short positions.

Trading Positions

Every other Friday, the Commodity Futures Trading Commission publishes the Commitment of Traders Report. It contains a breakdown of open interest for reportable and nonreportable traders in all futures as of the prior Tuesday close. The report shows the total number of open positions held by large-volume traders, speculators, and hedgers, as well as those held by market participants with smaller positions.

Technicians study these reports very carefully, noting in particular any unusual changes in the various trading categories that may indicate differences of opinion between large commercial and speculative interests and smaller speculators and hedgers.

Trading positions also allow analysts to determine the resiliency of the market. Small-position traders tend to be more unstable than large-position traders who have more market "staying power." That is because large-position holders are usually higher capitalized. As an example, a market that has been experiencing a price increase is more likely to break if there is a large amount of smaller-position traders in the market who will not be able to afford a market shift.

While many veteran traders avow that knowledge of the composition of the market—who is long and who is short—is the most useful of all clues to future price moves, it should be cautioned that the daily data available for determining this are less than ideal. Daily volume and open interest figures do not segregate particular trader categories or spreading activity. The Commitment of Traders Report, on the other hand, segregates spreads, but the small speculator figure is calculated by subtracting the number of positions held by large traders from the number of positions held by all traders.

Contrary Opinion

Similar reasoning is often applied to the opinions of market analysts who publish advisory services. The theory of contrary opinion holds that when more than 80 percent of these analysts are bullish, it can be assumed that they and their followers have taken long positions, leaving fewer potential additional buyers to absorb any selling that develops. Conversely, if 80 percent are bearish, the market is likely to become badly oversold, and a sharp price rally is likely to develop soon.

This theory often is applied after there has been a substantial move lasting an extended time period. And, it must be remembered that, after such a significant move, those who have opposed the move may be in financial difficulty. Thus, large moves tend to last longer than might reasonably be expected, and it can be very costly to take a contrary position too soon. This barometer is most useful as an early warning and is often used by prudent traders as the clue to take profits but not to reverse their positions.

CBOT Market Profile®

The Chicago Board of Trade's Market Profile is an information service that helps technical traders analyze price trends. CBOT Market Profile consists of a Time and Sales quotation ticker and the Liquidity Data Bank® (LDB)®.

The Time and Sales ticker is an on-line graphic service that transmits price and time information throughout the day to computer subscribers. The second half of the system is the LDB, which summarizes the entire day's trading activity including volume and a breakdown to the nearest 30 minutes of when specific trades were made. Traders use this information to recognize specific trends and forecast price movement.

Cyclical Theories

Cyclical theories are another growing area of interest for technical analysts. Cyclical theories are based on the premise that in nature certain phenomena have cycles and some analysts use this theory in forecasting price. One cyclical or wave theory that is used to project price movement and is attracting a lot of attention is the Elliot Wave Principle. (To learn more about this particular subject, check the Sources of Information in the Appendix.)

Combining Approaches

Traders frequently use a combination of fundamental and technical methods to forecast price. For example, many traders obtain a forecast of price movement using fundamental analysis and then choose the time for initiating or liquidating a position on the basis of technical factors.

But no matter what method or combination of methods for price analysis are used, none can be taken as foolproof. The process through which price is discovered in the futures markets represents the collective wisdom of all market participants trying to estimate future prices.

Futures markets provide a variety of trading opportunities. In addition to profiting from rising prices by purchasing futures contracts or from falling prices by selling futures contracts, there is the opportunity to profit from spreads. A spread refers to the simultaneous purchase and sale of two different futures contracts. When establishing or putting on a spread, a trader looks at the price relationship between contracts rather than the absolute price levels. The contract that is viewed as "cheap" is purchased, while the contract that is viewed as "expensive" is sold. If market prices move as expected, the trader profits from the change in the relationship between the prices of the contracts.

The economic contributions of spreading to the market are twofold: spreading provides market liquidity and restores prices to more normal relationships following a distortion in those relationships. An understanding of spread trading is important, therefore, to all market participants.

This chapter examines some of the underlying economic factors that account for the normal price relationships between different futures contracts. Also included are a few examples of spreading and explanations of some of the more common agricultural and financial spreads.

A trader initiates a spread when expecting the price difference between two futures contracts to change. To put on a spread, a

Using
Spreads
in
Futures
Markets

*Bulls,
Bears,
Butterflies*

11

155

July/Nov Soybean Spread
1989
Chicago Board of Trade

Source: *Custom Charts Inc., Chicago, Illinois*

trader simultaneously buys one futures contract and sells the other. He later liquidates his spread position following a change in the price relationship. Spread orders may specify prices at which the long or short positions should be put on, or the price difference at which the spread should be established.

Spreads are quoted as the price difference between two related contracts. As an example, to calculate a particular agricultural spread such as the July/November soybean spread, one would subtract the price of the November contract from the July contract. This difference would generally result in a positive number because ag commodity prices are typically lowest at harvest and trend higher during the marketing year* as storage, interest, and insurance costs accumulate. As a result, July soybeans (old-crop beans) are usually priced higher than November soybeans (new-crop beans).

Quoting Spreads

The July/November soybean 1989 spread graphed to the left illustrates the price difference between July 1989 soybeans and November 1989 soybeans.

The vertical axis of the chart represents the July/November beans spread value in cents per bushel; the horizontal axis is the trading day. The top line indicates the price of July futures, which fell approximately $1.90 between early July and late July 1988, then rebounded more than $1.50 by early September, but tumbled about $2.30 by July 1989. During the same period, the middle line, which indicates November futures, depicts a drop of about $1.10 in a choppy pattern between July and late November 1988. The same line also shows a temporary recovery of about 90 cents by mid-March before it plunged over $1.60 by July 1989. The actual spread between July and November beans is illustrated on the bottom of the graph.

For the spread between two contracts to change, such as July soybeans to gain on November soybeans, there are four possible market scenarios:

♦ In a bull market, July soybeans rise faster than November soybeans;

♦ In a bear market, July soybeans fall slower than November soybeans;

♦ July soybeans remain unchanged while November soybeans fall;

♦ July soybeans rise while November soybeans remain unchanged.

*The futures contract month of November represents the first major new-crop marketing month and the contract month of July represents the last major old-crop marketing month for soybeans. This is because the crop year tends to begin following harvest in the fall and end before the next year's harvest, e.g., the marketing year for soybeans begins September 1 and ends August 31.

**Reasons for Trading
Spreads**

There are many reasons why traders spread, but two important reasons are lower risk and attractive margin rates.

Lower Risk

Because of their hedged nature, spreads generally are less risky than outright positions. Since the prices of two different futures contracts for the same commodity exhibit a strong tendency to move up or down together, spread trading offers protection against losses that arise from unexpected or extreme price volatility.[†]

This "protection" occurs because losses from one side of the spread are more or less offset by gains from the other side of the spread. For example, if the short (sold) futures side of a spread results in a loss due to a price increase, the long (bought) side should produce a profit offsetting much of the loss.

Attractive Margin Rates

Because spreads usually are less risky than outright positions, spread margin rates are generally lower than those for outright positions. Lower margin rates allow traders to diversify their portfolios with a smaller amount of capital.

SPREADING IN AG FUTURES

Types of Ag Spreads

There are three basic types of spreads—interdelivery, intermarket, and intercommodity.

Interdelivery (or Intramarket) Spreads

The simultaneous purchase of one delivery month of a given futures contract and the sale of another delivery month of the same commodity on the same exchange—e.g., buy July wheat and sell December wheat at the Chicago Board of Trade.

Intermarket Spreads

The simultaneous sale of a given delivery month of a futures contract on one exchange and the purchase of the same delivery month and futures contract at another exchange—e.g., the sale of December wheat futures on the Chicago Board of Trade and the purchase of December wheat futures at the Kansas City Board of Trade.

[†]An intercommodity spread may not always be less risky than an outright position. For example, if a trader is long wheat and short corn, wheat prices might unexpectedly decrease and corn prices might increase during the life of the spread. If so, a trader would lose on both legs.

Intercommodity Spreads

The simultaneous purchase of a given delivery month of one futures market and the sale of the same delivery month of a different, but related, futures market—e.g., the purchase of July wheat futures and the sale of July corn futures.

The interdelivery spread is one of the most common types of spreads. An interdelivery spread position attempts to take advantage of the price difference between two delivery months of a single futures market when the difference is abnormal. Traders can describe interdelivery spreads as either bull or bear spreads. In an ag bull spread, a trader buys the nearby[‡] and sells the deferred[‡], expecting the nearby to gain on the deferred. The ag bear spread is just the opposite of a bull spread—a trader sells the nearby and buys the deferred, expecting the deferred to gain on the nearby.

Note: In a metals bull spread, one is short the nearby month and long the deferred month—just the opposite of an ag bull spread. In the ag markets, an increase in the cash price typically raises the nearby month more than the deferred month, while in the metals market an increase in price typically raises the deferred month price by more.

Carrying Charges

Among storable commodities, such as grains and metals, carrying charges have the greatest effect on the underlying futures prices of different delivery months.

Carrying charges are the combined costs of storage, insurance, and interest. The storage cost is the least variable of these three elements. For instance, the cost to store wheat, corn, soybeans, or oats in Chicago Board of Trade-approved elevators averaged 4.8 to 5.1 cents per bushel per month in 1991. This storage cost reflects general inflationary trends due to increased construction, labor, and energy costs.

Insurance costs vary with the price of the commodity. Obviously, it costs more to insure soybeans valued at $7.50 per bushel than it does for corn worth $2.50 per bushel. As an example, insurance per year for corn averaged about 1 cent per bushel and averaged about 3 cents per bushel for soybeans in 1991.

The most variable component of carrying charges has been interest rates. Historically, most agricultural production has been financed through loans based on deposits in savings and checking accounts from banks located in farm areas. For many years, the interest rate that local banks charged farmers was relatively insulated from fluctuations in the prime

[‡]Nearby futures month refers to the contract month closest to expiration and a deferred futures month refers to a contract month further from expiration.

rate—the rate that the large money-center banks charge their most creditworthy corporate customers. This has changed since the mid-1970s, however, as smaller customers have shifted funds from savings accounts at local banks to forms of savings and investments offering greater yields. Because of this loss of funds, local banks have become more dependent upon larger money-center banks for funds to loan to farm clients. The rates at which local banks borrow funds to lend to farmers are directly affected by fluctuations in the prime rate.

Full-Carry Markets

Theoretically, in a normal futures market—reflecting adequate supplies of the underlying cash commodity and sufficient storage capacity—the price of the nearby futures month and the price of the deferred futures month have a definite price relationship. The deferred futures price is usually more than the nearby futures price by approximately the amount of the cost of carrying the commodity from the nearby to the deferred month. Each futures delivery month price is usually higher than the previous month by the amount of the cost to store, insure, and finance the commodity from month to month. In the case of corn priced at $2.50 per bushel—with a base storage cost of 4.8 cents per bushel per month, insurance cost of .09 cent per bushel, and a prime rate of 10 percent—the carrying charge is 6.97 cents per bushel per month:

$$\frac{(\$2.50 \times 10\%)}{12} + \$0.048 + \$0.0009 = \$0.0697/bu/month$$

The theoretical spreads of futures prices at full carry are:

Dec	Mar	May	Jul
$2.50	$2.71	$2.85	$2.99

These prices reflect the corn crop year that begins September 1 and ends August 31. Consequently, December is considered the first new-crop futures delivery month, and July the last. Futures prices tend to be at their seasonal low right after harvest—October and November for corn. In a normal market, December futures (first contract month for the new corn marketing year) should be priced lower compared to deferred contract months as carrying charges accumulate in the deferred months.

Remember that these full-carry markets are theoretical. In practice, interdelivery futures price spreads only rarely attain the full cost of carry due to changing market conditions.

Let's take a look at the actual corn spreads at the Chicago Board of Trade from mid-November 1982. With the nearby December corn futures selling at $2.34½ per bushel and a prime rate of 11½ percent, the monthly carrying cost is about 7 cents.

Dec	Mar 1983	May	Jul	Sep
$2.34½	$2.45	$2.51½	$2.56¾	$2.60

These spreads are far from full carry. There are many different market variables that could have affected the spread between the delivery months:

♦ Expectations about the amount of corn planted by farmers during the next crop year
♦ Corn demand for animal feed, food, seed, and industrial uses
♦ Carryover expectations (remaining supplies of corn carried from one crop year to the next)
♦ Expected rate of inflation
♦ Interest rate fluctuations
♦ Availability of storage

Inverted Markets

Thus far, we have looked at interdelivery spreads in relatively normal carrying charge markets (in which the futures price of the nearby month is less than the futures price of the deferred month). In periods when a commodity is in short supply, the nearby futures contract trades at a premium to the deferred futures. Such a market is called an *inverted market*. The inversion represents, in effect, a negative return for holding inventories.

A common interdelivery spread is the intercrop—or old-crop/new-crop—spread. It involves buying futures in one crop year and selling futures in another crop year. Since prices are usually lowest at harvest, new-crop futures tend to be priced lower than futures from the previous crop year.

An Interdelivery or Carry Charge Spread

There are a number of factors to consider, however, when establishing an old-crop/new-crop spread. First, the trader should look at the price relationship—not absolute price levels—between the two contracts and determine whether the spread is expected to change. Then he should ask himself:

♦ How large are remaining supplies (carryover) from the last harvest?
♦ What is the outlook for the size of the next harvest?
♦ How does the rate of usage compare to previous forecasts?
♦ How strong is future demand expected to be?

Answering these questions will help a trader determine whether a spread will change over time. If he expects old-crop prices to rise relative to new-crop prices, the trader can buy the old-crop month and simultaneously sell the new-crop month. On the other hand, if he expects new-crop prices to gain relative to old-crop prices, the trader can buy the new-crop month and sell the old-crop month. Note that, in each case, both sides of the spread are usually executed in one step, not two.

A common intercrop spread is the July/December corn spread. July represents the old-crop month and December represents the new-crop month. The spread is calculated by subtracting the December futures price from the July futures price (July minus December).

As an example, assume in May 1986 a spread trader expects July prices to decline relative to December (i.e., spread to become less positive) because no new export business has developed during the month since the Chernobyl nuclear accident.

On May 28, the trader simultaneously sells one July 1986 corn futures contract at $2.37 and buys one December 1986 corn futures contract at $1.95. The spread on May 28 is 42 cents ($2.37 − $1.95). (This market position is considered a bear spread since he sold the nearby and bought the deferred.)

On July 2, the trader offsets both positions and closes out the spread. He buys one July 1986 corn futures contract at $2.05, for a gain on the July contract of 32 cents ($2.37 − $2.05). At the same time, the trader sells one December 1986 corn futures contract at $1.82, for a loss on the December contract of 13 cents ($1.95 − $1.82).

Jul Futures	Dec Futures	Spread
May 28 Sells 1 Jul corn futures at $2.37/bu	Buys 1 Dec corn futures at $1.95/bu	$0.42
Jul 2 Buys 1 Jul corn futures at $2.05/bu	Sells 1 Dec corn futures at $1.82/bu	$0.23
Result $0.32 gain/bu $950 on spread ($0.19 × 5,000 bu)	$0.13 loss/bu	$0.19

In this example, the spread became less positive moving from 42 cents to 23 cents, for a net gain of 19 cents per bushel ($0.42 − $0.23). Notice that this equals the 32-cent gain on the July contract less the

13-cent loss on the December contract. One futures contract equals 5,000 bushels, so this spread would have produced a $950 gain ($0.19 × 5,000 bushels) for the trader.

When a commodity is traded on two or more futures exchanges, price differences between contracts may reflect geographic relationships. Futures trading in wheat, for example, is conducted at the Chicago Board of Trade, the Kansas City Board of Trade, the MidAmerica Commodity Exchange, and the Minneapolis Grain Exchange. Spreading between markets might involve a long position in Kansas City wheat futures against a short position in Chicago Board of Trade wheat futures.

Intermarket Spreads

The intermarket spreader must analyze several factors that influence price differences between markets. Transportation costs are an important determining factor. Wheat prices are generally lowest in the primary producing areas and increase at least by the cost of transportation to areas where consumers are located.

A second factor influencing price differentials is the value of the class and grade of wheat deliverable on each exchange. While the different exchanges generally allow delivery of several classes of wheat (premiums and discounts allowed), each market has a tendency to reflect the prices of a particular wheat class. As an example, Chicago Board of Trade wheat futures prices tend to reflect the price of Soft Red Winter wheat, and Kansas City wheat futures prices tend to reflect the price of Hard Red Winter wheat. This is because the price at each market usually reflects the type of wheat grown nearby, i.e., Chicago and surrounding areas produce Soft Red Winter wheat, while Kansas and surrounding states produce Hard Red Winter wheat. It is also important for the spread trader to realize that different wheat classes tend to vary in price depending upon their use.

Market participants interested in spreading wheat watch the relationship between these two markets. When the price relationship becomes abnormal, spreaders tend to buy the underpriced contract and sell the overpriced contract. This occurred in October 1986 when Chicago wheat futures were trading nearly 40 cents higher than Kansas City wheat futures. The price discrepancy corresponded to a shortage of Soft Red Winter wheat in the cash market caused by a poor Soft Red Winter wheat crop coupled with heavy participation by wheat producers in the government programs.

In this market situation, spreaders bought Kansas City wheat futures and sold Chicago Board of Trade futures. When the price relationship reflected more normal market conditions, they closed their spreads by selling Kansas City wheat and buying Chicago Board of Trade wheat.

Opportunities for spreading between U.S. futures markets and foreign futures exchanges also exist. Some common international spread positions include New York versus London sugar, cocoa, or copper, and gold spreads between New York, Chicago, and London.

Intercommodity Spreads

An intercommodity spread is a spread between two different but related commodities. The two commodities can either be used interchangeably or have common supply and demand characteristics. Although it is not necessary in an intercommodity spread to spread the same months in both commodities, it is a common practice.

Wheat/Corn Spread

The wheat/corn spread is a popular intercommodity spread, and involves buying (selling) one or more wheat futures contracts and selling (buying) one or more corn futures contracts of the same delivery month. Since wheat prices are generally higher than corn prices, the spread is usually positive and quoted as wheat over corn—wheat minus corn.

Changes in the wheat/corn spread can be seasonal. The wheat/corn spread usually tends to become less positive sometime in May/June/July (following winter wheat harvest) when wheat prices are low and corn prices are high. On the other hand, a trader might expect the spread to become more positive in September/October/November during the corn harvest, when corn prices are low and wheat prices are high.

Given a "normal" spread relationship between wheat and corn, a trader can take advantage of an abnormal relationship returning to normal or a normal spread relationship becoming abnormal.

Suppose a trader anticipates a normal spread—wheat falling faster relative to corn until summer, then wheat gaining on corn in the fall. On June 29, the trader buys one wheat futures contract at $3.75 per bushel and sells one corn futures contract at $3.02½ per bushel in anticipation of the spread becoming more positive. The spread difference is 72½ cents a bushel ($3.75 − $3.02½).

On November 2, the trader offsets the position by selling one wheat futures contract at $4.01 per bushel and buying one corn futures contract at $2.49 per bushel for a difference of $1.52 per bushel ($4.01 − $2.49).

In this example, the spread moved from 72½ cents to $1.52, and the trader profited from both legs of the spread. His net gain on the position was 79½ cents per bushel ($1.52 − $0.72½) or $3,975 per spread ($0.79½ × 5,000 bushels).

Wheat Futures	Corn Futures	Spread
Jun 29 Buys 1 Dec wheat futures at $3.75/bu	Sells 1 Dec corn futures at $3.02½/bu	$0.72½
Nov 2 Sells 1 Dec wheat futures at $4.01/bu	Buys 1 Dec corn futures at $2.49/bu	$1.52
Result $0.26 gain/bu $3,975 on the spread ($0.79½ × 5,000 bu)	$0.53½ gain/bu	$0.79½

Commodity Versus
Product Spreads

A special type of intercommodity spread is the spread between a commodity and its products. The most common example, the spread between the soybean and its two products—soybean meal and soybean oil—is known as *putting on the crush* or a *crush spread.* This spread is often used by soybean-processing firms to hedge the purchase price of soybeans and the selling price of soybean oil and meal. It is established by purchasing soybean futures and selling soybean oil and soybean meal futures.

Putting on the Crush

The crush spread is used to minimize the financial risks of sudden increases in soybean costs and/or declining values of finished soybean oil and meal. To make a profit from soybean processing, soybeans must be purchased at a lower cost than the combined sales income from the finished oil and meal. The difference, or profit margin, is called the *gross processing margin (GPM).* Application of the GPM to the soybean, soybean oil, and soybean meal futures markets makes it possible for processors to buy soybean futures to hedge later purchases of cash soybeans and, at the same time, sell soybean oil and meal futures to hedge later sales of meal and oil. (For more information on the GPM, see Chapter 13 on agricultural commodities.)

Given a favorable price relationship between soybean futures and soybean oil and meal futures, the processor buys soybean futures and simultaneously sells oil and meal futures. He holds the long soybean portion of his hedge until he actually buys the required cash soybeans.

Suppose, as the processor feared, the price of soybeans in the cash market has risen. He is still relatively unaffected because the futures price of soybeans also rose in response to the same economic factors. He buys soybeans in the cash market and offsets his long soybean position—at the higher price—by selling an equal number of soybean futures contracts. This approximately offsets the increased cost of his raw material.

The processor holds the short side of his crush hedge—the sale of oil and meal futures—until he is ready to sell his finished oil and meal. If the cash market values of oil and meal decline, the futures prices probably will decline also. Although the processor receives less income from his cash market sale of the oil and meal, this loss is roughly offset by his equal purchase of oil and meal futures contracts at lower prices.

The hedge works in the same way and for the same reasons as do all well-placed hedges—because of the tendency of cash and futures prices, which are influenced by the same economic factors, to move in the same direction. But the crush spread is a uniquely effective hedge because it affords the soybean processor protection in three related markets.

Reverse Crush

The opposite of a crush spread is called a *reverse crush*. This spreading opportunity results from distortions in normal price patterns when the cost of soybeans is higher than the combined sales value of soybean oil and meal. The resulting unfavorable gross processing margin makes it unprofitable for the soybean processor to manufacture meal and oil.

When the GPM drops below a profitable level, a soybean processor may slow down or even stop his manufacturing operation, and at the same time possibly initiate a reverse crush spread—selling soybean futures and buying oil and meal futures. It is likely this firm would not be alone in this action, and the concerted pressure of reduced soybean meal and oil manufacturing and a reverse crush spread in the futures market will gradually reverse the price relationships to a more normal level.

SPREADING IN FINANCIAL INSTRUMENT FUTURES

Spread relationships exist between any number of financial instrument futures contracts and vary in reaction to and in anticipation of changes in economic circumstances. When price relationships are expected to shift, a spread trader puts on a trade to take advantage of these transitions.

Types of Financial Instrument Spreads

Within the financial markets, the three primary types of spreads are interdelivery, intermarket, and intercommodity.

Interdelivery or Calendar Spreads

Interdelivery or calendar spreads are between different delivery months of the same futures market on the same exchange—e.g., the sale (purchase) of December T-bonds and the purchase (sale) of March T-bonds.

Intermarket Spreads

Intermarket spreading involves taking opposite positions simultaneously in two similar markets at two different exchanges. Common intermarket spreads include the CBOT 10-year T-note/DTB German Government Bond futures—buying (selling) CBOT 10-year T-note futures and selling (buying) DTB German Government Bond futures—and the CBOT 10-year T-note/MATIF French Government Bond spread—buying (selling) CBOT 10-year T-note futures and selling (buying) MATIF French Government Bond futures.

Intercommodity Spreads

An intercommodity spread consists of buying one commodity and selling a different, but related, commodity—e.g., selling (buying) Municipal Bond Index futures and buying (selling) T-bond futures (commonly called the *MOB—Munis Over Bonds*), or buying (selling) 10-Year T-note futures and selling (buying) T-bond futures (referred to as the *NOB—Notes Over Bonds*).

A primary motivator in establishing an interdelivery spread in the financial markets is the implication of carry. Chapters 8 and 17 discuss carry and the financial markets in more detail.

Interdelivery or Calendar Spreads

In a financial bull spread, a trader is long the nearby contract month and short the deferred contract month. If prices increase, a bull spread is profitable if the nearby month rises faster than the deferred month. Conversely, if prices fall, the spread is profitable if the nearby month falls slower than the deferred month.

Bull Calendar Spread

For example, a trader has been watching the T-bond futures market for several months. He knows most market analysts call for higher interest rates in December, anticipating an increased demand for seasonal credit. This demand is expected to be only temporary and should not affect interest rates past year-end. For this reason, the price of March T-bond futures has remained relatively unchanged at 110-16, while December T-bond futures dropped from 111-25 to 111-08 by mid-October. The trader believes the price of the December T-bond contract has fallen too far, and the market has overreacted to the possibility of higher year-end rates. Since he thinks December T-bond futures are priced too cheap relative to March, he initiates a bull spread by purchasing 10 December contracts at 111-08 and selling 10 March contracts at 110-16, for a spread of 00-24 (December minus March).

By early December, the demand for credit has increased, but the increase has not been as great as generally anticipated. As the trader expected, the December/March spread became more positive: the price of the December futures contract rose sharply to 111-18, while March T-bonds rose slightly to 110-20, for a spread difference of 00-30. The trader unwinds the spread by selling the December position and buying the March position.

Dec Futures	Mar Futures	Spread
Oct 16		
Buys 10 Dec T-bond contracts at 111-08	Sells 10 Mar T-bond contracts at 110-16	00-24
Dec 3		
Sells 10 Dec T-bond contracts at 111-18	Buys 10 Mar T-bond contracts at 110-20	00-30
Result		
00-10 or $10/_{32}$ gain 10 × $31.25 × 10 contracts = $3,125	00-04 or $4/_{32}$ loss 4 × $31.25 × 10 contracts = −$1,250	00-06

Net gain = $1,875 on the spread
(6 × $31.25 × 10 contracts)

In this bull spread, the trader made a profit because the price of the nearby contract (December) rose faster than the price of the deferred contract (March).

Bear Calendar Spread

A bear spread is just the opposite of a bull spread. A trader is short the nearby contract month and long the deferred contract month. If prices rise, the spread is profitable if the nearby month increases at a slower rate than the deferred contract month. On the other hand, if prices are declining, the spread is profitable if the nearby falls at a faster rate than the deferred month.

Butterfly Spread

Another common calendar spread is a butterfly spread. A butterfly spread involves the placing of two calendar spreads in opposite directions with the center position common to both spreads. Two examples of a butterfly spread are:

♦ Long 3 Mar T-bonds/short 6 Jun T-bonds/long 3 Sep T-bonds
♦ Short 3 Mar T-bonds/long 6 Jun T-bonds/short 3 Sep T-bonds

A butterfly spread actually can be divided into two interdelivery spreads, e.g., long March T-bonds and short June T-bonds; short June T-bonds and long September T-bonds. The first example can be classified as a bull spread (long March bonds and short June bonds) together with a bear spread (short June bonds and long September bonds). The second example, on the other hand, is actually a bear spread (short March bonds and long June bonds) followed by a bull spread (long June bonds and short September bonds).

One reason a trader may be interested in establishing a butterfly spread is because he believes the price of the middle contract is out of line to the contract months on each side.

Butterfly spreads also can be established to take advantage of changes in the shape of the yield curve—using contracts with different maturities but the same delivery month. One example is a spread that includes December 2-year T-notes, December 5-year T-notes, and December 10-year T-notes.

Intermarket Spreads

Intermarket spreading involves taking opposite positions simultaneously in two similar markets at two different exchanges. As mentioned earlier in the chapter, there are a variety of financial intermarket spreads. An example of a stock index intermarket spread follows.

Stock Index Intermarket Spreads

All stock indexes reflect general market risk and, therefore, tend to move in the same direction over time. Because indexes tend to move in the same direction, spreaders base their trading strategies on the strength of one contract relative to another, rather than speculating on overall market direction.

A stock index contract is strong relative to another if it advances faster during a bull market rally or declines slower in a bear market. For example, if a trader anticipates the S&P 500 Index will be strong relative to the Wilshire Small Cap Index, he would buy the S&P 500 futures and sell the Wilshire Small Cap Index futures. The trader generally profits from this spread position when the S&P 500 advances faster in a bull market or declines slower in a bear market.

The performance of different stock index futures contracts varies in certain phases of the market due to the nature of the underlying stocks. The S&P 500, for example, is a blue-chip-oriented composite, while the

Wilshire Small Cap Index consists of smaller New York Stock Exchange and Amex stocks as well as NASDAQ issues. Historically, blue-chip stocks often tend to lead the rest of the market in the early stages of a bull market and, as the bull market matures, investors often buy the more affordable secondary and OTC issues. As the bull market nears its end, buying of blue chips levels off, while activity in secondary issues typically continues to increase. Because of these fundamental factors, the S&P 500 tends to move first in the initial stages of a bull (bear) market and, as the market matures, the Wilshire Small Cap Index increases (decreases).

Stock index intermarket spread trades are usually done in one of two ways: (1) by ratioing the contracts on a 1:1 basis, or (2) by matching total contract values (the dollar multiplier times the index point level).

As an example of an intermarket spread, assume a trader forecasts a bull stock market and expects the S&P 500 to gain on the Wilshire Small Cap Index. He buys two S&P 500 futures each at 447 and sells three Wilshire Small Cap contracts at 302. At a later date, the market moves higher and the trader closes his position by selling two S&P 500 contracts at 459 and buying three Wilshire Small Cap Index contracts at 307.

S&P 500 Futures	Wilshire Small Cap Index Futures
Now	
Buys 2 Dec S&P 500 contracts at 447	Sells 3 Dec Wilshire Small Cap Index contracts at 302
Later	
Sells 2 Dec S&P 500 contracts at 459	Buys 3 Dec Wilshire Small Cap Index contracts at 307
Result	
12 point gain × $500 × 2 contracts = $12,000 gain	5 point loss × $500 × 3 contracts = $7,500 loss

Net gain = $4,500 ($12,000 gain − $7,500 loss)

In this scenario, the trader made a profit because the S&P 500 contract, which gained 12 points, rose faster in the bull market than did the Wilshire Small Cap Index contract, which gained 5 points.

All spreading is a form of *arbitrage*—the purchase and sale of similar commodities in two different markets to take advantage of a price discrepancy. By performing this economic function, arbitrageurs increase the efficiency of the markets by narrowing the gap between bid and offer prices and minimizing price distortions between similar markets.

Typical arbitrage trading examples include cash and futures spreads between similar instruments, spreads between futures of the same type of commodity or security trading at different exchanges (e.g., Chicago Board of Trade gold versus COMEX gold), and spreads between markets in different countries (e.g., Chicago Board of Trade T-bonds versus London International Financial Futures Exchange T-bonds).

Intercommodity spreads normally are traded between two different, but closely related, futures markets. Two of the most actively traded intercommodity spreads among financial instruments are the MOB (Munis Over Bonds, i.e., Munis minus T-bonds) and the NOB (10-year Notes Over Bonds, i.e., 10-year T-notes minus T-bonds). Other commonly traded intercommodity spreads are the FOB (5-year T-notes Over Bonds, i.e., 5-year T-notes minus T-bonds); the FITE (5-year T-notes Over 10-year T-notes, i.e., 5-year T-notes minus 10-year T-notes); and different 2-year T-note spreads against 5-year T-notes, 10-year T-notes, or T-bonds.

The MOB (Munis Over Bonds) spread takes advantage of price differences between the Municipal Bond Index futures contract and Treasury bond futures.

The strategy consists of buying muni-bond futures and selling T-bond futures (buying the MOB) when an investor expects municipal bonds to gain on government bonds. Conversely, an investor anticipating government bonds to gain on municipal bonds would sell muni-bond futures and buy T-bond futures (selling the MOB).

Assume a spread trader has been observing a general rally in the long-term debt markets. Muni-bond issuance, however, has been picking up significantly. The trader expects an oversupply of munis to depress muni prices, while the Treasury market continues a strong rally. With December muni futures at 87-18 and December T-bond futures at 79-15, the spreader sold one muni contract and bought one T-bond contract. As expected, both contracts rallied, but T-bonds rose faster than munis. The trader then offsets the position by selling one T-bond contract and buying one muni-bond contract.

Arbitrage

Intercommodity Spreads

The MOB Spread

Muni-bond Futures	T-bond Futures	Spread
Now		
Sells 1 muni-bond contract at 87-18	Buys 1 T-bond contract at 79-15	08-03
Later		
Buys 1 muni-bond contract at 89-29	Sells 1 T-bond contract at 83-10	06-19
Result		
02-11 loss	03-27 gain	01-16

Net gain = $^{48}\!/_{32}$ or $1,500 on the spread
$\qquad$ (48 × $31.25 × 1 contract)

The NOB

The NOB refers to the spread between 10-year T-note futures and T-bond futures. Since intermediate-term note prices usually are higher than long-term bond prices, the spread is called the *NOB*—Notes Over Bonds (notes minus T-bonds).

NOB spread strategies take advantage of the different price sensitivities of 10-year notes and T-bonds to changes in interest rates—that is, bond prices are typically more sensitive than note prices to a given change in interest rates. Depending on interest rate expectations, a trader can either buy or sell the NOB. For example, to take advantage of an equal increase in yields along the yield curve—the spread becoming more positive—a spreader would buy the NOB (purchasing T-note futures and selling T-bond futures). On the other hand, an investor can take advantage of an equal decline in yields along the yield curve—a spread becoming more negative—by selling the NOB (selling T-notes and buying T-bond futures contracts).

The NOB Spread

Assume in April a trader anticipates the general level of interest rates to rise by about 20 basis points (.2 percent) over the course of the next few weeks for Treasury instruments of all maturities. Since the trader knows longer-term securities are more price-sensitive than shorter-term maturities, he buys the NOB spread to profit from the greater price sensitivity of T-bond futures relative to 10-year T-notes. With June 10-year T-note futures at 112-30 and June T-bonds at 112-22, the trader buys the NOB spread at 00-08 (10-year T-notes minus T-bonds) by purchasing ten 10-year T-note futures contracts and selling 10 T-bond contracts.

By late May, interest rates rise, as expected, by 20 basis points. The

NOB spread became more positive because the increase in interest rates had a greater impact on the price of T-bond futures compared to 10-year T-note futures. The trader offsets the spread by selling ten 10-year T-note contracts at 111-04 and buying 10 T-bond contracts at 110-08.

10-year T-note Futures	T-bond Futures	Spread
Apr 11		
Buys 10 10-year T-note contracts at 112-30	Sells 10 T-bond contracts at 112-22	00-08
May 28		
Sells 10 10-year T-note contracts at 111-04	Buys 10 T-bond contracts at 110-08	00-28
Result		
01-26 or $^{58}\!/_{32}$ loss 58 × \$31.25 × 10 contracts = −\$18,125	02-14 or $^{78}\!/_{32}$ gain 78 × \$31.25 × 10 contracts = \$24,375	00-20

Net gain = \$6,250 on the spread
(20 × \$31.25 × 10 contracts)

Because an equal increase in the level of interest rates had an unequal impact on the prices of T-bond and 10-year T-note futures, the trader made a profit from a long NOB spread position.

Conclusion

The information presented in this chapter just scratches the surface regarding the topic of spreads. Keep in mind that the primary purpose of this chapter is to give the reader a basic understanding of how spreads are established, the advantages of trading spreads, and the price relationships between different futures contracts. (For more information about the different types of spreads and their price relationships, see the Sources of Information in the Appendix. Options spreads are covered in Chapter 12.)

Options on futures contracts have added a new dimension to futures trading. Like futures, options provide price protection against an adverse price move. But unlike futures hedgers, option hedgers are not locked in to a specific floor or ceiling price, and can take advantage of a market trend. In addition, the variety of trading strategies available with options or in combination with futures makes options attractive to a wide base of investors.

Options on futures contracts were introduced in October 1982 when the Chicago Board of Trade began trading options on Treasury bond futures. They were initially offered as part of a government pilot program, and the success of this contract opened the way for options on agricultural and other financial futures contracts.

Trading in options is not new. Options traditionally have been used with underlying cash securities, such as stocks, as well as with physicals, such as precious metals and real estate. There was over-the-counter trading in options on shares of common stock long before the creation in the mid-1970s of centralized exchange trading in stock options. Participants in the stock options markets are primarily investors seeking to profit, on a leveraged basis, from anticipated movements in common stock prices. Many of the principles that apply to options trading in the cash market can be used effectively with futures contracts.

Options
on
Futures
Contracts

*Risk-Management
Alternatives*

12

OPTION BASICS

What Is an Option?

An option provides a choice. The buyer of an option acquires the right, but not the obligation, to buy or sell an underlying commodity (whether a physical commodity, security, or futures contract) under specific conditions in exchange for the payment of a premium. Within the futures industry, the underlying instrument is a futures contract.

Calls and Puts

There are two types of options: calls and puts. A *call option* gives the buyer the right, but not the obligation, to *purchase* a particular futures contract at a specific price any time during the life of the option. A *put option* gives the buyer the right, but not the obligation, to *sell* a particular futures contract at a specific price any time during the life of the option.

The price at which the buyer of a call has the right to purchase a futures contract and the buyer of a put has the right to sell a futures contract is known as the *strike price* or *exercise price*.

In options trading, it is important to understand that trading in call options is completely distinct from trading in put options. For every call buyer, there is a call seller; for every put buyer, there is a put seller.

Offset and Exercise

If someone purchases a call option, he can offset the position by selling the same call option contract. Conversely, if someone purchases a put option, he can offset the position by selling the same put option. The same is true for an option seller. If an option seller wants to offset his short position, he buys back an option at the same strike price and expiration date—a specific day preceding the futures contract delivery month.

Both buyers and sellers may offset an open option position any time prior to its expiration. However, only option buyers may *exercise* the contract, i.e., acquire a futures position at the option strike price. An option can be exercised on any trading day up to and including its last day of trading, which is usually the day before the actual expiration day of the option.

Once the buyer of a put or call exercises the option, the exchange where the contract is traded records an open futures position for the designated contract month at the strike price in the accounts of the buyer and the seller. The table on the next page illustrates the positions assigned to an option buyer and seller after an option is exercised.

Premium

In the case of either a call or put, the option buyer (option holder) must pay the option seller (option writer) a premium. This is the only

Futures Positions After Option Exercise		
	Call Option	**Put Option**
Buyer Assumes	Long futures position	Short futures position
Seller Assumes	Short futures position	Long futures position

variable of the contract and is determined on the trading floor of an exchange depending on market conditions, such as supply, demand, and other economic and market variables.

Regardless of how much the market swings, the most an option buyer can lose is the option premium. He deposits the premium with his broker, and the money goes to the option seller. Because of this limited and known risk, option buyers are not required to maintain margin accounts.

Option sellers, on the other hand, face risks similar to participants in the futures market.

For example, since the seller of a call is assigned a short futures position if the option is exercised, his risk is the same as someone who initially sold a futures contract. Because no one can predict exactly how the market will move, the option seller posts margin to demonstrate his ability to meet any potential contractual obligations.

Marking-to-Market

Following the conclusion of each trading session, each seller's option position is marked-to-market to reflect the gains or losses from that particular trading session. If there is a significant adverse price move, the seller may have to post additional margin before the start of the next day's trading to maintain the open position.

Furthermore, option margins are set by the exchange where the contract is traded at a level high enough to guarantee the financial integrity of the marketplace without unduly increasing the cost of participation to the investor. During conditions of high price volatility, futures exchanges raise margins; as price volatility decreases, these margins are lowered.

Margins

OPTION PRICING

Even though the marketplace is the ultimate determinant of how much an option is worth, there are some basic guidelines traders use to calculate option premiums. In general, an option premium is the sum of intrinsic and time value, which are influenced by volatility, the difference between a strike price and the underlying price, and time to maturity.

Intrinsic Value

Intrinsic value is the difference, if any, between the market price of the underlying commodity and the strike price of an option. A call option has intrinsic value if its strike price is below the futures price. A put option has intrinsic value if its strike price is above the futures price. Any option that has intrinsic value is referred to as being *in-the-money*.

For example, a corn call option with a $2.50 strike price gives the holder the right to purchase corn futures at $2.50 a bushel. If corn futures are trading at $3 a bushel and a trader exercises his $2.50 call, he realizes a 50-cent profit ($3 − $2.50). A call option with a strike price less than the current futures price is said to be *in-the-money*.

A corn put option with a $3.25 strike price, on the other hand, gives the holder the right to sell corn futures at $3.25. If corn futures are trading at $3 a bushel and an option holder exercises his $3.25 put, he realizes a 25-cent profit ($3.25 − $3). A put option with a strike price greater than the current futures price is said to be *in-the-money*.

A call option with a strike price above the current market price is said to be *out-of-the-money*. For instance, if an option buyer holds a $3.50 corn call option, he has the right to buy a corn futures contract at $3.50. But, if the futures price is $3, he would be better off to buy a corn futures contract at the lower price of $3 a bushel rather than exercising his option to buy at $3.50.

A put option with a strike price below the current market price is said to be *out-of-the-money*. If an option buyer holds a $2.50 corn put, he has the right to sell a corn futures contract at $2.50. But, if corn futures are at $3, his put option is not worth exercising, since he can sell a corn futures contract for a higher price in the futures market.

When the strike price of any put or call option equals the current market price, the option is said to be *at-the-money*. With corn futures at $3 a bushel, a $3 call or $3 put option is said to be *at-the-money*.

A summary of the intrinsic value of different put and call options is listed in the table on the next page.

Delta and Gamma

Two sensitivity measures associated with an option premium are delta and gamma. Delta measures how much an option premium changes, given

Calculating Intrinsic Value		
	Call Option	**Put Option**
In-the-Money	Futures > Strike	Futures < Strike
At-the-Money	Futures = Strike	Futures = Strike
Out-of-the-Money	Futures < Strike	Futures > Strike

a unit change in the underlying futures. Delta often is interpreted as the probability that the option will be in-the-money at expiration. Gamma measures how fast delta changes and is defined as the change in delta, given a unit change in the underlying futures price.

The second major component of an option premium is time value. *Time value* is the amount of money that option buyers are willing to pay for the protective characteristics afforded by the option. Of course, since there are sellers as well as buyers in the market, time value also reflects the price that sellers are willing to accept for writing an option.

In general, the more time remaining until expiration, the greater the time value. That is because the right to purchase or sell something is more valuable to a market participant if he has a year to decide what to do with the option rather than just six months. Conversely, an option buyer is asking the seller to face the risk of exercise, and a year's worth of risk costs more than six months' worth.

Some parallels can be drawn between the time value of an option premium and the premium charged for a casualty insurance policy. The longer the term of the insurance policy, the greater the probability a claim will be made by the policyholder, thus, the greater the risk assumed by the insurance company. To compensate for this increased risk, the insurer will charge a greater premium. The same is true with options on futures—the longer the term until option expiration, the greater the risk to the option seller, hence, the higher the option premium.

Volatility

Volatility of the underlying commodity is one of the more important factors affecting the value of the option premium. Volatility measures the change in price of a contract over a given time period. It is often expressed as a percentage and computed as the annualized standard deviation of percentage changes in daily prices.*

Time Value

---

*Vega is a measure of the net change in an option premium, given a 1 percent change in the volatility.

Time Decay

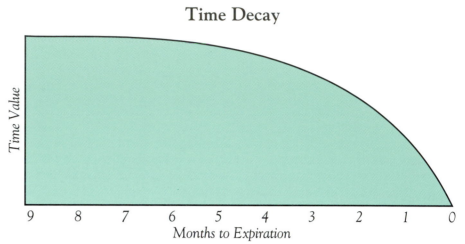

Months to Expiration

As the chart illustrates, when an at-the-money option approaches expiration, its time value erodes faster (all else being equal) because there is less time for the option to move in-the-money. At expiration, an option has no time value; its only value, if any, is intrinsic value. One option pricing derivative, theta, measures the rate at which an option value decreases with the passage of time, i.e., the slope in the time decay chart. Many traders use theta when selling options to gauge their potential profit or when buying options to measure their exposure to time decay.

While there are several mathematical models that compute volatility, the basic theory behind its influence on price is simple. Volatile prices of the underlying futures contract increase the probability that an option will move in-the-money, thereby increasing the option premium. The more volatile the price of the underlying commodity, the greater the chance of an adverse price move; thus, buyers are willing to pay more, and option sellers facing the risk of exercise require higher premiums.

For instance, if silver futures are trading for $6 an ounce and remain at that price for a year, there is little risk in selling a $6.50 call option. But, if silver futures trade between $5.25 and $6.75 an ounce during the same week, there is a greater risk that the $6.50 call will run in-the-money. The option seller must be paid for taking on the risk the option buyer requests, so the option premium should be greater than the same call in a less volatile market.

Option Pricing Models

There are many option pricing models that take these different variables—intrinsic value, time remaining to expiration, and volatility—into account (as well as other factors such as short-term interest rates) to calculate the theoretical value of an option. These theoretical values may or may not correspond to the actual market values in the marketplace, but are used by traders to make trading decisions.

One of the most prominent option pricing models was introduced by Fischer Black and Myron Scholes in 1973. Different option pricing models also calculate the value of delta, gamma, vega, and other pricing sensitivities. (While it is beyond the scope of this text to describe how the Black-Scholes or any other option pricing model works, several texts that cover this topic in depth are listed in the Appendix.)

OPTION STRATEGIES

Options are used in all market environments—bullish, slightly bullish, bearish, slightly bearish, and neutral. In no way can all of them be covered in this chapter, but, in reviewing those that are discussed, the reader will gain a basic appreciation of why call and put options are bought and sold daily.

Buying Call Options

Since a call gives the buyer the right to buy a futures contract at a fixed price, a call option buyer believes futures prices will rise by at least enough to cover the premium he paid. In some situations, a trader might buy a call to establish a price ceiling for the future purchase of a cash commodity or to protect a short futures position.

Using Calls for Protection Against Higher Prices

For example, a treasurer of an investment firm anticipates having funds available at a later date to purchase U.S. Treasury bonds. However, the treasurer is worried that between now and the time he purchases the bonds, interest rates may decline, raising bond prices. He would like to have temporary insurance against a sudden price increase, but also wants to avoid paying too much if bond prices decline. To achieve both price protection and an opportunity to purchase bonds at a lower price, the treasurer decides to buy a call option.

Suppose in May the price of a specific cash Treasury bond is 87-00. A September 86-00 call is purchased by the treasurer for $2,000. By August, interest rates on long-term Treasury bonds have declined and the price of the cash bond is 96-00, and the September 86-00 call is priced at $10,100. He decides to offset his position by selling the September 86-00 call.

By selling back his call option for $10,100, the treasurer makes an $8,100 gain ($10,100 − $2,000) and offsets most of the increased cost in the price of T-bonds.

Cash	Options
May	
Price of T-bonds is 87-00	Buys Sep 86-00 call option for $2,000
Aug	
Price of T-bonds is 96-00	Sells Sep 86-00 call option for $10,100
Result	
$9,000 (or 9-00) loss	$8,100 gain

A major advantage of this strategy is that the treasurer established an interest rate floor, but not a ceiling. Had interest rates increased instead of decreased, the treasurer could have purchased T-bonds at a lower price and either let the option expire or offset his option position to earn any remaining time value. The only cost for this price protection was the option premium.

Buying Put Options

Bearing in mind that a put is an option to sell a futures contract at a fixed price, a put option buyer expects futures prices to decline by enough to cover the premium. In many cases, a market participant might buy a put to establish a minimum price for the future sale of a cash commodity or to protect a long futures position.

Using Puts for Protection Against Lower Prices

Assume a feed manufacturer expects soybean meal prices to rise, so he contracts ahead for all his soybean meal needs during the spring and summer months. Prices do trend higher for a short time, but after hitting $165 per ton in mid-April, it appears that prices could drop sharply.

Fearing that competitors might pass along any cost savings to their customers and gain market share, the manufacturer buys an August $160 soybean meal put option for $4.40. By mid-June, soybean meal prices have fallen to $148, so the company sells back the put for $12.50 and makes a profit of $8.10 per ton.

Cash	Options
Mid-Apr	
Soybean meal price is $165	Buys Aug $160 put option for $4.40
Mid-June	
Soybean meal price is $148	Sells Aug $160 put option for $12.50
Result	
$17 loss	$8.10 gain

The feed manufacturer uses the $8.10 per ton profit from the put to keep his selling price for feed competitive. If soybean meal prices moved higher, the manufacturer could have let the put option expire or offset his option position to earn any remaining time value. The only cost for this price protection was the option premium.

Selling Call and Put Options

The primary reason for a trader to sell either a call or put option is to earn the option premium.

Generally, call options are sold by individuals who anticipate either little price movement or a slight decrease in prices. In any case, they hope the underlying futures price will not rise to a level that will cause the option to be exercised and result in a loss greater than the premium received.

Those who sell put options, on the other hand, generally expect prices to stay the same or increase only slightly. Sellers of put options hope the underlying futures price will not fall to a level that will cause the option to be exercised and result in a loss greater than the premium received.

Market Expectations for Option Buyers and Sellers		
	Call Option	Put Option
Buyer	Bullish	Bearish
Seller	Neutral to slightly bearish	Neutral to slightly bullish

Selling Calls to Earn the Option Premium

At a time when the futures price is 76-00 for Treasury bonds, an investor collects a premium of $3,000 by selling a six-month, at-the-money call. Since an at-the-money call, by definition, has no intrinsic value, the $3,000 premium is entirely time value. If the futures price at expiration is at or below 76-00, the option will expire worthless—with neither intrinsic value nor time value—and the investor's return will be the original $3,000 premium.

If the futures price at expiration is above 76-00, the option seller stands to realize some net return at expiration as long as the intrinsic value of the option is less than the premium received when the option was sold. Assume the futures price has risen to 78-00 by expiration. The option buyer exercises the call and the option seller incurs a $2,000 loss on the short futures position. However, since the initial premium received by the option seller was $3,000, his net gain is $1,000.

As stated earlier in the chapter, an option seller wishing to liquidate a position prior to exercise or expiration can make an offsetting option purchase at the prevailing premium. To whatever extent the erosion of the option's time value has reduced the cost of the offsetting purchase, the seller realizes a net profit.

What if three months after the investor sold the 76-00 call, the futures price is still 76-00, but the option's time value has declined to $2,000? By making an offsetting purchase at this price, the option seller realizes a net gain of $1,000. This purchase eliminates any further possibility of the option being exercised.[†]

Selling Puts for Limited Protection Against Higher Prices

When prices are likely to remain relatively stable, or when the expected price increase is fairly small, a hedger may find it worthwhile to sell a put option. By selling a put option, the seller receives a premium from the buyer and enters the hedge with a credit to his account. But the seller also faces the risk that the buyer may exercise the option if the futures price falls below the option strike price.

Suppose in late March a company that produces pet food and livestock feed expects soybean meal prices to move sideways in a fairly narrow range around the current price of $146 a ton. Wanting only limited protection against rising prices, the company sells a September $140 soybean meal put option and receives a premium of $8.55 a ton.

The market remains relatively quiet during the spring and summer

---

[†]An option can be exercised **only by the option buyer** any time before expiration. Although gains on in-the-money options are often realized through offsetting option sales, and the majority of exercises do not occur until at or near expiration, early exercise remains the prerogative of every option buyer.

months, with the price at $148 in early August. Therefore, the company pays 95 cents to buy back the put option for a gain of $7.60 a ton.

Cash	Options
Late Mar	
Price of soybean meal is $146	Sells Sep $140 put for $8.55
Early Aug	
Price of soybean meal is $148	Buys Sep $140 put for $0.95
Result	
$2 loss	$7.60 gain

Since the market price of soybean meal rose slightly, the company is able to buy back the put option at a lower premium[‡] and use the profit to partially offset the higher ingredient costs.

If futures prices had fallen, the premium of the put option would have risen. In this case, the option seller who buys back the put option could have suffered a loss. But ingredient prices also would have fallen, partially offsetting the potential loss on the option position.

Other Option Strategies

As the previous examples illustrate, there are a variety of ways options can be used to achieve either price protection or profits. While some option strategies can be as simple as either buying or selling one option, option strategies can become quite complicated and incorporate a combination of long and short options and/or futures and cash positions. Many of the more complicated option strategies fall under the category of spreads.

Option Spreads

An option spread is the simultaneous purchase and sale of one or more options contracts, futures, and/or cash positions. Since the prices of two different contracts for the same or related instruments have a tendency to move up or down together, spread trading can offer protection against losses that arise from unexpected or extreme price volatility.

[‡]The premium for a put option tends to move in the opposite direction from the price of the underlying futures contract.

This occurs because losses from one side of a spread are more or less offset by gains from the other side of the spread. For example, if the short (sold) side of a spread results in a loss due to a price increase, the long (bought) side should produce a profit, offsetting much of the loss.

While option strategies allow a trader to limit the amount of risk he is carrying, other reasons for establishing option spreads are to capitalize on a market environment where one option is overvalued or undervalued in relation to another, to hedge, or to enhance the return on investments.

Market participants have a variety of different option strategies at their fingertips to use in reaching their market objectives. These strategies can take into account different strike prices, futures prices, and expiration dates.

Vertical Spreads

Vertical spreads, sometimes referred to as *money spreads,* offer traders limited return with limited risk. They involve buying and selling puts or calls of the same expiration month but different strike prices. The four major types of vertical spreads are the bull put spread, the bull call spread, the bear put spread, and the bear call spread. Bull spreads are used when the trader expects a rising market, while bear spreads are used when the trader expects a declining market.

Bull call spread: Buying a call at one strike price and simultaneously selling a call at a higher strike price.

Bull put spread: Buying a put at one strike price and simultaneously selling a put at a higher strike price.

Bear call spread: Selling a call at one strike price and simultaneously buying a call at a higher strike price.

Bear put spread: Selling a put at one strike price and simultaneously buying a put with a higher strike price.

Example: Bull Call Spread for Moderate Price Protection

In late June, a baker is concerned that shortening prices might rise and reduce his expected profits from a cash contract he made to supply baked goods in December.

With the price of soybean oil at 17.2 cents a pound, he executes a bull call spread by purchasing a December 17-cent soybean oil call option for .96 cent a pound and simultaneously selling a December 18-cent soybean oil call option for .535 cent a pound.

By early September, soybean oil prices have risen to 17.8 cents, so he closes out the spread. He sells back the 17-cent call option for 1.285 cents, for a profit of .325 cent, and buys back the 18-cent call option for .55 cent, for a loss of .015 cent. When the results from both legs of the spread are combined, the hedger has a net gain of .31 cent a pound.

Cash	Options
Late Jun Soybean oil price is 17.2 cents	Buys Dec 17-cent call for .96 cent; sells Dec 18-cent call for .535 cent
Early Sep Soybean oil price is 17.8 cents	Sells Dec 17-cent call for 1.285 cents; buys Dec 18-cent call for .55 cent
Result .6-cent loss	.325-cent gain on Dec 17-cent call option; .015-cent loss on Dec 18-cent call; .31-cent net gain on spread

Horizontal Spreads

Horizontal spreads, also known as *calendar spreads,* offer traders the opportunity to profit from different time decay patterns associated with options of different maturities. Therefore, horizontal spreads involve the purchase of either a call or put option and the simultaneous sale of the same type of option with typically the same strike price but with a different expiration month. Because time value in a near-term option decays more rapidly than time value in a more distant option, a near-term option is often sold the same time a distant option is bought.

Horizontal spreads using calls often are employed when the long-term price expectation is stable to bullish, while horizontal spreads using puts often are employed when the long-term price expectation is stable to bearish.

Conversions

With a conversion, the trader buys a put option, sells a call option, and buys a futures contract. The put and call options have the same strike price and the same expiration month. The futures contract has the same expiration month as the options and its price is usually as close as possible to the options' strike price. If the futures price is above the call strike price before expiration, the short call is exercised against the trader, which automatically offsets his long futures position; the long put option expires unexercised.

If the futures price falls below the put strike price before expiration, the long put option is exercised by the trader, which automatically offsets his long futures position; the short call option expires unexercised.

Example: Conversion Spread to Take Advantage of Price Discrepancies

Assume a 90-day $3 wheat put option is underpriced by a quarter of a cent at 10¼ cents, while a 90-day $3 wheat call option is correctly priced at 10½ cents, with the underlying futures at $3.

The trader establishes a conversion by purchasing an at-the-money put option for 10¼ cents, buying wheat futures at $3, and selling an at-the-money call option for 10½ cents. Under this market scenario, he is guaranteed a profit of a quarter of a cent a bushel, or $12.50 on the position (based on a 5,000-bushel contract). He retains this profit no matter what the price of the underlying futures contract is at expiration** because the net debit†† or net credit†† from the conversion is always zero at expiration. See the calculations below.

		Credit (Debit)
Long 1 $3 put	$0.10¼	($512.50)
Short 1 $3 call	0.10½	525.00
Long 1 $3 futures	3.00	0
Net credit		$12.50

Futures price decreases to $2.50 at expiration:

		Credit (Debit)
Exercise 1 $3 put for 1 short futures	$0.50	$2,500
Abandon 1 $3 call	0.00	0
Offset 1 long futures by the exercise of the put option	2.50	(2,500)
Net debit/credit		0

Futures price remains at $3 at expiration:

		Credit (Debit)
Exercise 1 $3 put for 1 short futures	$0.00	0
Abandon 1 $3 call	0.00	0
Offset 1 long futures by the exercise of the put option	3.00	0
Net debit/credit		0

**There may be variation requirements that must be met prior to expiration.
††Net debit or net credit = (premium received − premium paid)

Futures price increases to $3.50 at expiration:

		Credit (Debit)
Exercise 1 $3 call for 1 short futures	$0.50	($2,500)
Abandon 1 $3 put	0.00	0
Offset 1 long futures by the call exercised against the trader	3.50	2,500
Net debit/credit		0

In this example, a conversion was initiated at a net credit. The return on a conversion can be calculated as follows:

    Return on conversion = (call premium − put premium) − (futures price − strike price).

Reverse Conversions

In a reverse conversion, the trader buys a call option, sells a put option, and sells a futures contract. The put and call options have the same strike price and the same expiration month. The futures price also has the same expiration month and its price is usually as close as possible to the options' strike price. If the futures price is above the strike price by expiration, the long call option is exercised by the trader, which automatically offsets his short futures position; the short put option expires unexercised. If the futures price falls below the strike price by expiration, the short put option is exercised against the trader, which automatically offsets his short futures position; the long call option expires unexercised.

Delta-Neutral Spreads

Delta-neutral spreads, also known as *neutral* or *ratio hedges*, involve offsetting the profit/loss potential in one option position with that in one or more options/futures/cash positions.

Ratio Hedge

Suppose an institution has scheduled several sales of Treasury bonds over the next few months even though bond prices are low and the weakness in the market is expected to continue.

The institution wants to obtain price protection against further declines in bond values that could sharply reduce proceeds from bond sales. In order to reach its market objective, the institution decides to employ a *ratio hedge*. In other words, put options are purchased and, subsequently, liquidated as cash bonds are sold and/or as bond prices change.

It should be recognized that this strategy requires continuous day-to-day management. As bonds are sold and as bond prices decrease or increase relative to the strike price of the options, the number of put options needed to maintain an effective hedge is subject to change. The complexity of the strategy can be justified, however, by its effectiveness when skillfully executed.

The management requirement consists of two components. The simpler and more obvious of these stems from the fact that once the institution no longer owns the assets, the institution no longer needs to protect its price. Thus, as bonds from a portfolio are sold, those put options purchased to provide protection can be sold. In effect, selling the puts cancels the protection.

Somewhat more involved are those adjustments required by changing bond prices. If bond futures prices decline, then fewer puts should be needed to maintain the hedge because the dollar value of the holdings is lower. Accordingly, some of the options can be sold.

The controlling variable (which an experienced options broker can explain in greater detail) is the option delta: the change in the option premium resulting from a one-unit change in the futures price. In general, the delta increases as an option moves in-the-money and decreases as an option moves out-of-the-money.

If the futures price decreases from 90-00 to 89-00 (a $1,000 decrease), it may be accompanied by a $500 increase in the premium of a put with a strike price of 90-00. The delta in this case is said to be .5. If there is a further decline in the futures price to 88-00 and the put option premium increases by $600, then the option delta would increase to .6.

The delta dictates the number of options needed to provide a "perfect" hedge, i.e., futures and options values move dollar for dollar. And as the delta changes, so does the necessary number of options for each bond being hedged. Specifically, the number needed to maintain a hedge at any given point in time is often calculated by dividing the conversion factor[‡‡] (for the particular bonds to be hedged) by the current option delta.

Assume the conversion factor for the bonds to be hedged (such as 10⅜ percent bonds of 2012) is 1.25 and that the option delta is .5. In this instance, 2.5 (1.25 divided by .5) puts per bond would be needed to provide a perfect hedge.

If a decline in the futures price results in an increase in the option delta to .7, then the number of options needed to maintain the hedge would be reduced to 1.8 (1.25 divided by .7). Some of the puts originally bought then could be sold.

A changing option delta in a delta-neutral hedge can work to the advantage of the institution, particularly if there is a significant movement in interest rates and bond prices. Reason: as bond prices fall below the strike price of the put options, an increase in the delta results in the

[‡‡]The value of each cash market T-bond eligible for delivery against the T-bond futures contract is adjusted using a conversion factor to reflect a standard 8 percent coupon value.

options rising in value by an amount greater than the decrease in the value of the hedged bonds.

Assume the futures price is 90-00 and the delta for an at-the-money put is .5. To hedge against a decline in the value of ten 10⅜ percent bonds, an investor buys 25*** at-the-money puts. Under these assumptions, each $1,000 decrease in the value of the bonds should be offset by a $1,000 increase in the value of the options, i.e., a perfect hedge.

Suppose, however, that the decline in bond prices is sharper than expected and that the option delta becomes .7. Each $1,000 decrease in the value of the bonds then would be offset by more than a $1,000 increase in the value of the options.

It is not uncommon for those learning about options to be overwhelmed by their complexity. Keep in mind, then, that the primary purpose of including specific options strategies in this text is to give the reader an idea of the market possibilities available with options, and not to make anyone an options expert.

While this text gives the reader just a few examples of how options are used, there are many other textbooks devoted to options and their uses. (Some of these texts are listed in the Appendix.)

More Information

***Conversion factor of 1.25 divided by delta of .5 multiplied by 10 bonds equals 25.

This chapter explains some of the economic, political, and market factors affecting the price of a variety of agricultural commodities traded on U.S. futures exchanges. The information discussed is a general overview and should not be viewed as an all-inclusive study of agricultural commodities. (For more information on particular commodities, see Sources of Information listed in the Appendix.)

AGRICULTURAL MARKETS

Grains,
Oilseeds,
Livestock

GRAINS

Several of the world's most important grains are traded on futures markets. They are commonly referred to as either *food* or *feed* grains. Grains such as corn and oats are used primarily as feed grains and, to a lesser extent, in manufactured foods. Rice is almost exclusively a food grain. Wheat also is generally grown and marketed for food uses, with a strong secondary demand as a feed grain.

Corn is unique among the grasses cultivated as grain cereals. It is used both for feed and as food, and is the only grain that originated in the Western Hemisphere. In fact, corn was unknown to the rest of the world until 1492, when Christopher Columbus returned to Europe with samples.

13

Within a generation, cultivation of corn spread to most farming areas of Europe; by the mid-1500s, corn was being grown in China. Worldwide, most corn is used for animal feed, but corn is a major part of the diet of the people of Mexico and Central America, and is raised by them mainly for food.

Corn

Varieties of Corn

There are 100 to 150 corn varieties; farmers and commercial users have developed a grading system based on kernel tests.

Dent corn is the most common variety, accounting for about 99 percent of U.S. corn production. Dent corn is named for the crease or trough that is formed in the top of the kernel by unequal shrinking of the starch components. Grain standards established for dent corn distinguish among Yellow, White, and Mixed. Yellow dominates all markets for livestock feed and for wet milling into flour and other products for human consumption and industrial uses. White corn is demanded by dry corn millers for flour production, for manufacturing hominy and grits, and for many industrial uses. Mixed corn—White and Yellow corn accidentally combined during storage—is seldom traded commercially and is used in livestock feed.

The other major American corn is Sweet corn; its kernels are predominately composed of starch, making it easy to chew. The chemical structure of still another type, Waxy corn, is well suited for certain wet milling processes. And, Squaw or Indian corn is used primarily for decorative purposes.

Corn Supply

Acreage and Yields

Acreage and yields are the major factors affecting corn production. The current practice by farmers of planting denser and narrower rows than in the past has resulted in a higher plant population per acre. The use of pesticides and herbicides has helped minimize crop damage caused by insects and crop diseases. Also, hybrid seed and fertilizer have increased yields by about 20 percent.

Two of the chief factors governing yields are moisture and temperature. To bring a large corn crop to successful harvest, an even amount of moisture is needed throughout the summer months. July and August are the critical weather months for corn. Higher-than-normal rainfall favors high yields. Below-normal rainfall, especially during July, and higher-than-normal temperatures, particularly during August, tend to reduce yields.

Growing Season

The length of the growing season can be an important production factor. During spring, late frosts or exceptionally wet weather can delay planting and reduce potential yields. And, early fall frosts can critically stunt development of late-planted seedlings.

Most U.S. corn production is centered in the area known as the Corn Belt, which includes Illinois, Indiana, Iowa, Minnesota, Missouri, Nebraska, Ohio, and South Dakota. Corn planting in most of these key production states begins in early May, with Minnesota and the Dakotas planting later. The corn plant reaches maturity in late August with one or two developed ears; harvest usually begins about October 15, just after the first hard frost. By mid-November, most of the corn in the United States has been harvested. Each year more corn is harvested prior to October 1 due to earlier planting in March or April, so the United States Department of Agriculture (USDA) now designates September 1 to August 31 as the official corn crop year. Because October is the principal harvest month, December is the first futures contract month for the new-crop year.

U.S. Government Farm Programs

The structure of the U.S. agricultural program has remained the same since its inception as part of the Great Depression reforms in the 1930s. The major program tools for domestic grains remain: price supports, target price deficiency payments, and production control programs.

In the nonrecourse loan program (price supports), farmers place grain under loan for less than one year. The *loan rate* is the amount lent per unit of the commodity. If the local cash price rises enough to pay back the loan and cover the interest cost, the loan is likely repaid and the farmer redeems the grain for sale in the cash market. If it is not redeemed, the Commodity Credit Corporation (CCC)* takes title to the grain and forgives the interest on the loan. Therefore, the CCC is a market of last resort, offering the farmer a guaranteed price.

In the case of target price deficiency payments, a target price above the loan rate is established for each commodity. If the market price fails to reach the target, the difference between the target and the five-month average market price (or between the target and the loan rate, whichever is less) is paid directly from the Treasury to the farmer. To become eligible for loan and deficiency payment programs, farmers may be required to set aside cropland.

Built into the government farm program is considerable discretionary authority for the Secretary of Agriculture and administering agencies. In many cases, the law establishes only minimum price levels for the most important programs, giving the Secretary of Agriculture authority to set higher price levels if warranted. Also, programs can be changed significantly from the original intent of the Congress. For example, the Payment-In-Kind (PIK) program of 1983 was not specifically authorized by

*The Commodity Credit Corporation (CCC) is a branch of the USDA that supervises the government's various farm loan and subsidy programs.

the Farm Bill of 1981, but was implemented using discretionary authority.

To participate in the 1983 PIK, farmers were required to comply with the voluntary acreage-control program and to set aside an additional percentage of acreage specified by the government. In return for not growing a particular crop, the government paid farmers in kind with government-owned stocks of grain or released the farmers' stocks, which were under loan, back to them.

The use of discretionary authority is a highly charged political issue. Typically, farm groups and segments of Congress pressure the Administration to make the programs more lucrative, while others exert pressure to use programs sparingly to hold down costs.

1990 Farm Bill

The 1990 Farm Bill, established under The Food Security Act of 1990, continues a market-oriented approach to farm policy initiated in the 1985 Farm Bill. U.S. farm policy attempts to support grain prices that avoid the costly buildup of huge supplies, thus depressing market prices and requiring publicly financed storage. Loan rates and target prices have been scaled down over recent years, enhancing the ability of U.S. commodities to compete abroad. For 1991-93, basic loan rates are based on 85 percent of the season price average received by producers during the five preceding marketing years, dropping the years with the highest and lowest prices. Target prices are frozen at 1990 levels for the five years, eliminating their downward trend under the 1985 Farm Bill.

Another feature of the 1990 Farm Bill is the authorization of an option pilot program designed to encourage farmers to buy put options as a marketing alternative to other farm subsidy programs.

Because of the discretionary nature of the U.S. farm bill and its myriad requirements, contact the USDA regarding the eligibility of corn for specific government programs.

Other countries also have specific policies regarding the production and price of agricultural commodities ultimately affecting the price of ag commodities worldwide.

There are countries that would like to get out of the subsidy business. As a matter of fact, trade officials from throughout the world have been meeting for years to negotiate a General Agreement on Tariff & Trade (GATT) aimed at reducing domestic farm subsidies and ending unfair trade practices. Because of the political nature of such an agreement, however, the future of GATT is an unknown. In the fall of 1992, talks broke down after six years of negotiations and it looked like GATT was history. Nonetheless, talks resumed and only time will tell whether or not an agreement can be reached.

Distribution of Corn in the United States
Millions of Bushels

| Year Beg. Sept. | HFCS* | Wet-Milled Use of Corn | | | Corn Starch | Total Wet Milling† |
		Glucose Syrup & Dextrose	Total Corn Sweetener			
1987–88	358	173	531		226	757
1988–89	361	182	543		223	766
1989–90	368	193	561		230	791
1990–91	379	200	579		232	811
1991–92	390	207	597		240	837

Year Beg. Sept.	Total Supply	Feed & Residual	Food, Alcohol, Seed & Industrial	Domestic Total	Exports	Total Use
1987–88	12,017	4,798	1,243	6,041	1,716	7,757
1988–89	9,191	3,941	1,293	5,234	2,026	7,260
1989–90	9,458	4,389	1,356	5,745	2,368	8,113
1990–91	9,282	4,663	1,373	6,036	1,725	7,761
1991–92	9,016	4,878	1,454	6,332	1,584	7,916

Note: Totals may not add due to rounding.
*High fructose corn syrup
† Does not include estimates for wet milled fuel ethanol.
Source: Economics Research Service, USDA

Consumption and Usage

Approximately 55 to 60 percent of the cash corn crop is used as livestock feed; in recent years, corn has accounted for 25 percent of all livestock feed. Because feed is typically the largest single cost item in raising livestock, the profitability of feeding corn is determined by its cost relative to the price of meat. When livestock-corn ratios are low, livestock feeders reduce their use of corn by adjusting the number of animals fed and the length of time livestock are kept on feed.

Two major factors account for the attractiveness of corn as an animal feed:

♦ It is generally good as a feed for fattening livestock and poultry because of its high starch content. In addition, it contains more oil than other cereal grains making it high in total energy.

♦ An acre of corn yields more animal feed in both grain and forage than any other crop, although it costs no more in labor to produce and harvest.

Because of the meat industry's traditional pattern of heavy corn consumption, any significant increase or decrease in animal production forces farmers to reevaluate their corn production.

Food and Industrial Uses

The manufacturing industry uses the entire corn plant to produce a variety of products. Paper and wallboard are made from the stalks. Husks are used as fillers. Cobs become fuel, charcoal, and industrial solvents. However, the grain kernel is the most valuable portion of the plant used commercially.

In wet milling, corn kernels are steeped or soaked in a solution of warm water and sulfur dioxide. Grinding and other operations then separate the hulls from the rest of the grain, which is further treated in various ways to produce corn oil, starches, dextrins, and syrups for human consumption, and adhesives, glues, textile fibers, soaps, sizings, paints, ethanol fuel, varnishes, explosives, and a host of other useful industrial products.

Dry milling, a process in which corn kernels are subjected to some spray or steam softening and then ground, is used largely for the production of cereals, flour, hominy, grits and feeds.

Exports

Supply and demand factors in the principal exporting and importing nations have a significant impact on corn and its price. For instance, a bumper world corn crop might reduce foreign demand, lead to increased competition between U.S. and foreign corn producers, or both. On the other hand, a smaller world corn crop can cause increased demand for U.S. corn exports. Livestock price levels in other nations are another important factor affecting U.S. corn export demand. Low livestock prices abroad discourage feeding and lessen the demand for U.S. corn, conversely, higher livestock prices tend to increase demand.

The USDA estimated worldwide corn production in 1990-91 at nearly 480 million metric tons. The United States was the largest producer with an estimated production of 201.5 million tons in 1990-91—about 42 percent of the total world supply. U.S. corn exports were 1.7 billion bushels, nearly 22 percent of production. Production in China, Brazil, Eastern Europe, and the European Community follows the United States, however, Eastern Europe and the European Community tend to also import large amounts of corn.

The largest buyers for U.S. corn are Japan, Taiwan, and the Commonwealth of Independent States (former Soviet Union).

Futures Markets

Corn futures and options on corn futures contracts are traded at the Chicago Board of Trade and the MidAmerica Commodity Exchange.

Wheat is one of the world's oldest and most widely used food crops. First cultivated in Asia Minor nearly 9,000 years ago, wheat production gradually spread across much of Europe, Asia, and Africa. Wheat was introduced to the United States in the 1600s by early colonists who brought seeds with them from Europe. Wheat is now grown on every continent except Antarctica. World production for 1990-91 was estimated at 593.1 million metric tons.

Types of Wheat

Wheat is divided into two major types: winter and spring. Winter wheat is planted in the fall, becomes dormant during the winter, resumes growth in the spring, and is harvested in the summer. Spring wheat is planted in the spring and is harvested in the fall.

The five main classes of wheat grown in the United States are Hard Red Winter, Soft Red Winter, Hard Red Spring, Durum, and White. Each class is adapted to a particular set of growing conditions, is raised in a specific region, and has unique milling and baking properties.

The predominant class of wheat grown in the United States is Hard Red Winter. During the 1990-91 crop year almost 1.2 billion bushels of Hard Red Winter were grown—accounting for almost half of all U.S. wheat produced that year. Hard Red Winter is grown in Kansas, Nebraska, Oklahoma, and the Texas Panhandle. The annual precipitation in this area of the country averages less than 25 inches, with frequent dry periods and winters that produce subzero temperatures. Flour from Hard Red Winter wheat is used primarily in bread.

The Soft Red Winter wheat belt extends from central Texas northeastward to the Great Lakes and then east to the Atlantic coast. Soft Red Winter wheat is generally grown in a subhumid climate, not conducive to the production of hard wheats. Soft Red Winter wheat production, estimated at 547 million bushels for 1990-91, accounted for about 20 percent of total U.S. production. Flour from Soft Red Winter wheat is used in cakes, cookies, crackers, snack foods, and pastries.

Hard Red Spring wheat is grown principally in northern states where the winters are too severe for winter wheat production. The principal Hard Red Spring wheat districts have a fairly deep black soil and dry, hot summers, both important factors in the production of a high-grade wheat suitable for milling as bread flour. Hard Red Spring wheat production was estimated at 554 million bushels for 1990-91, 20 percent of total U.S. production.

Durum, a spring wheat, is produced primarily in North Dakota and Montana. Durum kernels are extremely hard and contain the highest percentage of protein of any of the wheat classes.

Durum flour is used to make spaghetti, macaroni, and other pasta products and is not suitable for bread, cakes, or pastries. U.S. production

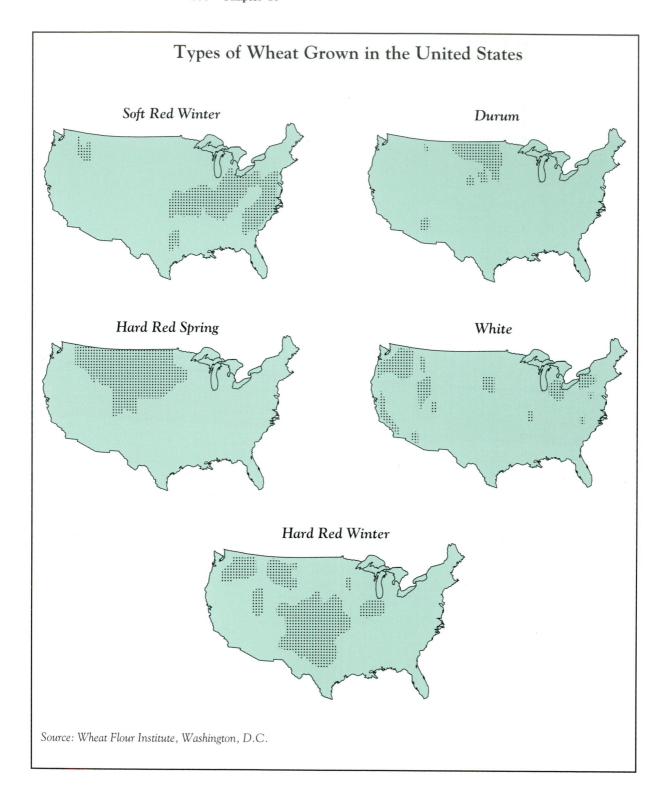

Types of Wheat Grown in the United States

Soft Red Winter

Durum

Hard Red Spring

White

Hard Red Winter

Source: Wheat Flour Institute, Washington, D.C.

of Durum wheat was estimated at 122 million bushels or 4 percent of total production for 1990-91.

White wheat can be either spring or winter type, and is grown mainly in southern Michigan, western New York, and the Pacific Northwest. It is used much like Soft Red Winter wheat and is available in both winter and spring varieties. Estimated U.S. White wheat production for 1990-91 was 313 million bushels, more than 11 percent of total U.S. production.

Production Factors

The crop year in the United States for wheat is June 1 to May 31. Winter wheat usually is seeded in September or early October, whenever the soil has sufficient moisture to germinate the seed. At this time of the year, the danger of the seed being damaged from insects such as the Hessian fly is considerably less than in late summer.

At freezing temperatures, winter wheat enters a period of dormancy that lasts until warm weather returns. Ideally, a blanket of snow should cover the fields to insulate and protect the plants. If adequate snow cover is not present, wheat sometimes heaves, i.e., the stem is severed from the root system, due to alternate thawing and freezing of the soil.

In the spring, the head, which contains the kernels, develops on top of the stem. After the kernels have fully developed and filled, the color of the plant begins to change from green to gold. When the heads are sufficiently dried, the fields are ready to be harvested; this begins in late May and is usually completed by the middle of July.

In the northern United States, where winters are too severe for winter wheat, spring wheat is planted as early as possible in the spring. The dormancy period is eliminated, the crop matures in August, and harvesting is usually completed by early September.

Yield

Wheat yields can vary substantially from one class to another and from one country or state to another. During the 1990-91 crop year, winter wheat produced an average yield of almost 41 bushels to the acre, spring wheat varieties yielded an average of about 37 bushels an acre, and Durum wheat yielded an average of 35 bushels an acre.

U.S. Farm Policy and Programs

As with other agricultural commodities, U.S. government programs—price support targets, acreage set-aside programs, and loan programs—can have a major influence on wheat production and price levels. (For more information on this topic, see U.S. Government Farm Programs under the Corn section in this chapter.)

Wheat Supply

Wheat Demand

Consumption and Usage

Approximately 30 percent of the U.S. wheat crop is milled domestically for flour; about 40 percent is exported; and less than 4 percent is set aside for subsequent crop plantings. The balance is used for animal feeds and in industrial products.

During the past decade, domestic wheat millers have produced over 350 million bags of flour annually. A 100-pound bag of white flour requires the milling of a little more than two 60-pound bushels of wheat. (This conversion factor varies according to wheat quality and flour type.)

Since World War II, domestic flour consumption has declined at the retail level. However, escalating standards of living have caused consumer demand for commercially prepared products using wheat flours to increase. In recent years, per capita flour consumption has leveled at about 109 pounds annually; per capita cereal consumption has remained steady at less than 3 pounds.

World Production

U.S. wheat production for 1990-91 was estimated at 2.7 billion bushels, more than 12 percent of the world's total. Forty percent of U.S. production was exported to other countries. China, the Commonwealth of Independent States, Japan, and Egypt are among the largest customers for U.S. wheat.

Other major wheat producers are the Commonwealth of Independent States, followed by the People's Republic of China, the European Community, India, and Eastern Europe.

Futures Markets

Wheat futures and options on wheat futures contracts are traded at the Chicago Board of Trade (Soft Red Winter wheat), the MidAmerica Commodity Exchange (Soft Red Winter wheat), the Minneapolis Grain Exchange (Hard Red Spring wheat and White wheat), and the Kansas City Board of Trade (Hard Red Winter wheat). While exchanges may designate a specific type and grade of wheat to be delivered against a futures contract, most will allow substitutions at differentials.

Oats

Oats, like other grains, belong to the grass family. Early records of oats indicate that they were first harvested as straw and used in mud bricks for Egyptian temples.

The ancient Romans used oats as a forage crop for grazing livestock nearly 3,000 years ago. However, it was not until the Middle Ages that oats were raised for their grain. During much of the intervening period, they were considered little more than weeds that infested fields of barley and other small grains.

Over the centuries, oats were recognized as an excellent grain for feeding livestock and poultry. They were introduced in the United States around 1600 by English settlers, who raised oats throughout the northern colonies. As the nation was settled and animal numbers increased, U.S. oat production also expanded.

Oat Varieties

Oats are divided into five major classes: White, Red, Gray, Black (including Brown), and Yellow. White oats comprise most of the U.S. production.

**Oat Production
Factors**

Oats are less exacting in soil requirements than any other cereal grain except rye. To produce top yields, oats need at least medium levels of the essential nutrients—nitrogen, phosphate, and potash. Oats grow best in temperate climates that have plentiful moisture and cool weather at maturity time.

Most domestically grown oats are sown in the spring—early April and late May—and harvested between mid-July and late August. Top oat-producing states are South Dakota, Minnesota, North Dakota, and Wisconsin.

The official U.S. crop year for oats is July 1 through June 30. U.S. oat production in 1991-92 was estimated to be 243 million bushels—the smallest in many decades. This represents a 32 percent drop in oat production compared to the previous year, and a 35 percent decline since 1989-90.

In fact, the number of acres planted to oats has decreased steadily since about 1920. During the early 1900s, oat production declined rapidly when horses and mules, which eat oats as a primary feed, were replaced by automobiles, trucks, and tractors. In later years, oat production fell again as rising milk production per cow led to a steady reduction in the number of dairy cattle.

Government Programs

The government programs available to oat producers are similar to those available to other grain producers. Because of the wide administrative latitude of the U.S. farm bill, commodity eligibility depends heavily on assumptions about how programs will be managed from year to year. (For more information on this topic, see U.S. Government Farm Programs under the Corn section in this chapter.)

**Consumption and
Usage**

Approximately 85 to 90 percent of the total oat crop is used as feed for livestock and poultry. About 6 to 7 percent is used for rolled oats, meal, ready-to-eat breakfast cereals, and oat flour; 7 to 8 percent is used as seed for upcoming crops.

World Production

In 1991-92, U.S. production has amounted to approximately 10 percent of the world total of 33 million metric tons; exports account for less than 1 percent of the U.S. oat crop. Oats are grown in most regions of the world. The Commonwealth of Independent States produces the greatest amount, followed by the European Community, Eastern Europe, and Canada.

Futures Markets

Oat futures and options are traded at the Chicago Board of Trade. The MidAmerica Commodity Exchange and the Minneapolis Grain Exchange trade oat futures.

Rice

Rice, an annual cereal grain, was probably first cultivated 5,000 years ago in China. Rice culture gradually spread westward and was introduced to southern Europe during medieval times. Since then, rice has been the most important food staple for most of the world's population.

Factors Affecting Rice Production

Rice is produced throughout the world in climates ranging from temperate to tropical. It is cultivated on wetlands that provide the necessary uniform moisture. Rice thrives under sunny, warm conditions and is highly vulnerable to either drought or unusually cool and overcast weather conditions. Cultivation practices vary widely among major rice-producing nations, reflecting differences in climate, other growing conditions, and levels of agricultural technology.

The harvested rice kernel, known as *paddy* or *rough rice*, is enclosed by the hull, or husk. Long, medium, and short grain are the three types of rice grown in the United States, and account for 69, 30, and 1 percent of total U.S. production, respectively. The 1990-91 U.S. rice production was estimated at 156.1 million hundredweights. Rice is grown in Arkansas, California, Louisiana, Texas, Mississippi, and Missouri. Arkansas is, by far, the largest rice producer, accounting for more than 38 percent of total U.S. output. The marketing year for rice in the United States is August 1 through July 31.

Government Programs

Rice production and marketing are covered by various government programs. One new government rice program, established under the 1985 Farm Bill, was designed to make U.S. rice competitive in world markets and to lower stockpiles. Under the rules of the program, rice farmers are allowed to borrow money from the government, using their crop as collateral, just as they have done under past government programs. When it is time to pay back the loan, they only need to repay an amount equal to the prevailing world price of rice (calculated by the USDA).

The uses of rice in the United States fall into three major categories: table rice (regular milled, parboiled, precooked, and brown rice); rice in processed foods (breakfast cereals, snacks, etc.); and brewers' rice. Approximately 56 percent of U.S. rice is consumed domestically.

Demand for Rice

Following harvest, rice is cleaned, sorted, and dried for further processing. Milling usually removes both the hull and bran layers of the kernel, and a coating of glucose and talc is sometimes applied to give the kernel a glossy finish. Rice that is processed to remove only the hulls is called *brown rice*. Rice that is milled to remove the bran as well is called *white rice* and is greatly diminished in nutrients. Parboiled white rice is processed before milling to retain most of the nutrients; enriched rice has iron and B vitamins added.

Rice Milling and Processing

The processing of precooked or quick-cooking rice is more complex and involves one of several methods, the most basic known as the *freeze-thaw process*. Raw milled rice is steeped, immersed briefly in boiling water, drenched in chilled water, slowly frozen, and then thawed. This results in a porous kernel that readily absorbs water and reduces the required cooking time.

By-products of rice milling (including bran and rice polish, a finely powdered bran and starch resulting from polishing) are used in a variety of manufactured goods. For example, broken rice is used in brewing, distilling, and in the manufacturing of starch and rice flour. Hulls are used for fuel, packing material, industrial grinding, and fertilizer manufacturing. Rice straw is used for feed, livestock bedding, roof thatching, mats, garments, packing material, and broomstraws.

World rough rice production was at 518 million metric tons for the 1990-91 crop year. China, India, and Indonesia were the three largest rice producers, accounting for an estimated 36.5, 22, and 8 percent of total world production, respectively. Other major producers include Bangladesh, Burma, Japan, South Korea, Pakistan, Thailand, Brazil, and the United States. U.S. rough rice production in 1990-91 was 7.1 million metric tons, and nearly 50 percent was exported. Major importers of U.S. rice are Brazil, the Netherlands, Saudi Arabia, Turkey, and Canada.

World Production and Exports

Rough rice futures and options on rough rice are traded at the MidAmerica Commodity Exchange.

Futures Markets

Canadian Grain Futures Markets

Two other important grains—barley and rye—have futures contracts trading on the Winnipeg Commodity Exchange. Both barley and rye are hardy and are grown around the world. In Canada, the planting of barley occurs during May and harvest occurs during August. On the other hand, most of Canada's rye crop is sown in September and October, lies dormant throughout winter, and is harvested in late July and August.

The amount of barley planted and its price are related to the level of production and the price of other feed grains. Barley is used chiefly as an animal feed for hogs and cattle. Another major use of barley is as a malt in beer. The largest barley producers are Russia, Germany, and Canada.

Rye also has several uses. It is the only cereal grass other than wheat that can be used to make bread. In Canada and the United States, rye is used for human food, animal feed, industrial applications, and seed. The milling and baking industries consume about 20 percent of the rye produced; approximately 35 percent is used for animal feed, although in the United States rye is not regarded as a primary livestock feed; and about 10 percent is used to manufacture whiskey.

Russia is the world's largest producer of rye followed by Poland and Germany. Canada is a modest producer of rye but is a major exporter.

OILSEEDS

Soybean Complex

It is nearly impossible to discuss soybeans without talking about soybean meal and soybean oil. The interrelationship between the soybean and its two principal by-products exists throughout the production, processing, and marketing phases. The term *soybean complex* refers to this interrelationship. This section presents the development of the soybean crop, its processing, and the intertwined supply and demand relationships of the soybean complex.

Soybeans

Soybeans were grown by the Chinese 5,000 years ago. Through cooking, fermentation, germination, and other methods, the ancient Chinese developed a wide variety of soy foods. The development of these foods encouraged the spread of soybean production across much of the Pacific Basin.

Historians believe Marco Polo may have introduced many of these soy foods to Europe, upon returning from his travels through China in the 13th century. During the next few centuries, limited quantities of these foods were carried west over the trade routes between Asia and Europe.

Until the early 1900s, there was little soybean production outside the Orient. At that time, the unique value of the soybean as a source of edible oil and high-protein meal, with secondary industrial and chemical applications, began to be recognized in the Western world.

Large-scale production of soybeans in the United States dates only from the mid-1930s. The rapid growth of soybeans as a crop in the United States was a result of the trade embargo by China in the 1930s that cut off soybean supplies. Acreage restrictions in cotton, corn, and wheat to curb oversupply in those commodities also stimulated increased soybean plantings. The production of less cotton reduced the supply of cottonseed oil—once the preferred domestic edible oil—and soybean oil became a logical substitute.

At the time of World War II, trade restrictions necessitated the development of a domestic oilseed industry, and this further stimulated soybean production. During the postwar recovery period, population growth and increased affluence in the United States, Western Europe, and Japan led to increased demand for meats and, therefore, for animal feeds, which increased soybean meal demand. These same factors were instrumental in the rising demand for both soybean oil and soybean meal from the 1950s to the present.

The 1990-91 U.S. soybean production was nearly 2 billion bushels accounting for over half of the world total. Soybeans is the third largest crop, following corn and wheat, in the United States, and a leading dollar-earner among U.S. agricultural exports.

World Production of Soybeans
1990-1991

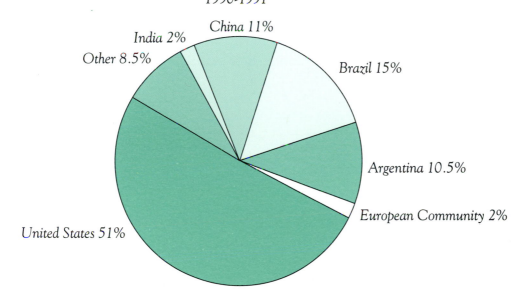

Source: U.S. Department of Agriculture

Factors Affecting Soybean Production

There are more than 150 varieties of soybeans grown in the United States, which vary according to soil and climate conditions from Arkansas to the Canadian border. The dominant class of soybeans in commercial markets is the Yellow soybean.

The soybean is a bushlike plant that grows to heights ranging from 12 inches to 6 feet. An extensive root system gives the soybean notable resistance to drought. After flowering, the plant develops several pods, each of which normally carries three seeds, or beans.

Soybeans grow best on fertile, sandy loam suitable for cotton or corn. Planting takes place in late May or June following corn planting, and harvest usually runs from early September through October.

The soybean plant is photoperiodic, which means that the flowering and opening of the pods are controlled by the length of daylight. Also, because of this photoperiodic growth habit, the soybean plant will mature within a few days of a given calendar date, regardless of planting time. Increased worldwide demand and higher overhead costs have prompted farmers in many cereal- and cotton-producing areas to double-crop using a short-term soybean hybrid. Illinois and Iowa are the two major soybean-producing states, followed by Indiana, Minnesota, Missouri, and Ohio. The important growing areas are more concentrated, and roughly coincide with the central and southern sections of the Corn Belt. As a result, soybeans must compete with corn and cotton acreage.

Farm Programs

Although there is a loan program for soybeans, it is used to a much lesser extent than those for most other commodities. (For more information on the loan program, see U.S. Government Farm Programs under the Corn section in this chapter.) In addition, there is no target price for soybeans and therefore no deficiency payment. There also is no acreage-diversion program for soybeans.

Soybean Demand

Whole soybeans have limited uses. They are held as seed for the coming crop, or baked, puffed, roasted, or steamed for dairy animal feed. The greatest demand for soybeans is as meal and oil.

Soybean Meal

Feed

Approximately 98 percent of soybean meal is used as poultry and livestock feed to satisfy basic protein and amino acid requirements. Therefore, demand for soybean meal is closely related to the number of livestock and poultry on feed.

An attempt to forecast consumption of soybean meal focuses on the demand for animal protein—meat and poultry products—which is influenced by such factors as consumer preferences.

Soybean meal faces competition from various animal and vegetable products. In the animal category, fish meal and tankage—dried by-products of meat packing—compete with soybean meal. Vegetable oilseed meals include those produced from rapeseed, cottonseed, flaxseed, and sunflower seeds. There is a tendency to substitute them for soybean meal when they are priced more favorably.

Food and Industrial Uses

Approximately 2 percent of the soybean meal consumed in the United States is used directly in food and industrial production. The food uses are the more significant of the two categories, and include high-protein derivatives of soybean meal consumed in relatively small amounts in cake mixes, waffles, cereals, breads, snack foods, blended meat products, soups, and baby foods. Higher concentrations of soybean meal products are found in dietetic, health, and hypoallergenic foods and cosmetics, and in antibiotics.

The greatest demand for soybean oil is in the form of edible oil products—such as shortening, margarines, salad oils, and cooking oils. To a lesser extent, soybean oil is used to manufacture chemicals, paints, varnishes, sealants, lubricants, and adhesives.

In food and industrial markets, soybean oil faces competition from a variety of animal and vegetable oils. Soybean oil competes with such animal oil products as butter, lard, and fish oils, and with vegetable oil products such as cottonseed oil, rapeseed oil, sunflowerseed oil, flaxseed oil, olive oil, coconut oil, and palm oil. Because of the competition among these fat and oil products, soybean oil accounts for about 25 percent of the total world oil consumption.

Soybean Oil

Oil

Over the years, there has been a radical change in the technology of soybean processing methods—a shift from mechanical extraction to chemical extraction. Oil and meal were originally extracted from soybeans by hydraulic crushing, a method that left about 4 to 15 percent of the oil and solvent in the soybean flake or cake. (The cake is what remains after the extraction of the oil and solvent.)

Today, nearly all U.S. and foreign processing plants use a chemical extraction method that leaves only 1 percent of the oil in the cake. In this hexane-solvent extraction method, the soybeans are first crushed and flaked. The oil is then extracted, and the solvent removed from it by evaporation and saved for reuse. In the refining process, crude oil can be degummed, refined, bleached, deodorized, or hydrogenated, depending on the end use.

Processing Methods

Meal

After extraction, the soybean flake is toasted and ground into soybean meal containing 48 percent protein. If a lower protein content is desired, the hulls are mixed back into the meal to lower protein content to 44 percent. Approximately half of all U.S. soybean meal is 48 percent protein, and is used primarily for high-performance feeds.

Gross Processing Margin

To make a profit from soybean processing, soybeans must be purchased at a lower cost than the combined sales income from the finished oil and meal. The difference, or margin, is called the *gross processing margin* (*GPM*). The GPM is a critical key to the profitability of a soybean processing plant.

The first step in calculating a processor's GPM is to determine the oil and meal dollar value in one bushel of soybeans. To calculate these values, each processor has specific conversion factors he uses to determine the GPM for his plant. These factors vary slightly among processing facilities due to (1) differences in plant efficiencies, and (2) the soybeans a processor typically purchases. (The protein and oil content of soybeans vary depending upon the environmental conditions of where the legume was raised.)

For purposes of explanation, however, standard conversion factors of 11 pounds of oil, 44 pounds of high-protein meal, 4 pounds of hulls, and 1 pound of foreign matter (dirt, stones, seeds) per soybean bushel are used in the following example. By the way, these are the same standards used by hedgers when calculating a futures "crush" margin, which is described later in the chapter. (The average weight of a bushel of soybeans is 60 pounds and hulls and foreign matter factors are not included in the example.)

Gross Processing Margin Example

Oil prices are converted to a bushel equivalent by multiplying the oil price by 11. If soybean oil is selling at $18.24 per hundredweight, or $0.1824 per pound, the value of oil in a bushel of soybeans would be $0.1824 × 11 or $2.0064. Similarly, the value of meal per ton is converted to the bushel equivalent by multiplying the price per ton by the conversion factor of .022 (44 pounds divided by 2,000 pounds (one ton) = .022). With meal selling at $182.70 per ton, the meal conversion would be $182.70 × .022 = $4.0194 the value of soybean meal per bushel of soybeans.

If the price of soybeans is $5.27 per bushel, and given the above values for soybean oil and soybean meal, the gross processing margin would be computed as follows:

$ Amount × Conversion Factor

Oil value ($0.1824 × 11)	=	$2.0064/bu
Meal value ($182.70 × .022)	=	+4.0194
Combined sales value		$6.0258
Less soybean cost		−5.2700
Gross processing margin		$0.7558/bu

Frequently, there is a seasonal pattern in processing margins, reflecting a favorable GPM after the fall harvest when soybeans are in abundance and priced low. During this same period, there tends to be a growing demand for feed in anticipation of colder weather, lack of grazing, and heavier livestock feeding requirements. Thus, the combination of lower soybean prices and strengthening soybean meal demand tends to increase the processing margin.

Processing margins tend to decline later in the crop year for two primary reasons. First, as demand for feed declines, soybean meal prices drop. Second, soybean prices tend to rise as the crop year progresses, due to lower supplies and the accumulation of carrying costs.

Crush Hedge

Application of the GPM to the soybean, soybean oil, and soybean meal futures markets makes it possible for processors to buy soybean futures to hedge later purchases of cash soybeans and, at the same time, sell soybean oil and meal futures to hedge later sales of meal and oil. This market position—long soybean futures and short soybean oil and meal futures—is known as a *crush spread* or *board crush*. The processor holds the long soybean portion of his hedge until he buys the required cash soybeans and the short portion of the hedge until he sells soybean oil and meal. An example of a crush hedge is given in Chapter 11 on Spreading.

Reverse Crush Pattern

The opposite of a crush hedge is a *reverse crush*. This spreading opportunity results from distortions in normal price patterns. It may occur when the cost of soybeans is higher than the combined sales value of soybean oil and meal. The resulting unfavorable gross processing margin makes it unprofitable for the soybean processor to manufacture meal and oil. When the GPM drops below a profitable level, a processor may slow down or even stop crushing soybeans, and at the same time possibly initiate a reverse crush spread—selling soybean futures and buying oil and meal futures. A decline in soybean processing eases the demand on tight soybean supplies and tends to curb rising soybean prices. At the same time, reduced processing tends to lead to tighter supplies of oil and meal, increasing their price levels. As the soybean price is held down, the cost/price relationship may change with a more favorable GPM being reestablished.

Futures Markets

The Chicago Board of Trade trades soybean, soybean oil, and soybean meal futures and options. The MidAmerica Commodity Exchange trades soybean and soybean meal futures and options on soybean futures. Soybean futures are also actively trading on the Tokyo and Osaka grain exchanges.

Canadian Oilseed Futures Markets

Flaxseed and rapeseed are two oilseeds that, like soybeans, can be crushed into meal and oil. The Winnipeg Commodity Exchange trades flaxseed futures and options as well as futures and options on canola, which is a high quality rapeseed.

The largest producer of flaxseed is Canada, followed by Argentina, India, and the Commonwealth of Independent States. Flaxseed is grown in temperate climates in drained sandy loam. Canadian flaxseed is generally sown in May and June and harvested in September and October. Most flaxseed is crushed to produce linseed oil and meal. Linseed oil is used as an industrial oil—as a drying oil in outside paints, printing inks, and varnishes. Linseed meal is a valuable supplement in livestock and poultry feed.

With rapeseed, China is the largest producer, followed by India and Canada. In recent years there has been an upward trend in rapeseed production, which can be attributed to an increase in the use of rapeseed, including canola, as an edible oil. Rapeseed meal is used as a feed supplement.

LIVESTOCK

Meat is the major source of protein in the diet of Americans and persons of other developed nations. It is also a growing source of protein in the diet of those living in developing nations. In 1991, Americans spent more than $570 billion on all food; approximately 12.5 percent of this—$71 billion—was spent on beef and pork products.

Pork Commodities

The public's attitude toward pork and its consumption has changed over the years. Pork was once regarded as part of the rich man's diet. Now, increased production efficiency has made pork readily available. A shift away from the fat-type hog—reflecting a decline in the use of lard—and a corresponding emphasis on production of a lean, meat-type hog has boosted demand for pork. In 1991, the commercial slaughter of hogs was 88 million head, up 4 percent from 1990, yielding over 16 billion pounds of pork.

Pork Production

Pork production is concentrated in the Corn Belt; Iowa, Illinois, Indiana, and Ohio account for about 50 percent of total U.S. pork production. Other major producing states include Minnesota, Nebraska,

Virginia, South Dakota, Michigan, Missouri, and North Carolina.

Historic price patterns and current price trends are among the most important influences on the level of pork production. Hog producers, as do producers of most other commodities, tend to cut back on production when the price outlook is bearish. However, cutbacks in periods of weakening prices are not as pronounced as they were previously. Hog-feeding operations tend to be larger than they once were; therefore, operators attempt to feed at or near capacity to offset the higher fixed costs of automated feeding facilities.

Feeding Costs

Feed is the primary cost in livestock production operations. Feed cost, in relation to the sales value of finished market-weight hogs, is the primary determinant of how much pork will be produced. In addition, feed prices may influence the producer's decision of when and at what weight to market hogs. Generally, when feed costs are high relative to the sales value of finished hogs, producers tend to breed, feed, and market fewer hogs, at lighter weights, than they would in periods of lower feed costs. When the cost-to-sales-price ratio is more favorable, breeding, feeding, marketing, and average market weights of hogs increase.

Hog/Corn Ratio

The hog/corn ratio is used to express the relationship of feeding costs to the dollar value of hogs. It is measured by dividing the price of hogs ($/hundredweight) by the price of corn ($/bushel). For instance, if the price of hogs in Omaha was $49.50 per hundredweight and the Omaha price of #2 Yellow corn was $3.20¼ per bushel, the hog/corn ratio would be 15.5 ($49.5000 divided by $3.2025 = 15.5). In other words, 15.5 bushels of corn have the same dollar value as 100 pounds of live pork.

When corn prices are high relative to pork prices, fewer units of corn equal the dollar value of 100 pounds of pork. Conversely, when corn prices are lower in relation to pork prices, more units of corn are required to equal the value of 100 pounds of pork. A hog/corn ratio of 13.3 would indicate higher corn costs and perhaps weaker hog prices than a ratio of 22.5. Thus, the higher the ratio, the more profitable it is to feed hogs.

Production-Marketing Schedule

By closely controlling breeding and feeding operations, hog producers can be relatively certain about the number and weight of hogs they will have ready for market at a given date. The producer's first decision is how many sows to breed. In making this decision, he takes into account the gestation period of nearly four months and the average yield of 7.3 pigs per litter. By knowing the number of sows bred and then multiplying that number by the average litter size, the producer is able to accurately project feeding requirements and develop a marketing plan. Depending on his feed plan and seasonal factors that can affect weight gain, the producer normally can bring newly born pigs to market weight in five to seven months.

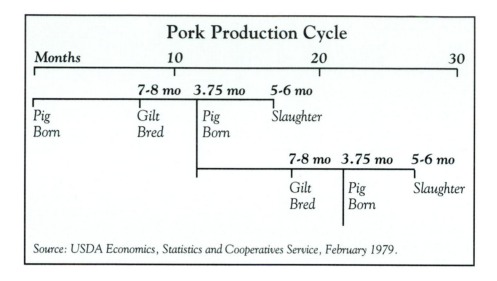

Pork Production Cycle

Source: USDA Economics, Statistics and Cooperatives Service, February 1979.

He makes this kind of calculation not only in terms of his own production but, based on reports from the USDA, applies it as well to total U.S. hog production in an attempt to get a reasonably sound picture of total production, available market supply, and probable price outlook.

Seasonal Pattern

Hog production usually follows a seasonal pattern, however, seasonal production trends are now of less importance than they once were. The largest number of farrowings (pig births) occurs during March, April, and May, and, ordinarily, the smallest number occurs during December, January, and February. Since it takes five to six months to bring newly born pigs to market, spring pigs farrowed in March, April, and May come to market from August through December. Because the hog supply is greatest during this period, pork commodities are traditionally at the lowest price level of the year from August through December.

In the past, most sows were bred only twice a year; now they are commonly bred three times a year, which tends to even out the number of hogs coming to market throughout the year. Better management, improved feeding programs, and higher fixed costs (such as heated production facilities) make it desirable to maintain production at near-capacity level throughout the year.

Long-term Price Cycles

Along with the historic seasonal trends in production, there are long-term cycles in hog prices, which may last up to five or six years. They occur chiefly because of producers' reactions to price levels. Relatively high prices stimulate hog production for several years thereafter. Increased production then leads to depressed prices; this then influences producers to cut production. Volatile feed prices have affected these patterns also. As in the beef industry, hog price cycles now tend to be shorter in duration than in the past as a result of better price forecasting, greater production planning, and the trend toward more even production levels.

Various long- and short-term factors affect the supply situation for both pork bellies and other pork products—hams, loins, and butts. Some factors have greater impact upon the supply and price level of pork bellies than they do on other cuts of pork. The most important long-term factors affecting supplies include the current livestock situation—feed costs and profitability considerations—general consumer-income levels, the number of hogs and pigs on farms, and the birth of new pigs.

Supply Factors for Pork Products

In the short run, the current rate of weekly hog marketings at major markets tends to be the strongest influence on both the supply and price of pork products. In addition to current hog marketings, weekly bacon slicings and cold storage figures are most important in forecasting pork belly supplies and price levels.

The demand for pork—such as chops, hams, bacon, and in prepared meat products—is most strongly affected by the price relative to general income and to the price of competitive meat products. The trend to greater weight consciousness has increased the demand for leaner pork products, particularly those made from hams and loins. Hams and loins account for 20 percent and 16.9 percent of carcass weight, respectively.

Demand for Pork

Pork bellies, the end product of which is cured sliced bacon, account for 15 percent of the carcass weight of hogs. The demand for bacon has risen due to increasing demand for pork in general, and increases in population and per capita consumption. Bacon is rather unique among meat products in that it has relatively few substitutes. Consumption tends to remain stable from one year to the next, except in situations of major price changes.

Demand for pork, particularly bacon and processed meats, reaches its peak in the summer and early fall. The convenience of these items is particularly well suited to vacationing families; and their lower seasonal prices tend to stimulate consumption.

Futures Markets

The Chicago Mercantile Exchange trades futures in live hogs and frozen pork bellies, and options on both contracts. The MidAmerica Commodity Exchange trades futures on live hogs.

Beef Commodities

The U.S. cattle/calf inventory peaked in the mid-1970s, and was 132 million head on January 1, 1975. By 1980, it had decreased to about 111 million head. It then gained about 4 million head during the early 1980s. Liquidation resumed in the mid-1980s, because of volatile financing costs and shifts in consumer tastes. By January 1, 1991, the cattle/calf inventory had dropped to 98,900,000 which was one of lowest inventories in 30 years. And in 1991, cattle feedlots in the United States marketed 32 million head of cattle, yielding almost 23 billion pounds of beef.

Factors Affecting Beef Supply

U.S. Beef Production

The production of beef involves breeding and raising cattle. At specific stages of development, cattle are sent through the three sectors of the cattle industry. The first sector is the cow-calf operation, which produces calves, or feeder cattle. The second is the feedlot or cattle-feeding system. A cattle feeder buys calves and feeder cattle from Western ranchers and commercial breeders and then feeds them to a desired market weight in the surplus feed grain production areas of the Corn Belt and the Great Plains. The third is the meat packer, who slaughters cattle for beef.

The major beef-producing states are Nebraska, Kansas, and Texas. The level of beef production is affected by many interrelated factors, the most influential of which are current and recent-past price levels. When prices are high, commercial breeders increase their breeding programs in anticipation of increased demand for feeder cattle. When prices are low, feeders cut back their production, and breeders reduce the number of feeder cattle produced. In periods of extremely low prices, breeders may liquidate some of their breeding stock.

Drought and crop failure in the Corn Belt may reduce feed-grain production and cut back cattle feeding. Sustained periods of excessively hot, cold, or rainy weather slow the rate of weight gain and increase feeding costs. Conversely, less extreme weather generally results in better feed-grain yields, creating cheaper feed supplies and improved profits for the cattle feeder.

Feeding Costs

The cost of feed in relation to the market price of beef is an important influence on the level of production, and is determined by the steer/corn ratio. The ratio, released monthly by the USDA, is calculated by dividing the price of cattle ($/hundredweight) by the price of corn ($/bushel). For instance, if the price of Choice steers in Omaha is $66.69 per hundredweight and the Omaha price of #2 Yellow corn is $3.20¼ per bushel, the steer/corn ratio would be 20.8 ($66.690 divided by $3.2025 = 20.8). In other words, 20.8 bushels of corn are equal in dollar value to 100 pounds of Choice steer beef.

When the value of corn is high in relation to the sales value of beef, fewer units of corn equal the dollar value of 100 pounds of beef. Conversely, when corn prices are lower in relation to beef prices, more units of corn are required to equal the value of 100 pounds of beef. A steer/corn ratio of 17.6 would indicate higher corn costs and weaker beef prices than a ratio of 22.5. Thus, the higher the ratio, the more profitable it is to feed the cattle.

Beef production requires a lengthy start-up time. A heifer, a female that has not yet produced a calf, is normally not bred until it is 14 to 18 months old, and the gestation requires another nine months. At 6 to 8 months of age, calves are weaned from their mothers and are either sent directly to a feedlot or to an intermediate stage wherein they are fed roughage. This phase lasts 6 to 10 months at which time cattle are sent to feedlots. Both steers and heifers are placed in feedlots, although fewer heifers are placed because their retention is necessary to maintain cow herds. To bring feeder cattle to a desired market weight requires another six to nine months. Because of the time required from breeding to finished market weight, adjustments in beef breeding and feeding to meet demand and price changes are difficult.

Production Cycles

Cattle Cycle

The cattle cycle—a cyclical change in the size of the cattle herd— arises from several factors including a lengthy start-up time, changes in demand for beef, and the availability and cost of feed. Since 1896, there have been seven cattle cycles. As of 1992, the cattle industry was beginning an expansion phase signifying the start of an eighth cycle. The length of the cycles averages about 12 years, but ranges from 9 to 16 years. On average, 7 years of the cycle are herd expansion and 5 years are herd reduction.

The expansion phase of a typical cattle cycle begins when producers decide to expand their breeding stock in response to rising prices or expectations that prices will rise. Breeding stock is held back to expand herds and, as a result, prices rise. Rising prices also keep calves, yearlings, and steers out of the market and on feed to an older age and a heavier weight. When the large number of new calves from the expanded herds matures, slaughter begins to increase because fully finished steers must be marketed. Prices then start to drop because of the oversupply of cattle. The slaughter of cows and calves is then increased, because herd expansion is no longer desirable, thus depressing prices further. Eventually, herds become so small that prices go up, and cattle producers realize that the bottom of the cycle has been reached.

Seasonal Effects

Despite the seasonal breeding and feeding patterns, beef production has only a small seasonal trend, tending to rise slightly from the second to the fourth quarter, after declining slightly from the first to the second quarter.

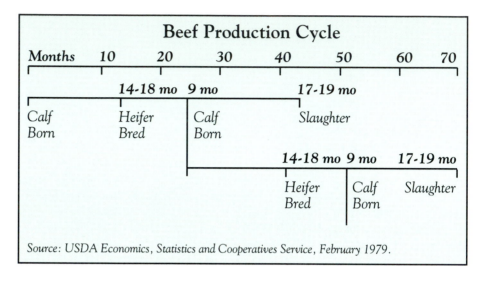

Similarly, there is a fairly weak seasonal trend in prices, tending to reach a low in February and peak in August.

Government Influences

Various government regulations, programs, and information, particularly from the USDA, impact the production and marketing of beef. The effect of the government is first felt in the overall annual farm program, which may use acreage controls or crop-production incentives to influence the amount of feed grain raised during a given crop production/marketing year. The dairy program also can greatly affect beef supply. For instance, if the government initiates a program to reduce milk production, farmers participating in the program will be required to reduce dairy cattle numbers. In turn, more dairy cattle will be slaughtered, increasing beef supplies. This action ultimately forces beef prices down.

Other government actions are aimed directly at beef production. In periods of depressed meat prices, for example, the government has attempted to stimulate demand through subsidized school lunches and other donation programs. At other times, the government uses export or import quotas of beef products to influence domestic beef production and price levels.

The USDA also provides information on cattle and livestock inventories, the number of cattle and calves on feed, and production and stocks data on competitive meat and poultry. This information is watched closely by the cattle-breeding, feedlot, and meat-packing segments of the industry to enable them to anticipate future beef demand and price trends.

Demand
Considerations

The amount of U.S. beef produced depends on domestic demand factors. Meat consumption tends to increase as a result of population growth and rising affluence. Production has barely kept pace with the demand for Choice beef and has never exceeded demand for any significant time period. In inflationary periods and in times of steeper feed costs, however, consumers tend to avoid the more expensive beef varieties in favor of cheaper cuts. At such times, a change in diet—the substitution of poultry or pasta products—is not uncommon.

Competitive Meat Products

Since 1985, the annual per capita consumption of beef has declined from 79 pounds (retail weight) to about 67 pounds in 1992, while the annual per capita demand for chicken has increased from 58 to 79 pounds. Pork consumption, on the other hand, has remained fairly steady through the years at an annual rate of around 52 pounds.

One reason for the decrease in beef consumption is consumers' preference toward white meat products—fish and poultry. Another reason for the increase in chicken consumption is the development of more convenience foods that include chicken.

Price Considerations

Although beef historically has commanded higher prices than either pork or poultry, price movements for the three commodities are somewhat parallel, as they are all affected by the general availability and cost of feeds, chiefly corn. However, when beef supplies are scarce, higher beef prices tend to lead to greater consumption of lower-priced meat products—pork, poultry, and fish.

Import, Export
Trade

Except for the relatively small number of live cattle imported and exported to improve breeding herds, most beef in international trade is either frozen or canned. Imports and exports tend to be of the lesser grades of beef—Standard, Utility, Cutter, and Canner.

Futures Markets

Live cattle futures and options on futures, as well as feeder cattle futures and options are traded on the Chicago Mercantile Exchange. The Chicago Mercantile Exchange also trades broiler chicken futures and options in addition to their beef and pork contracts. Live cattle futures are traded on the MidAmerica Commodity Exchange.

Futures contracts in gold, silver, copper, platinum, and palladium are traded on various commodity exchanges throughout the United States. The following chapter covers the supply, demand, current production, known reserves, and U.S. policies for these metals.

GOLD

Gold is primarily used for jewelry and monetary investment purposes. It is therefore regarded as a precious metal rather than an industrial metal. However, gold has industrial qualities—durability, electrical conductivity, and indestructibility. It also is used to a small extent in electronic applications.

For centuries, gold has been used for domestic and international exchange, but it was not until the mid-1800s that gold became the formal standard of exchange. In modern history, the first formal monetary role for gold was established when England made the gold sovereign the primary monetary unit in 1816. By the mid-1800s, the economies of many nations were based on the gold standard, including the United States, as provided for by the United States Coinage Act of 1873.

METALS
FUTURES
AND
OPTIONS

Gold,
Silver,
Copper,
Platinum,
Palladium

14

The gold standard system, in its pure form, specified that payments between nations be made in gold, either bullion or coins. This system worked until World War I when Britain suspended payments in gold. The United States, however, sought to continue the gold standard; but, later, the economic strains of war caused the United States to abandon gold as its means for international settlement.

Gold Exchange Standard

In 1922, the United States modified the pure gold standard by creating the *gold exchange standard*, which allowed international payments in both gold and U.S. dollars. This was possible because the United States continued to honor its commitment to redeem the dollar in gold on demand.

By 1931, in the midst of worldwide economic depression, Britain came off the gold standard. Two years later, to lend stability to U.S. banks, Franklin Roosevelt broke the link between the dollar and gold by banning gold hoarding and public exporting of gold bullion. In 1933, the official price of gold was changed from $20 an ounce—a level at which it had been since 1869—to $35 an ounce, the level at which it remained until 1971.

Changing Economic Policies

Bretton Woods Agreement

The world's major trading nations, anticipating the severe economic and financial problems that would follow World War II, met at Bretton Woods, New Hampshire, in 1943, to deal with separate proposals by the United States, Britain, Canada, and France for a new international system of payments. A compromise between U.S. and British plans resulted in the Articles of Agreement International Monetary Fund (IMF), signed in July 1944. Central to this system, which functioned until 1972, was the concept that each IMF member nation's currency would have a par value relation to the gold content of the U.S. dollar.

Throughout most of the 1950s, the Bretton Woods system worked comparatively well, despite the economic disruption of the Korean War and the Suez crisis. A general problem on the part of less-developed nations was the shortage of money because they tended to spend more for imports than was generated from their exports.

In the 1960s, the economies of the less-developed nations strengthened. At this time, the United States began to experience a slight balance-of-payments deficit rather than a surplus, and U.S. foreign expenditures outdistanced export income. (A balance-of-payments deficit occurs when a nation's foreign purchases exceed its foreign sales.)

In 1968, a two-tier gold market was developed. Gold had an official price of $35 an ounce to be used in all international settlements and a free market price to be used in all other transactions.

At the same time, the Special Drawing Right (SDR) was created as a new international medium of exchange. SDRs are issued by the IMF to its member nations. Initially the SDR was priced at 35 SDRs per ounce of gold reflecting the then current price of gold. After 1973, the link to gold was severed and the SDR was based on the weighted value 16 (in 1974) and now 5 member-nation currencies.

New U.S. Economic Policies

U.S. inflation and balance-of-payments deficits continued to worsen, and, in the spring of 1971, the United States announced the suspension of converting dollars to gold bullion, along with an anti-inflationary effort using wage and price controls. At the same time, a formal devaluation of the dollar to $\frac{1}{38}$ ounce of gold raised the official price of gold to $38 an ounce.

With the balance-of-payments deficit approaching $6 billion in 1973, the United States again devalued the dollar to $\frac{1}{42}$ ounce of gold; the resulting official value of gold applied to international payments between central banks. On December 31, 1974, the U.S. ban on the ownership of gold bullion by private citizens was lifted, and the first gold futures contract began trading.

From 1975 through 1979, the IMF and U.S. Treasury continued efforts to eliminate the use of gold as a monetary standard. Both, for example, increased gold sales significantly during this period. In 1978, official gold sales accounted for 20 percent of total world gold supplies, compared to 1971 when official gold sales accounted for only 7 percent of total sales.

In 1982, the question of the role of gold in the international monetary system received attention once more with the formation of the Gold Commission by President Reagan. But, this panel voted against any move to return to the gold standard.

In 1991, for the 12th consecutive year, world gold mine production exceeded the previous year with production estimated at over 2,100 metric tons. However, the growth rate slowed compared with the strong growth rates of the mid-1980s. Also, the total supply of gold to Western World markets fell, for the first time since 1983, by more than 3 percent from 1990 available supplies.

South Africa was the largest producer of gold in the world, mining

*Information from U.S. Department of the Interior and Gold Fields Mineral Services Ltd., London

more than 600 metric tons. The United States was the second largest producer with close to 290 metric tons produced. Of this total, Nevada produced 61 percent. Just behind the United States was the Commonwealth of Independent States (former Soviet Union) and Australia producing 240 and 230 metric tons, respectively.

The slowdown in world production rate was due to a variety of factors including the increasing difficulty in attracting financing for marginal properties, plus the depletion, scaling-back, or closure of some older mines, thereby offsetting gains in new capacity elsewhere. Gold prices, having fallen to the lowest level in real terms since the early 1970s, impacted both investors and gold mines. Although many mines were able to adapt to the lower prices through production cost reductions, the savings gained were often accompanied by lower production.

Lower gold prices, reduced mine development, and other factors reversed the popularity of gold loans[†] and the net affect was, that for the first time, repayments of gold loans exceeded the demand for new loans by 11 metric tons. Forward sales added only 51 metric tons to the overall supply or about 200 metric tons less than 1990.

Other components of 1991 supply figures included net sales of gold from centrally planned economy countries at 226 metric tons, down 47 percent from 1990; official or central bank sales to the market at 105 metric tons compared to the previous year when these institutions absorbed 66 metric tons; supplies of old gold scrap added 410 metric tons to supplies, down 16 percent from 1990; and inferred disinvestment, which showed the greatest turnaround during 1991, when the private sector disposed of 241 metric tons during 1991, up nearly 70 metric tons from 1990. Most disinvestment was attributed to private investors in Europe and the United States.

Gold jewelry fabrication demand rose by 4 percent in 1991, marking the fifth consecutive year of rising demand for that sector. The 1991 increase was the result of inventory buildups by jewelry distributors and retail outlets, mainly in Europe and the Gulf countries. Gold usage in electronics and industrial applications was 147 metric tons, essentially unchanged from 1990. This was attributed to a sharp decline in computer sales and the first sign of weakening military equipment orders. Dental gold usage rose 5 percent, continuing a trend begun in 1988. Gold use in medals and invitation coins rose 20 percent to 23 metric tons while gold used in striking official coins was 150 metric tons—32 metric tons higher than the year before. Although identified bar hoarding rose 12 percent during 1991, if the masking effects of unusual events in Brazil during 1990 and 1991 are factored out, demand in this category actually peaked in 1989 and has declined since.

[†]Gold loans is defined as gold lent to the market by producers in return for development capital.

World Gold Supply and Private Investment
1987-1992

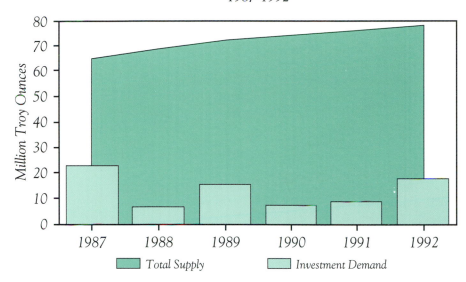

Total Supply   Investment Demand

Source: CPM Group, New York

U.S. gold consumption in 1991 was more than 114 metric tons. Jewelry manufacturers were by far the largest consumers of gold accounting for 74 percent of all U.S. gold consumption—84 metric tons. Industrial demand was the second largest user of gold representing 19 percent of consumption.

Futures markets in gold are conducted at the Chicago Board of Trade, the Commodity Exchange, Inc. (COMEX), and the MidAmerica Commodity Exchange. Options on gold futures are traded at COMEX and the MidAm. And, the Tokyo Commodity Exchange actively trades gold futures.

Futures Markets

SILVER

For centuries, silver has been used in coins, ornaments, and jewelry. But, recently, these uses have accounted for 15 to 20 percent of total world silver consumption.

Today, the electronics and photography industries have taken the lead, consuming the majority of the world's silver. Silver is highly attractive to these industries due to its properties including light sensitivity, malleability, ductility, high electrical and thermal conductivity, and resistance to corrosion.

Silver Supply

Mine production is the primary source of silver with more than 50 percent of silver recovered as a by-product of the mining of other metals, such as copper, gold, lead, nickel, and zinc. As a result, the demand and price of these other metals directly influences the amount of silver produced and, in turn, the price of silver. An important but smaller percentage of silver is produced by mines where silver is the main product. While mining is the primary source of silver, secondary sources include scrap production and stocks.

World Production

Estimated total world production for silver reached nearly 473 million ounces in 1991. Nearly half of all silver is produced in the Western Hemisphere. Mexico, the world's leading silver producer, produced 71 million ounces, or about 15 percent of the world total. The United States was second at 59 million ounces followed by Peru and Canada at 57 and 45 million ounces, respectively.

Outside the Western Hemisphere, the two leading silver producers are Australia and the Commonwealth of Independent States.

Demand

World consumption of silver in 1991 was more than 540 million troy ounces (510 milion troy ounces for industrial uses and 30 million troy ounces for coinage).

Western Europe was the world's largest consumer of silver using nearly 190 million troy ounces, followed by the United States and Japan consuming 128 million troy ounces and 110 million troy ounces, respectively. Total 1991 imports of silver by the United States were nearly 133 million ounces, an increase of 24 percent from the previous year.

World Total Silver Supply
1992

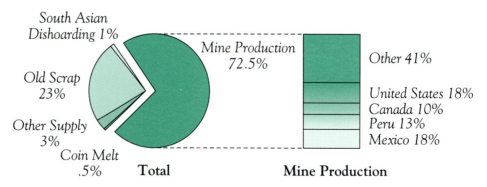

Source: CPM Group, New York

Monetary

Historically, silver has been used for monetary purposes. In the United States, silver, like gold, has been used in coins and its price has been supported by the government. However, its uses and value for monetary purposes have decreased significantly since 1968.

In 1965, the U.S. Coinage Act stopped the use of silver in quarters and dimes and cut back the amount of silver in half-dollars from 90 to 40 percent. Two years later, the U.S. Treasury stopped selling silver at $1.2929 per fine ounce, and the price of silver immediately increased to $1.87 per ounce. The coins became worth more than their face value, and a ban on melting down coins was issued. In the middle of 1967, Congress authorized the Secretary of the Treasury to rule that outstanding silver certificates worth about $150 million were either lost, destroyed, or privately held and would not be redeemed. And, by 1968, holders of U.S. silver certificates could no longer redeem them for silver. The international demand for silver also has declined and Britain, Canada, and Australia no longer use silver coinage.

In today's markets, the price of silver is determined primarily by its industrial applications, and to a lesser extent by its use in jewelry; its value is not based on monetary purposes.

Industrial Applications

In 1991, industrial purposes accounted for about 90 percent of U.S. silver consumption; the remaining 10 percent was used for coinage.

As mentioned earlier, the photography film, plate, sensitized paper, and photocopying machine industries comprise the largest single market for silver in the United States today. In 1991, 66 million troy ounces were used by the photographic industry, which also is the leader in reclamation and recycling of silver, primarily from waste solutions from film development.

Because silver is a thermal and electrical conductor with high heat resistance, the electrical and electronic industries are major silver consumers. Silver electrical contacts are used in practically every on-off switch and electrical appliance. Silver also is used in computer, telephone, and aviation systems. In 1991, these industries accounted for 18.3 million ounces of the total U.S. silver consumption.

Coinage

The use of silver in U.S. Coinage Fabrication reached 9 million troy ounces in 1991. The amount of silver used in coins has remained fairly stable over the years.

Uses of Silver

Factors Affecting Price

Substitutable Commodities

Stainless steel, pewter, and aluminum are popular substitutes for silver tableware. Aluminum and rhodium are used as substitutes for silver in reflectors, and tantalum is substituted in surgical sutures, plates, and pins.

Substitutes for silver in the electrical and electronic fields are available, but at the moment are costly and somewhat inferior to silver.

Futures Markets

Silver futures are traded at the Chicago Board of Trade, the Commodity Exchange, Inc. (COMEX), and the MidAmerica Commodity Exchange. Options on silver futures are traded at the Chicago Board of Trade and COMEX.

COPPER

Geological evidence shows that open-pit mining of copper and the use of copper in primitive weapons, tools, and utensils dates back to prehistoric times. Copper was probably first discovered and used by people living in a European region.

A nonferrous metal, copper is a highly versatile substance valued for its excellent conductivity, noncorrosiveness, and heat resistance. It has many applications in automotive, electrical/electronic, communications, and construction products, as well as lesser uses in jewelry, decorative arts, and housewares.

Mining and Processing

Copper is obtained from mining and from secondary recovery of scrap. Approximately 80 to 90 percent of copper is mined in open pits; the remainder is mined by various underground methods. Most mined copper comes from base-metal sulfide ores that contain varying amounts of other metals, including gold, silver, nickel, lead, zinc, platinum, and palladium. As a result, a rather complex processing that includes milling, smelting, and refining is necessary to obtain pure, refined copper. The milling process involves crushing the ore and using water, chemicals, and air to concentrate the copper and isolate it from other metals and waste.

In the smelting process, the copper concentrate that results from milling is roasted, melted, and treated with air. Prior to smelting, the concentrate is only 20 to 30 percent copper. At the end of the three-part smelting operation, the resulting product, called *blister copper*, is 98.5 percent pure.

Refining

Copper can be refined by two different methods—electrolysis and firing. Electrolytic refining is used to produce nearly 90 percent of all refined copper. In this process, the blister copper is melted in a furnace and cast into anodes (positive terminals of an electrolytic cell). The anodes are then placed in tanks of electrolytic solution with thin sheets of copper called *cathodes*. When an electrical charge is run through the electrolyte solution, pure copper is deposited onto the cathodes, leaving impurities behind in the tank and solution. The pure copper cathodes can then be melted and cast into ingots.

Manufacturing

To manufacture finished copper products, ingots of various kinds and sizes are normally rolled to produce sheets, melted and extruded for wire products, or melted and recast to make parts of many shapes and sizes.

Throughout the world, there are only a few large companies that mine, refine, and manufacture copper; they vary greatly in the type of functions they perform. Some firms are involved in all stages of copper production, from mining copper through the manufacturing process, while others specialize in refining or manufacturing.

Supply

World and U.S. Production

The world mine production of copper in 1990 totaled nearly 9 million metric tons, and total refined copper, which is close to 99 percent pure copper, was almost 11 million metric tons.

The leading copper-producing countries in 1990 were the United States and Chile. During 1990, the United States and Chile accounted for 18 percent each of world mined copper production. Arizona totaled 61 percent of the 1.2 million metric tons mined in the United States. Other leading states in copper mining included New Mexico, Michigan, Montana, and Utah. The United States and Chile were also leaders in refined copper production with the United States producing 2 million metric tons (19 percent), and Chile producing 1.2 million metric tons (11 percent).

The United States also imports copper for consumption, with total imports reaching 773,670 metric tons in 1990. Of this total, 261,670 metric tons were refined.

Newly refined copper, however, is not the only source of supply. In 1990, secondary recovery—the reclamation of old copper scrap—accounted for 25 percent of the total U.S. consumption of copper.

Demand

The major refined copper-consuming countries or areas, of the world in 1990 were Western Europe (28.5 percent), the United States (19 percent), Japan (14 percent), the Commonwealth of Independent States (10 percent), and China (5 percent).

Uses

Copper is used in a wide range of products. The electrical industry is the primary user of copper, accounting for 72 percent of U.S. demand.

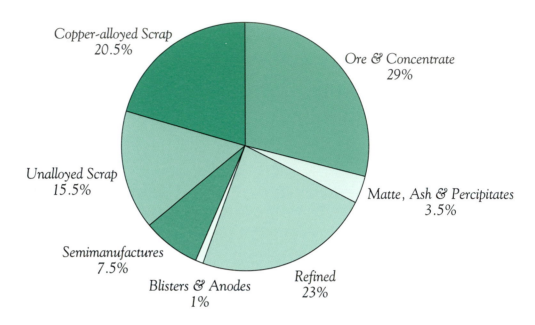

U.S. Copper Exports
1990

Copper-alloyed Scrap
20.5%

Ore & Concentrate
29%

Unalloyed Scrap
15.5%

Matte, Ash & Percipitates
3.5%

Semimanufactures
7.5%

Blisters & Anodes
1%

Refined
23%

Source: U.S. Bureau of the Census

Also consuming large amounts of copper are the construction, industrial machinery, and transportation industries.

The construction industry accounts for 15 percent of total U.S. demand and uses it in roofs, plumbing fixtures and pipes, hardware, and decorative products. However, copper faces some competition from aluminum for use in roof construction, and plastic, which is used in place of copper pipes.

Because copper is resistant to corrosion and has the ability to conduct heat, it is used in motors, power generators, batteries, fans, and heating and refrigeration equipment, and accounts for 5 percent of U.S. consumption. Copper also is used in a variety of communications equipment, such as telephones, telegraphs, televisions, radio receivers, and communications satellites.

The transportation industry consumes about 4 percent of all U.S. copper and is used to manufacture motors and turbines in automotive, rail, and aircraft applications, and in steering, air-conditioning, switching, and signal devices.

Copper also is used in military equipment, coins, and jewelry. These uses of copper account for approximately 4 percent of total copper demand.

Because copper is used in a variety of products, its price is highly sensitive to fluctuations in supply and demand.

Copper futures and options on copper futures are traded on the Commodity Exchange, Inc. (COMEX). The London Metals Exchange also trades copper futures.

Platinum Group

Six metals comprise the platinum group: platinum, palladium, iridium, osmium, rhodium, and ruthenium. Of these, platinum and palladium are the most important, accounting for about 90 percent of the total metal refined in the United States from this group of platinum ores.

Platinum and palladium have many similarities and common metallurgical characteristics; often they are used in combination with one another. Both have excellent electrical conductivity and are noncorrosive. Platinum, particularly, is used in settings for fine jewelry.

Nearly 292 metric tons of platinum-group metals were produced worldwide in 1991. South African-mined platinum-group metals totaled 147 metric tons, accounting for 50 percent of world production. The second largest producer of platinum-group metals was the Commonwealth of Independent States mining more than 120 metric tons or nearly 42 percent of the world's production. Canada, a smaller producer of the platinum-group metals, produced nearly 11 metric tons—approximately 4 percent of the 1991 world production.

World reserves of platinum-group ores are estimated at 56,000 metric tons. Platinum-group ores are found either in placers (glacial deposits that contain particles of valuable minerals), loose rock formations shifted by glacial movements, or in deposits in rock fissures.

Both South Africa and the Ural Mountain region of the Commonwealth of Independent States are rich in platinum-group ores, with reserves estimated at 50,000 metric tons and 5,900 metric tons, respectively. There are smaller, but significant, reserves of platinum-group ores in Canada and the United States with each holding 250 metric tons.

Platinum-group metals are used primarily in the automotive industry, in particular to manufacture catalytic converters. The automotive industry accounted for 41 percent of platinum consumption in 1991.

Properties of platinum, used in the catalytic converter, help break down poisonous carbon monoxide and hydrocarbon emissions into harmless oxygen and hydrogen. The use of platinum metals by the auto industry has

U.S. Platinum-Palladium Consumption
1991

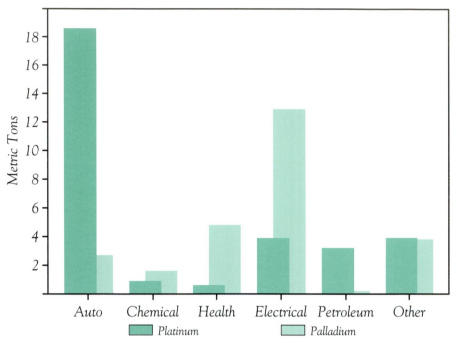

Source: U.S. Bureau of Mines

grown in recent years due to the strict government exhaust-emission standards.

Platinum and palladium can be used in combination or singly as catalysts in the production of nitric acid, an important element used to make fertilizers and explosives. In addition, both platinum and palladium are used as catalysts in the production of pharmaceuticals, high-octane gasoline, and other petroleum products.

Platinum, in particular, is used in the manufacturing of blown glass, pressed glass, and glass and synthetic fibers. The use of palladium in low-voltage electrical contacts is far greater than the use of platinum in these products. Due to their excellent electrical conductivity, both platinum and palladium are important products used in the manufacturing of telephones, other telecommunications equipment, and industrial controls.

Though highly valued as precious metals in settings for jewelry and other decorative pieces, use of platinum and palladium for these purposes is small, representing less than 1 percent of total world demand.

As a major consumer of platinum and palladium with only light domestic mine production—nearly 8 metric tons in 1991—the United States relies heavily on secondary refining and imports. In fact, the net import reliance as a percent of consumption was 89 percent.

In 1991, the United States consumed close to 46 metric tons of platinum and 57 metric tons of palladium.

Large supplies of platinum in the mid-1970s decreased prices and stimulated cutbacks by major producing nations. In addition, the Soviet Union reduced platinum sales in 1978. The sales reduction was believed to reflect the channeling of domestically produced platinum by the Soviets toward the production of commemorative coins for the 1980 Moscow Olympics. It also reflected delays in increasing platinum-group metal production and related nickel mining and refining.

The reduced Soviet sales, coupled with an approximate 18 percent increase in the world industrial demand, were major factors behind the world supply deficit of 400,000 to 500,000 ounces in 1979, which sent platinum prices sharply higher.

Part of the sharp rise was caused by increased gold prices related to inflation and currency considerations. Prices continued to climb through 1980 and 1981. In early 1980, for example, platinum exceeded $1,000 an ounce, and palladium was over $300. More recently, prices of both metals have fallen. By 1991, the average dealer price of platinum was $371 per troy ounce and palladium was $87 per troy ounce. Palladium prices are significantly lower than platinum prices mainly because palladium is a less effective catalyst in industrial applications.

Futures markets for platinum are conducted on the MidAmerica Commodity Exchange. Palladium and platinum futures trade on the Commodity Exchange (COMEX) and the New York Mercantile Exchange. COMEX and the New York Mercantile Exchange also trade platinum options. The Tokyo Commodity Exchange trades platinum futures.

U.S. Production and Consumption

Price History

Futures Markets

This chapter covers the basic economic and political factors that affect the price of lumber, cotton, orange juice, sugar, cocoa, and coffee. All of these commodities are traded on U.S. futures exchanges.

The information presented here is a general overview and is not meant to cover all the factors affecting commodity prices. (For additional information on these commodities, see the Sources of Information listed in the Appendix.)

FOREST

Forests are among the country's most valuable national resources. Timber provides a wide variety of wood products that are used in housing, nonresidential construction, furniture, packaging, transportation, and paper products.

Although timber is regarded as an agricultural commodity, a renewable resource, it differs greatly from crops that have annual growing seasons; timber grows for years before it is ready to harvest and mill into wood and paper products.

FOREST,
FIBER,
AND
FOOD
CONTRACTS

*Lumber,
Cotton,
Orange Juice,
Sugar,
Cocoa,
Coffee*

15

The first section of this chapter discusses two-by-four lumber—a commonly used timber product.

Lumber

Forestlands

Ownership of commercial forestland is divided among private individuals, lumber firms, local and state governments, and the federal government. There are three major forest areas in the United States—the Pacific Northwest, the Rocky Mountain, and the Southern regions. A variety of hardwood and softwood timber is grown in the Pacific Northwest and Rocky Mountain regions, while nearly all timber produced in the Southern region is southern yellow pine. The Pacific Northwest and the Rocky Mountain regions are sometimes referred to as the coastal and inland regions, respectively. The primary species of timber grown in the Pacific Northwest are the Douglas fir and hemlock pine. The Rocky Mountain region forests are populated by white fir, Douglas fir, larch pine, Engelmann spruce, and lodgepole pine.

Lumber Production

The production of lumber is generally not affected by seasonal considerations; levels are determined primarily by the rate of demand and price. Most lumber mills operate five days a week, two shifts a day, as long as prices are sufficient to produce a profit. This puts a continuous supply of lumber into the distribution pipeline. To produce two-by-four lumber, sawlogs are fed through the automated sawmills onto planing machinery. From there, the lumber is transferred to boxcars and flatcars and transported to where it is sold.

The sawmills that make two-by-fours also produce other lumber products. When prices for two-by-four lumber production are weak, sawmill equipment can be realigned to produce lumber products of other dimensions with better profit potential.

Price Factors

Demand for Lumber

Approximately 40 percent of all dimensional lumber produced in the United States is used in residential construction—framing applications, including external and internal walls, rafters, roofing, and floor joists.

The second highest demand for dimensional lumber, about 30 percent, is in repairs and remodeling followed by nonresidential construction applications, approximately 14 percent. The remainder of dimensional lumber is used in material handling, furniture manufacturing, and other wood products.

U.S. Timberland Ownership

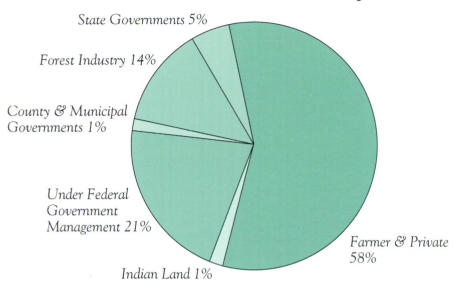

State Governments 5%

Forest Industry 14%

County & Municipal
Governments 1%

Under Federal
Government
Management 21%

Indian Land 1%

Farmer & Private
58%

Source: U.S. Department of Agriculture

Housing Starts and Mortgage Rates

Because lumber is used primarily in residential construction, the monthly housing starts report, compiled by the U.S. Department of Commerce, is the most critically watched indicator of lumber demand. In 1992, new housing starts were at 1.2 million—about the same as the previous year.

In addition to housing starts, a variety of other economic factors indicate lumber demand. In particular, mortgage interest rates, which increased in 1980, caused construction of single-family housing to decrease with a corresponding decrease in lumber demand.

Substitutes, such as steel and aluminum, which are being used more and more in place of lumber for residential construction, also influence lumber demand.

Lumber Exports

In recent years, the export level of U.S. lumber products has been a major factor in the overall demand and price for two-by-four lumber. This was particularly true in the mid-1970s when Japan imported large quantities of U.S. lumber. Although U.S. exports have declined somewhat, there is still significant foreign demand for plywood, lumber, and sawlogs.

Futures Markets

The Chicago Board of Trade trades Structural Panel Index futures and the Chicago Mercantile Exchange trades random-length lumber futures and options.

FIBER

Cotton

Cotton, one of the oldest fibers known to man, is the world's leading natural textile fiber. For the past 20 years, the demand for cotton has grown significantly because of population increases and the desire for quality fabrics.

While world cotton consumption has continued to grow over the years, the introduction of synthetics such as rayon and polyester has affected U.S. demand. As a matter of fact, in 1982, U.S. cotton consumption was at its lowest point since 1911. More recently, U.S. consumers have begun to value the superior quality of cotton as a textile, and U.S. demand has begun to rise.

Production

World Cotton

Cotton is produced in more than 75 countries and on every continent in the world except Antarctica. World cotton production in 1990-91 was 87 million bales. (One bale of cotton weighs 480 pounds.)

The People's Republic of China, the leading cotton producer during the 1990-91 marketing year, produced about 20 million bales of cotton. The United States followed China with more than 15 million bales. The Commonwealth of Independent States (former Soviet Union), India, and Pakistan also are leading cotton producers.

U.S. Production

The cotton crop year in the United States begins on August 1 and ends on July 31. Planting begins in March and continues through mid-June depending on the area of the country where cotton is grown. Ninety-nine percent of all U.S. cotton is grown in four major regions: the Delta produces approximately 39 percent, followed by the West at 24 percent, the Southwest (Texas/Oklahoma) at 23 percent, and the Southeast at 13 percent.

The U.S. Department of Agriculture (USDA) releases a cotton planted acreage intentions report in the spring and an actual planted acreage report during mid-July. Production estimates are published monthly, August through January, or until harvest is completed.

Factors Affecting Production

The price of cotton and the number of acres planted to other crops each year have a great effect on cotton production. For instance, when cotton is priced low and other crops are priced high, fewer acres of cotton are planted. On the other hand, when cotton is priced high and other crops are priced low, more acres of cotton are planted.

Cotton production also is sensitive to weather and insects. Extremes in temperature and rainfall during planting, growing, and harvesting can affect the quantity and quality of cotton.

Government Policies

Government policies play an important role in the supply and price level of cotton.

U.S. government production and price programs for cotton began in 1929 when the Agricultural Marketing Act established a loan rate for cotton. During the 1940s, 1950s, and 1960s, U.S. cotton carryover grew under government programs. Basically, farmers were producing cotton for the government, and artificially high price levels made U.S. cotton unattractive on the world market.

In the 1970s, the government moved toward a free-market system but several government-support programs for cotton continue today, including acreage-reduction, Payment-In-Kind, and export programs.

One new government cotton program, established under the 1985 Farm Bill, was designed to make U.S. cotton competitive in world markets and lower stockpiles. Under the rules of the program, cotton farmers are allowed to borrow money using their crop as collateral, just as they have done under past government programs. But when it comes time to pay back the loan, they only need to repay an amount equal to the prevailing world price for cotton (calculated by the USDA).

This marketing program has made U.S. cotton prices competitive in foreign markets and, as a result, U.S. cotton carryover has fallen drastically. The USDA reported that cotton carryover stocks dropped from over 9 million bales in 1985 to 5 million bales in 1987 and to a little over 2 million bales in 1991.

The marketing route for cotton starts with the farmer. He sells his crop to the local gin, uses it to redeem a government loan, or sells it to cotton merchants or large textile mills where it is eventually processed into fiber and oilseed.

Marketing Chain

Cotton Processing

At a gin, the cotton is cleaned, and fiber, called *lint*, is removed from the seed and pressed into 480-pound gross weight bales. The cottonseed is usually sold to oil mills where it is processed into a variety of edible and industrial oil products and cottonseed meal, an animal feed ingredient.

After cotton is processed, its quality and grade are determined. Quality is established by the grade, staple length, and fiber fineness. Merchants then classify the cotton and price it according to similar types.

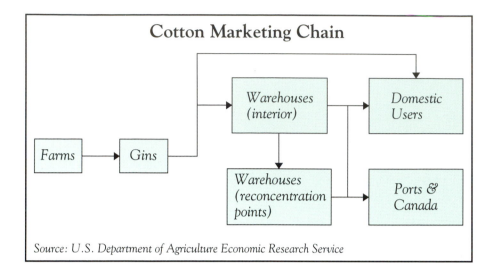

Cotton Marketing Chain

Farms → Gins → Warehouses (interior) → Domestic Users

Warehouses (reconcentration points)

Ports & Canada

Source: U.S. Department of Agriculture Economic Research Service

Cotton is graded according to color, brightness, foreign matter, and the ginning preparation that determines the smoothness of cotton. Actual grading and classifying are done by trained classers, who are licensed and supervised by the USDA.

Both the grade and class tell a buyer how a specific lot of cotton will perform under further manufacturing.

Cotton Uses

Cotton represents approximately 30 percent of the U.S. fiber market. The greatest use of cotton is for apparel, followed by household items such as linen goods, upholstery, draperies, and carpeting.

Futures Market

U.S. cotton and Cotlook World Cotton™ futures and options are traded on the New York Cotton Exchange. Cotton yarn futures trade on the Tokyo Commodity Exchange.

FOOD

Orange Juice

Oranges are grown in several countries, and the United States and Brazil are among the top producers.

The popularity of frozen concentrated orange juice (FCOJ) has skyrocketed since World War II, causing orange production and the development of frozen concentrated orange juice to increase significantly.

The U.S. crop year for oranges runs from December through November. Florida is the dominant orange-producing state and its production runs from January through mid-June or July, with a break in late February and early March. Frozen concentrated orange juice (also known as *pack*) is processed from mid-December through mid-July.

Orange juice production is directly related to the number of oranges each tree yields. Yield is measured in gallons of juice per box, and one box equals 1.55 gallons of Florida FCOJ.

Yield varies according to the age of the tree and weather conditions. An orange tree requires more than four years of intensive care before it begins to bear fruit. A 5-year-old tree, for example, can be expected to yield only one box of oranges per year, while a mature tree (20 to 45 years old) yields about six boxes each year. Weather affects yield; cold spells, sudden heat, dryness, and strong winds all can damage orange growth and production. The sweetness depends on the length of time the fruit remains on the tree—the longer an orange is on the tree, the sweeter it will be. Processors measure sweetness by the yield of pounds solids. Solids, which are mostly sugar, are what remain when the water is evaporated from the orange juice.

Factors Affecting Yield

U.S. Orange Production
1991-1992

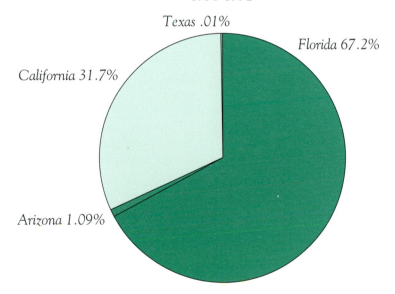

Texas .01%
Florida 67.2%
California 31.7%
Arizona 1.09%

Source: U.S. Department of Agriculture

Production

World production of oranges doubled between 1965 and 1985, reaching 40 million metric tons during the 1985-86 crop year. The United States produced about 16 percent of the world's oranges that year, an estimated 6.8 million metric tons.

In 1991-92, the United States produced more than 8 million metric tons of oranges. Florida produced the most oranges with nearly 140 million boxes.* California followed with 66 million boxes, and the remainder were grown in Texas and Arizona.

Other Sources of Supply

Supply is influenced not only by current production, but by the number of stocks on hand and the movement of FCOJ to retail outlets.

Demand

Ninety-three percent of Florida oranges is processed into various food products and 80 percent of that is made into frozen concentrated orange juice and consumed domestically. While the FCOJ market has been primarily a domestic market, it appears it could become more international in the future as more oranges are imported from Brazil to meet U.S. consumer demand.

The best measure of demand is found in the movement of pack (FCOJ) from Florida processors to wholesalers, supermarket chains and other distributors, and manufacturers of food products that use the concentrate as an ingredient. This figure is released every Thursday by the Florida Citrus Processors.

The federal government also is a large consumer of frozen concentrated orange juice because of its purchases for school-lunch and various food programs.

U.S. exports are another measure of demand. In 1990-91, U.S. exports accounted for 11 percent of all U.S. orange juice produced with Canada, the European Community, and Japan being the largest customers.

Although it has become a staple breakfast item over the years, FCOJ has not escaped competition from market competitors such as artificial orange juice products, other pure fruit juices, and diluted fruit drinks.

Futures Markets

A futures contract in frozen concentrated orange juice and options on that contract are traded on the New York Cotton Exchange, Inc.

Sugar

Historically, sugar has been an important item of international trade because it is considered a luxury item and produced in many countries

---

*The size of one box of oranges varies per state. Florida: one box = 90 pounds; Texas: one box = 85 pounds; Arizona and California: one box = 75 pounds.

throughout the world. Over the past 20 years, sugar consumption has grown about 2 percent per year. The fairly steady year-to-year expansion in sugar use on a global basis generally reflects population growth, as well as the stability of the human diet, and sugar's role as a basic staple in most of the world.

Much of the growth has taken place in wealthy countries, which consume most of their own production. About 80 percent of the world's sugar is consumed in the same country where it is grown. In 1991-92, more than 116 million metric tons of sugar were produced worldwide.

India, Brazil, China, Cuba, and the Commonwealth of Independent States were the top five sugar producers during 1991-92. The United States also is a large producer of sugar and follows the Commonwealth of Independent States.

Sugar is produced from both sugarcane and sugar beets. Except for the United States and China, which raises both sugarcane and sugar beets, most areas of the world produce sugar from only one type of plant. Although the nature and location of production as well as the processing techniques for sugarcane and sugar beets are different, refined sugar from each is indistinguishable.

Sugarcane and Sugar Beets

Sugarcane, a bamboolike grass that grows in tropical and semitropical climates, can be harvested approximately 18 months after planting and continues to produce for several years. Sugarcane is usually harvested from fall through spring.

India, Brazil, China, and Cuba are large sugarcane producers. In the United States, sugarcane is grown predominantly in Florida, Louisiana, Hawaii, and Texas.

Sugar beets are white, tapering roots that are about 12 inches long and weigh approximately 2 pounds. They are planted in early spring and harvested before the first winter freeze. The sugar beet plant produced about 33 percent of all sugar in 1991-92. Sugar beets are grown in temperate zones with the majority produced in Europe and the Commonwealth of Independent States. The United States produces about 9 percent of the world's sugar beets. Minnesota, Idaho, California, and North Dakota are the major sugar beet-producing states.

There are several economic and political factors that affect the supply and demand of sugar, which, in turn, affect price.

Supply/Demand

Income, Population Growth

On the demand side, per capita income and population are two important economic factors influencing price. Increases in the level of income and population growth in Third World countries, for example, have led to an increase in sugar demand. In recent years, however, sugar demand has fallen slightly due to the use of corn sweeteners.

Production

Variables affecting production and, eventually, the supply of sugar include weather, the number of acres of sugar beets and sugarcane planted, and disease problems.

Among the other variables that affect sugar prices are government stocks, protective agreements, and government policies. Reports of sugar stocks, which measure the balance between supply and demand, are an important indication of total supply and expected price levels.

Marketing Agreements

Most of the world production remaining after domestic consumption is sold internationally under special protective agreements. This accounts for most of the sugar sold to major importers, such as Russia, the United States, the European Community, Japan, and China.

Approximately 20 percent or less of the world sugar production trades in the world market at the world price. The remainder is sold in the country where it is produced, usually at a price higher than the world

U.S. Sugar Deliveries
Thousands of Short Tons, Refined

Year	Bakery, Cereal & Allied Products	Confectionery	Ice Cream & Dairy Products	All Other Food Uses	Non-Food Uses	Industry Uses
1987	1,513	1,146	449	1,144	149	4,400
1988	1,541	1,107	394	1,120	121	4,283
1989	1,532	1,187	426	1,194	126	4,465
1990	1,607	1,277	460	1,200	107	4,651
1991	1,632	1,276	439	1,159	89	4,595

Year	Hotels, Restaurants & Institutions	Wholesale Grocers	Retail Grocers	All Other Deliveries	Non-Industry Uses	Total U.S.
1987	91	2,040	996	72	3,199	7,599
1988	89	2,200	940	86	3,316	7,598
1989	106	2,051	1,026	75	3,259	7,723
1990	106	2,121	1,071	75	3,374	8,024
1991	99	2,078	1,182	107	3,467	8,063

Note: Totals may not add due to rounding.
Source: U.S. Department of Agriculture, Sugar Market Statistics

price or traded under special trade agreements, such as the U.S. tariff rate quota or European Community import quota. The International Sugar Organization (ISO), a voluntary alliance of sugar exporting and importing countries, monitors the world sugar trade. The ISO was formed in 1937 to maintain a stable, orderly, free world sugar market.

U.S. sugar supplies are governed by a quota system, established by the USDA, wherein domestic production is supplemented by imports. Each exporting nation is given a quota for which the United States will pay a certain price, usually above the world market price.

The top four sugar exporters are Cuba, the European Community, Thailand, and Australia. The United States exports virtually no raw sugar, but is an exporter of refined sugar.

U.S. Quota System

World sugar, domestic sugar, and white sugar futures and options on world sugar futures are traded on the Coffee, Sugar & Cocoa Exchange, Inc. Raw sugar futures trade on the Tokyo Sugar Exchange.

Futures Markets

Cocoa is produced from the cocoa or cacao tree, a tropical plant that bears cantaloupe-sized pods. The pods contain cocoa beans that are processed into cocoa, cocoa butter, and various sweetened and unsweetened chocolate products.

The cocoa plant was originally cultivated in Central and South America and introduced to the European explorers of the Western Hemisphere in the 16th century. Until the 20th century, most cocoa production continued to come from Central and South American countries. Since then, various African nations have become major cocoa producers, and Asian and Oceanian nations have begun production.

Cocoa

World cocoa bean production in 1991-92 was more than 2.2 million metric tons, down 10 percent from the previous crop-marketing year.

In 1991-92, Africa produced more than 1.2 million metric tons, or about 54 percent of the total world cocoa bean production, with the largest crop coming from the Ivory Coast. Alone, the Ivory Coast accounted for 33 percent of world production. South America was the second largest cocoa producer, with 468,000 metric tons, or 20 percent of world production. Brazil and Ecuador grew the most cocoa of the South American countries. Asia and Oceania also raised close to 20 percent of the world's cocoa in 1991-92; Malaysia and Indonesia were the two largest producing nations.

World Cocoa Production

World Cocoa Production
1991-1992

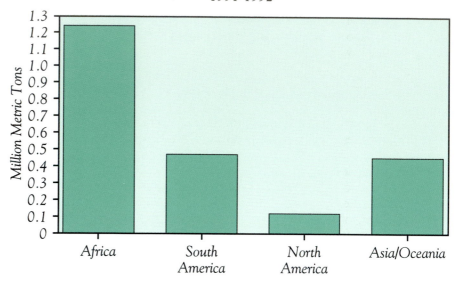

Source: *U.S. Department of Agriculture*

It takes several years to produce cocoa, because the cocoa tree does not produce enough beans to harvest until it is at least 5 years old. After that, the amount of beans produced increases until the tree reaches its peak yield at 15 years and maintains that yield for another 15 years. A tree's production begins to decline after 40 or 50 years until the tree can no longer be used for commercial production.

Harvest

Beans ripen from October through August with two crops being harvested. The main crop runs from October through March and produces approximately 80 percent of the world total. The mid-crop runs from May to August and produces the balance of the world's total.

After the cocoa pods ripen, they are cut from the trees, opened, and the beans are removed. The beans are fermented, dried, packed into bags, and transported to a processing plant.

In processing, beans are roasted, separated from the husks, and ground into a liquid known as *chocolate liquor*. As the liquor cools, it hardens into a cake. To produce cocoa, most of the fat or cocoa butter is removed from the liquor by hydraulic presses. In the manufacturing of chocolate, however, additional cocoa butter is mixed with the cocoa.

The International Cocoa Organization estimated 1990-91 world cocoa consumption at a record 2.21 million tons, nearly 6 percent higher than the 1989-90 level. The United States was the largest consumer, accounting for about 25 percent of the total, followed by Germany with 12.5 percent; the United Kingdom, 8.3 percent; France, 7.1 percent; Japan, 5 percent; and the Commonwealth of Independent States, 4.2 percent. However, on a per capita basis, Switzerland retained the number one position with 5 kilograms.

Consumers

Virtually all of the major bean producers—the African and South American countries, Malaysia, and Indonesia are exporters of cocoa.

Supply

Government Policies

Governments of the countries that produce the largest quantities of cocoa designate the amount of cocoa to export. However, the marketing and sales policies of these nations differ considerably. In Ghana, Nigeria, and other West African countries, for instance, government marketing agencies purchase cocoa from farmers and then sell the exports to buyers at predetermined prices. Announcements of the size of the holdings by the marketing agencies, especially those by the Ghana Cocoa Marketing Board, are important indicators of the current crop size and of available supplies for export.

By contrast, Brazilian cocoa is sold through free markets, although the government may establish minimum selling prices and export quotas.

Visible and Invisible Supplies

Cocoa bean stocks are either visible or invisible. Visible stocks are held in public warehouses and these supply figures are available to the public. However, a larger portion of cocoa bean stocks is invisible and held in private warehouses. Because these stocks are privately held, invisible supply figures are difficult to estimate.

Cocoa futures and options on cocoa futures are traded at the Coffee, Sugar & Cocoa Exchange, Inc. Cocoa futures also are actively traded at the London Futures and Options Exchange.

Futures Markets

The Ethiopians were probably the first people to use coffee during ancient times. Its popularity spread from Ethiopia to various Arabian countries and into Europe in the Middle Ages. In the 1600s, coffee was the main nonalcoholic drink of most of Europe and the Americas. As coffee demand continued to grow in the United States and Western countries before World War II, coffee was mainly imported from South and

Coffee

Central America. Since then, several African countries have become major producers.

Coffee is one of the most internationally traded commodities. A primary reason for this is that coffee production is concentrated in subtropical and tropical climates while the major consumers tend to live in the United States and Europe.

Coffee Production

There are two types of coffee: high and low quality. The high-quality group includes the mild coffees of Brazil, Colombia, and other South and Central American countries. The low-quality coffees are lower priced and are grown primarily in Africa.

Coffee trees, or bushes, are grown from hybrid seeds, and they begin to produce fruit about five years after planting. They thrive in subtropical climates at altitudes from 500 feet to more than 2,000 feet above sea level.

Mature trees, 8 to 30 years old, produce about 1 pound of marketable coffee per year. Yield is adversely affected by frost, high wind, drought, excessive rain, and various insects and diseases.

Harvest and Processing

To harvest the coffee berries, which are the seeds of coffee beans, they are picked by hand and soaked in water. The coffee beans are removed from the pulp by friction and fermentation. Beans are then dried and peeled before being sized and packed in 60-kilogram bags to protect the coffee from foreign odors and moisture.

Coffee that is processed and ready for shipment and storage is known as *green coffee*. Green coffee can be stored for long periods of time with little change in quality. At a later time, the coffee beans are blended, roasted, and packaged for consumer sales.

Importers/Exporters

The United States produces very little coffee, but consumes and imports more than any other country in the world. In 1991-92, U.S. green coffee imports totaled almost 19 million bags—nearly 19 percent of the world green coffee production which was 100.5 million bags.

Coffee is consumed almost entirely as a beverage in the United States, but also is used as a flavoring in food products. U.S. coffee is sold as beans or ground into a variety of processed forms, such as instant, decaffeinated, or freeze-dried. Coffee bean oil, extracted during processing, is used to manufacture soaps, paints, shoe polish, and medicine. Coffee also is used to produce a type of plastic called *cafelite*.

Other major coffee-importing countries include Germany, Japan, France, Italy, Spain, the Netherlands, and the United Kingdom.

Imports are largely from Central America, South America, and the Caribbean. During the late 1980s and early 1990s, these areas have produced approximately 70 percent of the world's total.

World Green Coffee Production
1991-1992

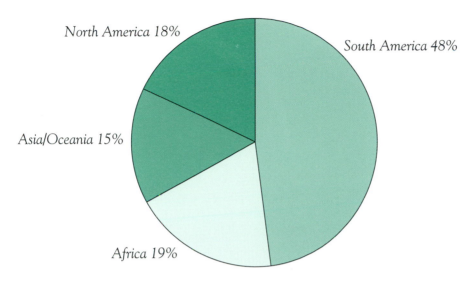

North America 18%

South America 48%

Asia/Oceania 15%

Africa 19%

Source: U.S. Department of Agriculture

Marketing

The International Coffee Organization (ICO), a voluntary alliance of coffee exporting and importing countries, sets export and import quotas in an effort to maintain market stability. The ICO evaluates current world supply and demand, and determines production and marketing policies.

The Coffee, Sugar & Cocoa Exchange, Inc. trades Brazil-differential coffee and coffee "C" futures and options on coffee "C" futures.

Futures Markets

This chapter covers some of the basic supply and demand factors that affect the price of crude oil, heating oil, gasoline, and natural gas. (To find out more about each, see the Sources of Information listed in the Appendix.)

CRUDE OIL

Crude oil is petroleum in its natural state. The word *petroleum*, derived from Latin and Greek, means *rock oil*. Petroleum is a generic term applied to oil and oil products in all forms, such as crude oil and petroleum products.

Petroleum probably was used 5,000 years ago to coat the hulls of wooden ships and for religious and medical applications. It was not until approximately 2,000 years ago that its value as a source of light and heat began to be understood. And, the first oil well dug deliberately to obtain crude oil, in Titusville, Pennsylvania, dates only from 1859. In less than 130 years, crude oil exploration has spread around the world to the Middle East, North and South America, Europe, and Africa.

ENERGY
FUTURES
AND
OPTIONS

*Crude Oil,
Heating Oil,
Gasoline,
Natural Gas*

16

World Market

Since the mid-1970s, changes in crude oil pricing and supply have been more frequent and more pronounced. These changes, resulting from political and economic factors, increased competition and limited profits throughout the petroleum marketing chain.

In the early 1970s, the price structure of crude oil changed dramatically due to the Organization of Petroleum Exporting Countries (OPEC).* OPEC emerged as the major pricing power in 1973, when the ownership of oil production in the Middle East transferred from the operating companies to the governments of the oil-producing countries or their national oil companies.

At the same time, OPEC, led by the world's largest oil producer, Saudi Arabia, was the major supplier to the United States, Western Europe, and Japan. Due to increased oil demand, by the mid-1970s, OPEC was supplying two thirds of the free world's oil and more than half of U.S. petroleum imports.

With OPEC's new authority came tremendous price increases and supply changes influenced by political and economic events within the OPEC countries. After successive price hikes during the 1970s brought the average annual price of crude oil to a peak in 1981—$31.77 a barrel—oil prices began trending downward in 1982 and plummeted to $12.51 in 1986. Of the many factors contributing to the unprecedented decline in crude oil prices during 1986, the most important was excess worldwide production—primarily by OPEC members seeking to regain market share. After 1986, crude oil prices fluctuated. In 1990, the Iraqi invasion of Kuwait drove up the price of crude oil to $20.03. In 1991, the ability of oil producing nations to replace Iraqi and Kuwaiti oil, coupled with an economic recession that restrained petroleum demand, caused the price to decline to $16.54 per barrel.

Production

World production of crude oil in 1991 averaged 60 million barrels per day. (Barrels per day are the maximum number of barrels of crude oil that can be processed during a 24-hour period. One barrel equals 42 U.S. gallons.) The Commonwealth of Independent States (the former Soviet Union) was the world's leading producer of crude oil in 1991 with 9.55 million barrels per day, approximately 16 percent of the world total. Saudi Arabia was just behind the Commonwealth of Independent States, producing just over 8 million barrels a day.

U.S. Consumption

Producing more than 7 million barrels of crude oil per day, approximately 12 percent of the world's total in 1991, the United States

*OPEC members: Algeria, Ecuador, Gabon, Indonesia, Iran, Iraq, Kuwait, Libya, Nigeria, Qatar, Saudi Arabia, the United Arab Emirates, and Venezuela; Arab OPEC members: Algeria, Iraq, Kuwait, Libya, Qatar, Saudi Arabia, and the United Arab Emirates

was the third largest oil producer and one of the largest oil importers in the world.

In 1991, the United States consumed an average of 16.7 million barrels of petroleum per day to meet its great energy demands, especially for heavy industry, manufacturing, and transportation. However, the 1991 figure marks a decline from the amount consumed during the 1970s, which peaked at 19 million barrels per day in 1978. By 1983, consumption had declined to 15 million barrels per day. This decline in consumption was the result of changes in the world's economy and U.S. policies and practices to conserve more oil. After 1983, lower crude oil prices tended to promote consumption, reaching 17.3 million a day in 1989. In 1991, however, a warm winter and a stagnant economy combined to restrain petroleum consumption.

U.S. Petroleum Imports by Source
1960-1990

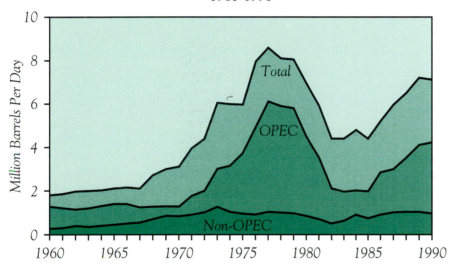

Source: Energy Information Administration, Annual Energy Review 1991

U.S. dependence on petroleum net imports peaked at 47 percent of consumption in 1977, then fell in 1985 to 27 percent, the lowest level since 1971. By 1990, dependence on petroleum net imports had risen to 42 percent. In 1991, a record level of petroleum product exports, lower petroleum imports, and restrained petroleum consumption lowered U.S. dependence on petroleum net imports to 40 percent. That year, Saudi Arabia, Venezuela, Canada, Nigeria, and Mexico were the primary foreign suppliers of petroleum to the United States.

Demand

The demand for energy from crude oil and its refined products is generally broken down into three sectors: residential/commercial, transportation, and industrial, which includes electrical utilities. In addition, petrochemical ingredients are used to manufacture various products, such as plastics, fertilizers, insecticides, waxes, adhesives, foods, cosmetics, pharmaceuticals, and textiles.

Futures Markets

The New York Mercantile Exchange trades crude oil futures and options. Crude oil futures also are actively traded on the International Petroleum Exchange.

HEATING OIL

Petroleum is refined into six basic product groups—kerosene, jet fuel, diesel fuel, motor gasolines, and residual and distillate fuels.

Distillate fuels are primarily used as fuels for heating, diesel engines, railroads, and agricultural machinery. Heating oil, used to heat homes, accounts for about 20 percent of total distillate fuel consumption, and follows natural gas and electricity as an energy source of residential heating.

Demand for Heating Oil

Generally speaking, the short-run demand for heating oil is relatively inelastic,[†] but given time, heating oil demand responds to changes in oil prices. Individuals will alter their conservation habits, build more energy-efficient homes, use more insulation, etc., to combat rising oil prices. During the 1980s, for example, consumers reduced their use of heating oil as a result of rising costs, and switched to less-expensive fuels.

While the short-run demand for heating oil is relatively inelastic, situations occur where heating oil prices will respond to short-term market conditions. For instance, a particularly harsh, cold winter can increase the demand for heating oil substantially, leading to large price increases; whereas a particularly mild winter can result in lower demand and lead to a price decline.

In 1991, U.S. distillate fuel oil consumption fell 3 percent from the previous year to 2.9 million barrels a day. The decline was due to lower industrial production, which caused a decline in demand for transportation use of diesel fuel, and to warm winter weather, which depressed residential and commercial demand for heating oil.

[†]Inelastic: Buyers' responsiveness to a change in price is relatively small.

U.S. Energy Consumption by Sector
1970-1990

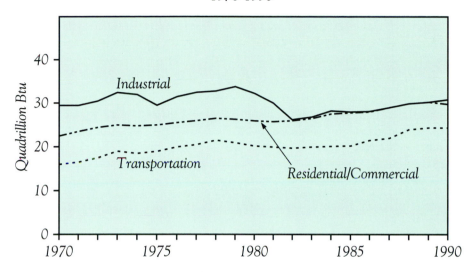

Source: Energy Information Administration, Annual Energy Review December 1991

Heating oil futures and options are traded on the New York Mercantile Exchange.

Futures Markets

GASOLINE

Gasoline includes premium and regular grades, both leaded and unleaded, gasohol, and other refinery products.

Gasoline is the largest petroleum product refined in the United States. Nearly 75 percent of gasoline is used by individuals, peaking during the summer when people travel more, and reaching lows during the winter. Total U.S. motor gasoline consumption averaged about 7.4 million barrels a day in 1991. More than 90 percent of that total was used for transportation, and the remaining 10 percent was used for construction and agricultural purposes.

The introduction of unleaded gasoline has heralded an important change in the gasoline market over the past decade. Production of unleaded gasoline increased as more and more cars using unleaded fuel were sold. In 1977, unleaded gasoline consumption was less than 30 percent of production. By 1987, unleaded gasoline comprised 75 percent of the total U.S. gasoline production, and, in 1991, the unleaded gas market was 96.5 percent of production.

Supply and Demand

Gasoline demand is influenced by summer driving conditions, winter heating oil needs, and governmental fuel efficiency regulations such as pollution-control devices.

Factors that affect the supply of gasoline include refiners' production ratios, storage capacity, cost of crude oil imports, international events, and government regulations.

Refining

Because gasoline and heating oil demands are inversely related—heating oil demand is greatest during the winter months and gasoline demand is highest during the summer—refineries can alter their production to meet changes in demand.

Gasoline is refined from lighter molecules of crude oil, and distillate fuels from heavier molecules. The heavier molecules can be transformed into lighter-end gasoline products by a catalytic cracking process. If gasoline demand increases, then refiners can run the catalytic cracking at higher levels, increasing the production of lighter-end gasoline products.

Futures Market

Unleaded regular gasoline futures and options contracts are traded on the New York Mercantile Exchange.

NATURAL GAS

Most scientists believe natural gas has been forming under the earth's surface for hundreds of millions of years, and the forces that created natural gas also created petroleum. Because of this, natural gas tends to be found with or near oil deposits. The term *natural gas* is often confused with the shortened term for *gasoline* or *gas*. But gasoline is a liquid whereas natural gas is a gaseous form of matter.

Supply and Demand

The Commonwealth of Independent States was the largest producer of natural gas in 1990—39 percent of the world's total or 29 trillion cubic feet. The United States followed, producing 18 trillion cubic feet. Consumption patterns are similar with the Commonwealth of Independent States, the largest consumer of natural gas, followed by the United States.

Natural gas is best known as fuel for cooking and heating in homes. U.S. natural gas consumption in 1991, despite the economic recession, reached 20 trillion cubic feet—the highest level since 1980. The largest consumer of natural gas by sector was industry, 44 percent, followed by residential use at 23 percent. Due to different federal and state rate structures, there are many price categories for natural gas. In addition,

U.S. Energy Production by Major Source
1950-1990

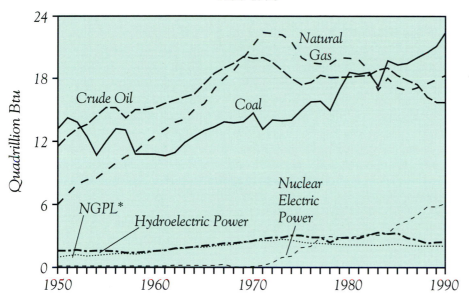

*NGPL–Natural Gas Plant Liquids
Source: Energy Information Administration, Annual Energy Review December 1991

prices to consumers vary considerably by region due to different factors such as transportation costs. Keeping these facts in mind, the estimated average wellhead price per thousand cubic feet declined from $1.71 in 1990 to $1.59 in 1991.

Natural Gas Liquids

Certain chemical compounds can be obtained in liquid form from natural gas. Natural gas liquids, also called *NGL*, are widely used as fuel and in the manufacturing of petrochemicals. Detergents, drugs, fertilizers, paints, plastics, man-made rubber, acrylic, nylon, polyester, and other synthetic fibers, are some of the many products manufactured using petrochemicals.

Natural gas liquids, classified as light hydrocarbons, become liquid when they are put under pressure. The liquid takes up much less space than the original gas and is easily transported in small pressurized containers. As the fuel is used, normal air pressure changes the liquid back to gas.

Two of the primary NGL compounds are propane and butane. Propane, butane, or a combination of the two (also known as *liquefied petroleum gas (LPG)*, *LP gas*, or *bottled gas*) is used as a heating fuel in industry and homes. Those who live in mobile homes, farm areas, or other locations far from gas pipelines can purchase liquefied petroleum gas for cooking, heating, and other uses. Liquid petroleum gas represents approximately 4 percent of residential heating use, whereas nearly half of all homes use natural gas as a heating source. In addition to being produced from certain compounds in natural gas, LPG can be produced from gaseous compounds in petroleum.

Futures Market

The New York Mercantile Exchange trades natural gas futures and options and propane futures. The Chicago Board of Trade trades anhydrous ammonia (NH_3) futures, a fertilizer contract in which natural gas is a major ingredient. The other fertilizer contract traded at the Chicago Board of Trade is diammonium phosphate (DAP) futures, which is produced from NH_3.

In addition to trading futures contracts related to physical commodities, exchanges also trade futures based on commodity indexes. Examples include CRB Index futures and options traded on the New York Futures Exchange and Goldman Sachs Commodity Index futures and options traded on the Chicago Mercantile Exchange.

Financial futures make up more than 80 percent of the world's futures trading volume. Their growing recognition and use by financial managers during the past two decades as risk-management tools is a reflection of unprecedented market volatility as well as the many types of financial instruments available on the market today. Whether a financial manager is protecting an investment from adverse price changes in the debt, equity, or currency markets, futures and options on futures contracts provide a vehicle to manage these risks. An overview of the cash market forces underlying these major futures markets is provided in this chapter.

FINANCIAL MARKETS

Debt Instruments, Stock Indexes, Currencies

OVERVIEW OF FINANCIAL MARKETS

Like commodities, financial instruments are an integral part of one's life. Every time an individual makes a deposit at a bank or borrows money using a credit card, one is using a financial instrument. And, every time a company issues shares of stock or a government sells a bond, they too are participating in the financial markets.

As familiar as these practices are, they differ from the goods and services markets where money is exchanged for food, shelter, clothing, etc. In the financial markets, participants invest their money in bonds, stocks,

17

and other instruments, storing their purchasing power until needed sometime in the future.

The role of the financial markets within a market economy can best be illustrated by examining the major participants and the flow of goods, services, and funds among them.

Market Economy

A competitive market society can be divided into households, businesses, and governments with each trading something with the other. For example, in the goods market, households purchase food, clothing, and other goods from businesses. Within the resource market, businesses hire labor to produce goods and services.

Beyond providing for its immediate needs, society plans for the future. Households save a portion of their income for retirement, home purchases, education, and other needs. Businesses borrow money to construct office buildings or power plants, to develop new products, and so on. Governments need money to finance various projects and services when their spending exceeds tax revenues.

Financial markets provide the means for households, businesses, and governments to transfer funds from savers to spenders. With their excess funds, households purchase securities, such as bonds or stocks, from businesses and governments. Corporations and governments use these funds to finance upcoming projects. A flow chart depicting a market economy is shown on the next page.

This economic picture is oversimplified as households are not the sole source of funds, and businesses and governments are not the only sources of securities. In general, however, U.S. households are net providers of funds and businesses and governments are net users of funds. Also absent from the picture is the international flow of funds. Despite these missing elements, this economic overview illustrates that financial markets are at the heart of a competitive market society.

Characteristics of Financial Instruments

Within the financial markets, there are many types of instruments with different characteristics. Some are debt-related, others are equities. Financial instruments can be traded directly or indirectly. The maturity and quality of the instruments also vary as well as how they are issued.

Debt vs. Equity

There are two basic types of financial instruments—debt or equity. Debt instruments are loans with an agreement to pay back the funds with interest. Depending upon the terms of the debt instrument, the interest payment can be either fixed or variable as determined by a set formula. Examples of debt securities include bonds, notes, and mortgages.

Circular Flow: An Overview of a Market Economy

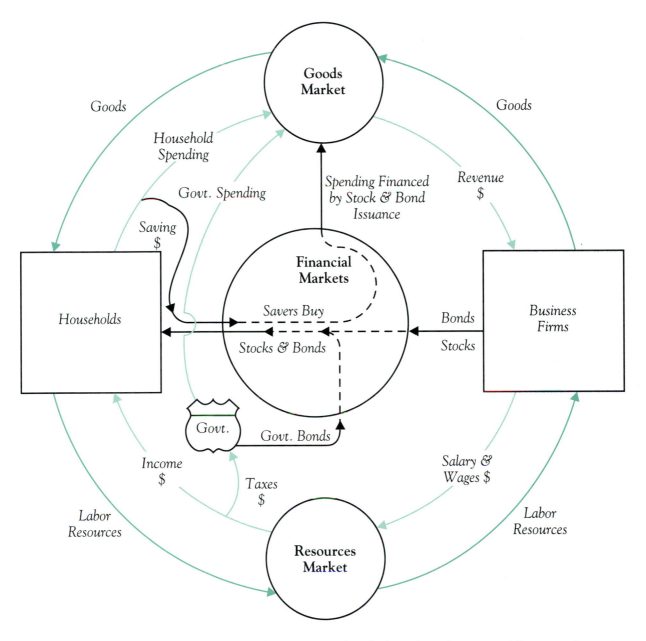

The combined activities of households, businesses, and governments produce the flows of a market economy. The outer circle, running *counterclockwise*, illustrates businesses channeling goods to households through the goods market. In turn, households offer their labor skills to businesses through the resource market. The inner circle, running *clockwise*, depicts money payments—income dollars to households; households spending dollars to pay for goods; businesses taking sales revenues back to their firms; and businesses paying employees. The very center shows the financial markets' role—providing the means by which households with surplus dollars transfer savings to corporations, governments, and other spending units.

In contrast, equity securities are shares of stock in a company. Those who purchase equity securities become owners in a company. As owners, they are entitled to a share of the company's profits, typically in the form of quarterly dividends. If for some reason the company is not profitable or it winds down operations, stock owners are last in line to receive a portion of the company's assets; whereas, those who purchase debt securities are lenders and have a higher priority of claim on assets and a legal right to interest compensation. Equity holders give up the certainty of debt-security income for the prospect of realizing higher returns.

Direct vs. Indirect Exchange of Funds

Securities can be traded directly or indirectly. Direct exchange occurs when the source of funds, say, a household saver, trades directly with the ultimate user of funds, say, a corporation or a government. For example, as a private investor, you successfully bid in a U.S. Treasury auction for 90-day Treasury bills. In return for your money, the government issues a T-bill and repays the loan plus interest in 90 days.

While securities can trade directly between the user and the source of funds, many do not because of the minimum size of transactions, brokerage fees, and research costs. In the case of the T-bill auction, the minimum size is $10,000, which is out of reach for many small savers. Transaction costs also can be prohibitive. For a million dollar trade, a $500 transaction fee is nominal, but for a purchase of a $1,000 bond, a $500 fee is prohibitive. Research costs are another impediment to trading directly. The cost of evaluating the quality and terms of each security is too expensive for most small private investors. However, a firm with a large portfolio worth hundreds of millions of dollars can spread these costs over the entire portfolio, thereby achieving a lower cost per dollar of securities purchased.

In fact, these hurdles—minimum size, transaction costs, and research costs—have given rise to the indirect trading of securities. Banks, credit unions, insurance companies, savings and loans, pension funds, mutual funds, money market funds, and other "middlemen" facilitate the flow of funds between savers and users of funds, giving small savers a way to participate in the financial markets.

These financial intermediaries have reduced the size of the minimum investment as well as related costs, thus attracting funds from savers. Having pooled the funds of many savers, these firms buy debt and equity securities from governments and corporations. As the following chart summarizes, financial intermediaries have transferred billions of dollars.

Financial Institutions Ranked by Asset Class
end of 1990

	Assets Billions of $	Percentage of Total Assets
Commercial Banks	3,334.0	30.5
Private Pension Funds	1,505.8	14
Life Insurance Companies	1,367.4	12.5
Savings & Loans	1,096.8	10
Finance Companies	772.1	7
State and Local Retirement Pension Funds	751.5	7
Mutual Funds	602.1	5.5
Other Insurance Companies	529.2	5
Money Market Funds	498.4	4.5
Mutual Savings Banks	263.8	2
Credit Unions	217.0	2
TOTAL	10,938.1	100

Source: Flow of Funds Accounts, *June 1993, Board of Governors of the Federal Reserve System*

Maturity of Securities

Securities have different maturities ranging from overnight to 30 years or more. Some securities, such as Treasury bills, mature in 90 days, whereas others mature only after decades, like the 50-year bonds issued by the Tennessee Valley Authority. Equities have no stated maturity, continuing until the corporation no longer exists.

Security	Maturity
U.S. Treasury bills	13 weeks/26 weeks/52 weeks
U.S. Treasury notes	2, 3, 5, 10 years

Bonds (many types—
    corporate, municipal,
    state, federal, government
    agencies)
	10 years and over

Corporate stock	Nonapplicable

Besides the debt and equity securities listed above, there are other interest-bearing instruments, such as Eurodollar deposits with a stated maturity, and checking accounts, which are payable upon demand.

Rating Debt Instruments

Debt instruments are rated according to an issuer's ability to pay back a loan. Two of the most prominent debt-rating agencies in the United States—Moody's Investors Service and Standard and Poor's (S&P)—give

debt instruments a rating ranging from the best, Aaa or AAA, to the worst, C or DDD. (See table below.) These agencies determine ratings for thousands of debt instruments by analyzing the history, previous borrowing and repayment records, and other economic factors of the issuers. Ratings are not fixed. If a debt issuer's economic condition changes in the estimation of either Moody's or S&P, they adjust the issuer's credit rating.

Ratings are important to both borrowers and lenders. Borrowers with high ratings can sell their debt at lower interest rates than borrowers with low ratings. Ratings are important to lenders because they provide a snapshot view of the overall financial conditions of the firm they are lending to.

Debt Ratings			
		Moody's	Standard & Poor's
Investment Grade	Highest Quality	Aaa	AAA
	High Quality	Aa1, Aa2, Aa3	AA+, AA, AA−
	Upper Medium Grade	A1, A2, A3	A+, A, A−
	Medium Grade	Baa1, Baa2, Baa3	BBB+, BBB, BBB−
High Yield or "Junk" Debt	Predominately Speculative	Ba1, Ba2, Ba3	BB+, BB, BB−
	Low Grade	B1, B2, B3	B+, B, B−
	Default Likely	Caa1, Caa2, Caa3	CCC+, CCC, CCC−
	Very Speculative	Ca	CC
	Lowest Quality	C	C
	In Default	DDD	

Primary Market vs. Secondary Market

When a company or government first sells a stock or bond in the marketplace, it is issuing a security in the primary market. Often, the issuer turns to investment banking firms that underwrite the new issue by purchasing it in bulk. Then, through their sales force, investment banks sell the security to the institutional and retail markets. Alternately, an issuer of a new security can hold an auction in which bids are accepted and the winning bidders receive the securities. In either case, the company or government issuing the securities receives the proceeds of the sale.

Once securities make their debut in the primary market, they trade from that point on in the resale or secondary market through an interdealer network or on an organized exchange, such as the New York Stock Exchange or American Stock Exchange. While any security can trade on the secondary market, there is no guarantee a security will have an active, liquid secondary market.

DEBT INSTRUMENTS

Since debt instruments are loans, they must state the terms agreed upon by the lender and borrower. Debt instruments identify the borrower; the amount loaned; when repayment is due; the rate of interest; and how the interest is to be paid. This section gives an overview of the cash markets for those debt instruments that have futures contracts associated with them. With today's menu of interest rate futures contracts, which span the entire yield curve, banks, insurance companies, savings and loans, and other institutions can hedge debt instruments of virtually any maturity.

Eurodollar Deposits

Eurodollar deposits are U.S. dollar-denominated deposits held in banks outside the United States. Because these nonnegotiable, fixed-rate deposits are held in banks outside the United States, Eurodollar deposits are not subject to U.S. banking regulations.

Originally, most of these dollar-deposits were held in Europe, but now the name *Eurodollar* is applied to dollar-deposits offered by banks throughout the world. The interest rate banks pay on Eurodollar deposits is the London Interbank Offer Rate (LIBOR), which is paid using the add-on method. With this method, if $100 was deposited for one year at 5 percent, the bank would add $5 to the account balance at the end of 360 days (a year for money market calculations), and the depositor could withdraw $105.

The origin of Eurodollars is just one example of financial market innovation in response to changing economic conditions and government regulations. During the Cold War, the Soviet Union, its Eastern European satellites, and the People's Republic of China feared the United States would someday freeze their bank accounts and confiscate dollar balances held in New York City banks. Anticipating this possibility, the Soviets transferred their dollar balances from New York to London and other European financial centers. This transfer of funds was achieved via the Soviet bank in Paris, Banque Commerciale pour l'Europe du Nord, also known as *Eurobank*. The term *Eurodollar* emerged from this incident.

Factors accelerating the creation of dollar-denominated deposits outside the United States were regulatory controls, including the Fed's Regulation Q (which limited interest banks could pay on deposits), and the Fed's

Short-term Money Market Instruments

requirement that its member banks hold cash reserves against deposits. These controls imposed costs and restrictions making it attractive for banks to offer Eurodollars and, at the same time, providing depositors with higher interest rates than possible on domestic deposits.

Today's Eurocurrency market is so large that financial intermediaries hold not only Eurodollars, but other currencies from outside their borders, such as the Japanese yen (Euroyen) and the German Deutsche mark (Euromarks).

Federal Funds

The Federal Reserve requires banks and other depository institutions in the U.S. to meet reserve requirements based on their customers' deposits and loans. Complicating matters, bank loan and deposit customers change their balances. This results in some banks having excess reserves and others having insufficient reserves. So, banks with excess reserves lend to banks needing funds to meet reserve requirements. Funds in excess of reserve requirements lent to other banks needing reserves are referred to as *fed funds*. Fed funds are generally lent overnight, but longer maturity lending occurs, known as *term fed funds*.

Larger money center banks are typically net borrowers of fed funds and smaller banks net lenders of fed funds. Interest is paid using the add-on method, the same as with Eurodollars. The fed funds rate is closely watched by the financial community since it is continuously changing throughout the day due to demand and supply for bank reserves as well as Federal Reserve monetary actions. As such, it serves as a benchmark for other short-term rates.

U.S. Treasury Bills

Treasury bills are probably the most liquid instruments paying interest in today's money markets. The dollar amount of marketable U.S. Treasury bills has increased substantially through the years. In 1972, there were $94.6 billion in T-bills outstanding and by 1992 the T-bill market had grown to $634.3 billion.

Brand-new 13- and 26-week T-bills are publicly auctioned every Monday, except holidays, and issued three days later. Treasury bills with 52-week maturities are auctioned every fourth Thursday and issued the following Thursday. Minimum bids are for a $10,000 face value T-bill with larger purchases in multiples of $5,000.

T-bills have become increasingly popular with individuals and corporations worldwide for several reasons. For one, T-bills are extremely liquid instruments. Secondly, like all securities issued by the U.S. Treasury, T-bills are free of credit risk. Also, interest received on Treasury securities is free from taxation by state and local governments.

Treasury bills pay interest using the discount method, which is different from the add-on method used by Eurodollars, fed funds, or personal savings accounts. Rather than adding interest onto the principal, Treasury bills subtract the interest from the face amount of the bill at the time of issue, then pay the face amount at maturity. The difference between the purchase price and the redemption value is the interest. For example, in one auction the U.S. Treasury sold $11.043 billion face value of 13-week bills. The average price of the 13-week bills was 99.272 percent of par or $9,927.20 for a $10,000 face value T-bill. Thirteen weeks later when the T-bill matures, the investor receives $10,000.

The interest rate or discount yield in this example equals 2.88 percent and is calculated using the following formula. (**Note:** The T-bill in this example matures in 91 days.)

$$\text{Discount yield} = \frac{\text{par} - \text{price}}{100} \times \frac{360 \text{ days}}{\# \text{ days}}$$

$$= \frac{100 - 99.272}{100} \times \frac{360 \text{ days}}{91 \text{ days}}$$

$$= .00728 \times 3.956$$

$$= .0288 \text{ or } 2.88\%$$

As the previous example illustrates, discount yield is calculated as a percent of face value using the 360-day year, which is customary for securities with an original maturity of a year or less. Debt instruments with original maturities greater than one year compute yield based on the price paid, rather than the face value, using a 365-day year. To adjust for these differences, investors calculate the bond equivalent yield of the T-bill. This way they can compare the discount yield of a T-bill with the yield of a bond.

$$\text{Bond equivalent yield} = \frac{\text{par} - \text{price}}{\text{price}} \times \frac{365 \text{ days}}{\# \text{ days}}$$

$$= \frac{100 - 99.272}{99.272} \times \frac{365 \text{ days}}{91}$$

$$= .007333 \times 4.010989$$

$$= 2.94\%$$

U.S. Treasury Notes and Bonds

Governments around the world issue longer-term debt instruments to finance their borrowing needs. In Germany, the securities are referred to as *bunds*, in England as *gilts*, and in the United States as *Treasuries*.

The U.S. Treasury market is enormous and has grown dramatically over the years. In 1973, for instance, there were $263 billion in

Long-term Debt Instruments

outstanding securities. Nearly 20 years later, it had exploded to more than
$2 trillion. While there has been growth in all maturity categories, there
has been a sizable shift from T-bills to longer-term T-notes and T-bonds,
especially the intermediate-term T-notes. U.S. Treasury notes accounted
for nearly 60 percent of all marketable Treasury debt in 1992, up from 46
percent in 1973.

    Treasury notes and bonds are considered capital market instruments
because they represent the medium- to long-term segment of the maturity
spectrum. Notes are issued at maturities between 1 and 10 years, but most
often with maturities of 2, 3, 5, and 10 years. Bonds may be issued at any
maturity greater than 10 years, but are currently issued for 30 years.
Treasury notes with original maturities of less than 4 years are usually
issued in minimum denominations of $5,000, while notes and bonds
maturing in 4 years or more are typically issued in minimum
denominations of $1,000.

    Some T-bonds are callable, which means the Treasury may, at its
discretion, redeem or call-in the bond before its designated maturity.
(T-notes are not callable.) In the case of a 30-year callable T-bond, the

Marketable U.S. Treasury Debt

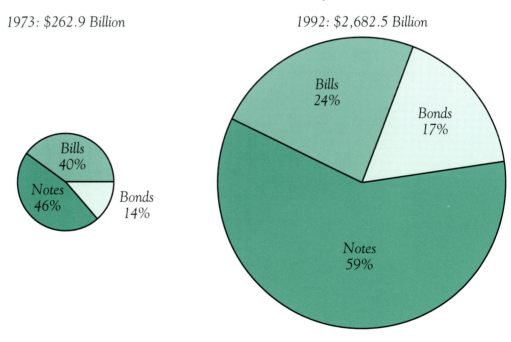

1973: $262.9 Billion

1992: $2,682.5 Billion

Bills 40%

Notes 46%

Bonds 14%

Bills 24%

Bonds 17%

Notes 59%

Source: Economic Report of the President 1993 *and the Federal Reserve*

call feature typically can be activated at any time during the 5-year period preceding the bond's maturity date. In financial newspapers, the maturity of a callable bond could be written as May 2009-14, meaning it matures in May of 2014 but it is callable beginning May of 2009. Although there are callable T-bonds trading, no callable T-bonds have been issued since 1982.

The annual interest payment—or coupon—is known when the bond or note is issued and determined by multiplying the coupon rate (expressed as an annualized percentage, say 8.5 percent) by the face value of the instrument. Since neither the coupon rate nor the face amount of the instrument change, interest payments do not change during the life of the note or bond; hence, the name, *fixed-income security*.

The term coupon is a holdover from earlier times when bond holders received certificates with interest coupons attached. Bond holders clipped these coupons and presented them to the issuer to receive their interest. However, due to the rising cost of printing and distributing debt certificates and the growing use of computers, there is a move toward issuing *book-entry securities*. In these instances, debt issuers ask a transfer agent, typically a commercial bank or trust company, to electronically transfer interest payments to a creditor's bank account. For Treasuries, this process began with U.S. Treasury bills issued in 1979. By 1986, all marketable Treasury debt was issued by electronic book-entry.

T-note and T-bond prices are quoted as a percent of the face value of the instrument or par and 32nds of a percent. For example, a $1,000 face value bond priced at 90-16 (90 and $^{16}\!/_{32}$ percent of par) is a bond whose current market price is $905 (90.5% × $1,000). This quoted price excludes any interest due. Since holders of T-notes and T-bonds receive interest payments at six-month intervals, most purchases and sales must account for interest that has been earned but not yet paid to the holder—commonly called *accrued interest*. If a bond or note is sold in the secondary market between interest payments, it is understood the buyer pays the quoted price plus accrued interest.

Municipal, Corporate, and Zero-Coupon Bonds

Long-term debt instruments also are issued by city and state municipalities. Local governments sell municipal bonds to generate funds to finance new developments and local improvements. Investors are attracted to munibonds because the interest earned is exempt from federal taxes and, in some cases, state and local taxes.

Municipal bonds are issued in minimum denominations of $5,000 and in increments of $5,000. They are priced as a percent of par and 32nds, like T-bonds.

Corporate bonds have similar features to municipal and Treasury securities. However, interest received on corporate bonds is not exempt from federal, state, or local income taxes. Corporate bonds typically pay higher interest rates than Treasuries with the same maturity due to their investment rating. Corporate bonds are priced in points and eighths of a point. A bond with a $1,000 face value quoted at 95⅜, for example, has a price of $957.50.

Another type of debt instrument is pure discount bonds, also known as *zero-coupon bonds*. These long-term bonds with maturities up to 30 years do not pay interest periodically. Rather, the interest on a zero-coupon bond is reflected in the difference between the initial purchase price and eventual redemption at face value, similar to T-bills. In other words, the coupon rate on the bond is zero, hence, the name *zero-coupon bond.*

Zero-coupon bonds emerged in the mid-1980s as an innovative response to market conditions. At that time, brokerage firms began separating or stripping coupons from the principal of a Treasury bond, packaging enough coupons with coupons and principals with principals to make market-sized bundles—$1 million lots at the dealer level—and selling them. This process was profitable as the pieces of the bond could be sold for more than the cost of the whole bond.

Today, the market trades these instruments as STRIPs (Separate Trading of Registered Interest and Principal) since the Treasury facilitated the strip market—giving each T-bond principal an identification number and each individual coupon payment an identification number. Individuals use zero coupon bonds as vehicles to save for college and retirement. Insurance companies and pension funds use zeroes as a way to match their long-term payment obligations with sure, long-term cash inflows.

Yield and Its Relationship with Price

For all debt securities with fixed interest payments, including T-bills and zero-coupon bonds, the security's price and its yield—return on invested capital—are inversely related. That is, when the yield of a fixed-income security rises, price falls; and, when the yield falls, price rises.

Price/Yield Inverse Relationship

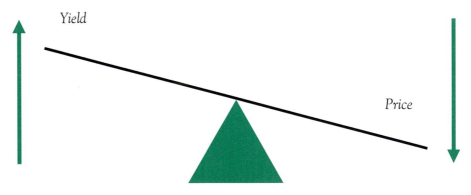

Yield

Price

Fixed Amount
of Interest & Principal

This inverse relationship holds true because the interest payment and principal are fixed, while market conditions and the demand for credit are continuously changing. For example, if current market yields are hovering around 10 percent when a debt security is issued, then borrowers issuing a $10,000 face-value bond would set the coupon rate at 10 percent to be competitive in the market.

As time passes, financial conditions change causing market yields to rise, say, to 15 percent. But if newly issued bonds with a 15 percent coupon are paying $1,500 of interest a year, what happens to the existing 10 percent coupon bonds paying $1,000 a year? To remain competitive in the market, the price of the 10 percent coupon bond must fall.

To see why the price of the 10 percent bond falls, consider the choice buyers have when purchasing a $10,000 face value bond. They can either earn $1,500 of interest per year purchasing a newly issued 15 percent coupon bond or $1,000 a year in interest buying the older 10 percent coupon bond. If the two bonds were priced the same, everyone would buy the newer 15 percent coupon given its higher interest payment. However, competitive market pressures force sellers of the older bond to reduce its price to attract buyers.

Current Yield

Several formulas are used by market participants to determine the price of a fixed-rate bond when yields change. The simplest of these is current yield—the ratio of annual interest receipts divided by the current price of the security.

$$\text{Current yield } (Y) = \frac{\text{annual interest received } (C)}{\text{current price } (P)}$$

Recalling the inverse relationship between price and yield, if an investor holds a $10,000 bond with a 10 percent coupon and current yield rises to 15 percent, then the price of the bond falls below $10,000. Using the current yield formula, the price is $6,666.66:

$$15\% = \frac{\$1,000 \text{ (interest received on 10\% bond)}}{\text{current price}}$$

$$= \frac{\$1,000}{\$6,666.66}$$

The table on the next page illustrates the inverse relationship for a 10 percent bond at three different yield levels using current yield calculations.

Current Yield	Annual Interest Payment of 10% Bond (10% coupon rate × $10,000 face value)	Market Price
5%	$1,000	$20,000.00
10% (par)	$1,000	$10,000.00
15%	$1,000	$ 6,666.66

The table also shows that the same change in yield does not result in the same change in price. A 5 percent yield increase (from 10 percent to 15 percent) causes the price to decrease by $3,333.34 (from $10,000 to $6,666.66); whereas a 5-percent yield decrease (from 10 percent to 5 percent) causes the price to increase by $10,000 (from $10,000 to $20,000). This differing price response for the same change in yield suggests the complexity of the inverse relationship. And, the magnitude of the differing results also reveals a drawback in the current yield formula—namely, that the formula does not account for key factors such as an instrument's maturity and timing of coupon payments. Because of this, the market uses a more sophisticated formula called *yield to maturity*.

Yield to Maturity

Yield to maturity (YTM) is used to determine the rate of return an investor receives if a fixed-income security is held to maturity. To do this effectively, YTM must account for several variables including time remaining to maturity, the amount and timing of coupon payments and principal repayment, as well as two other income sources not accounted for in current yield: (1) capital gains or losses (the difference between the price paid for the debt instrument and the amount received at maturity); and, (2) the interest earned on reinvested coupons. Yield to maturity assumes coupons received are reinvested at the YTM rate.

Yield to maturity is the rate that satisfies the following formula, which appears imposing but is easily calculated with financial calculators:*

$$P = \frac{C_1}{(1+YTM)^1} + \frac{C_2}{(1+YTM)^2} + \cdots + \frac{C_n}{(1+YTM)^n} + \frac{F}{(1+YTM)^n}$$

where:
P = price of instrument
C = annual coupon payments
n = number of years to maturity
YTM = yield to maturity
F = face value of instrument

*For simplicity, the yield to maturity formula used here accounts for annual coupon payments even though Treasury bonds have semiannual coupon payments. The formula becomes more complicated when using semiannual payments, however, one can calculate YTM either way.

To see how this formula is used, consider a $10,000 face value bond with a 10 percent coupon paying $1,000 annually, and three years left until maturity. If the bond's yield to maturity is currently 15 percent, an investor would solve for price using the formula:

$$P = \frac{\$1,000}{(1+.15\,)^1} + \frac{\$1,000}{(1+.15)^2} + \frac{\$1,000}{(1+.15)^3} + \frac{\$10,000}{(1+.15)^3}$$

$$= \$8,858.39$$

In this equation, price equals $8,858.39. (Alternately, given a target price, the formula can be used to compute a security's yield to maturity.) As shown in this example, the inverse relationship between price and yield exists in yield to maturity calculations as well as current yield calculations. As yields rose from 10 percent to 15 percent, the price of the bond fell from $10,000 (par value) to $8,858.39.

Price Sensitivity

This inverse relationship depends most heavily on two major factors: the instrument's maturity and its coupon.

The longer the time to maturity, the greater the effect a yield change has on the price of a security. For example, given a 30-year T-bond and a 5-year T-note with the same coupon rate of 8 percent, the bond will experience a greater price change for a given change in yield. The shaded half of the chart below indicates the price of the 5-year T-note would fall $14/32$ if yield increased by .1 percent, whereas the 30-year T-bond with the same coupon rate would fall $36/32$ if yield increased by the same amount of .1 percent. The differing price sensitivity of T-bonds versus T-notes is an important consideration to many traders of yield curve spreads in the cash and futures markets. NOB (notes over bonds) traders, for example, frequently weight their positions in each futures market to adjust for the difference in price sensitivity.

Maturity	Coupon	Yield	Price	Price Impact of .10 Yield Change
5-year T-note	8%	8.00	100-00	
5-year T-note	8%	8.10	99-18	$-14/32$
30-year T-bond	8%	8.00	100-00	
30-year T-bond	8%	8.10	98-28	$-36/32$

The differing price sensitivity of debt instruments is also evident when comparing coupon rates. With all else equal, low-coupon instruments are more sensitive to a given change in yield than high-coupon instruments. As an example, as yield rises .1 percent, the price of a 10-year T-note with a 2 percent coupon priced at par falls $^{29}\!/_{32}$ whereas a 10-year T-note issued when current yields were 14 percent, falls only $^{17}\!/_{32}$.

Maturity	Coupon	Yield	Price	Price Impact of .10 Yield Change
10-year T-note	2%	2.00	100-00	
10-year T-note	2%	2.10	99-03	$-^{29}\!/_{32}$
10-year T-note	14%	14.00	100-00	
10-year T-note	14%	14.10	99-15	$-^{17}\!/_{32}$

A third variable affecting the price sensitivity of debt instruments is credit risk. (More information about credit risk and other factors influencing the price sensitivity of debt instruments is available in several textbooks. Some of these texts are listed in Sources of Information.)

Yield Curves

Fixed-income analysts study the relationship between yield to maturity and the time to maturity of debt instruments of the same quality using a yield-curve graph. By plotting yields against maturity, a yield curve provides a snapshot view of the current interest rate environment.

The U.S. Treasury yield curve is the most commonly watched yield curve in the industry as (1) U.S. Treasuries are rated the highest quality since they are backed by the U.S. government; (2) it encompasses a full range of maturities; and (3) the Treasury market is very liquid with prices determined throughout the day. For these reasons, the Treasury yield curve serves as a foundation from which other yield curves can be built as well as a base from which other securities are priced.

Shown in the Treasury yield curve on the next page, as maturity rises, YTM rises—indicating long-term yields are greater than short-term yields. This yield curve is referred to as a *positively sloped yield curve*, also called a *normal yield curve* because its shape is the most common.

Yield curves also can be flat, where yields are the same at every maturity. Or they can be negatively sloped with short-term yields greater than long-term yields. A negatively sloped yield curve is referred to as an *inverted yield curve*.

Financial economists have several explanations why the yield curve is shaped a certain way, but many believe its shape is influenced by the market's expectation of future interest rates. That is, by analyzing a yield curve, one can get an idea of what the market currently expects interest rates to be in the future. Rates extracted from a yield curve and expected to prevail in the future are known as *forward rates*.

Yield Curve

Percent, Weekly Averages, on February 26,1993

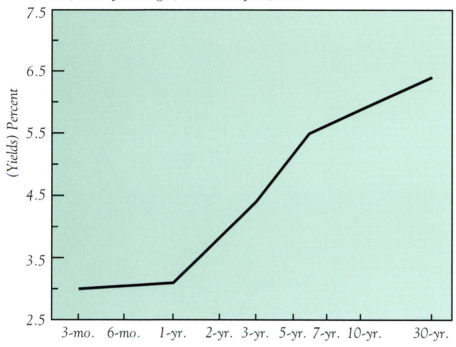

Source: Board of Governors of the Federal Reserve System

Forward rates are important for the Eurodollar, Treasury bill, and fed funds futures markets because these futures markets price according to the forward rates embedded in the yield curve.

Market yield reflects the current price of credit and fluctuates with changes in (1) the behavior of demanders and suppliers of credit, (2) the expected inflation/deflation during the life of the loan, and (3) the creditworthiness of the borrower. (Since there is no credit risk associated with U.S. Treasuries, this topic is not covered here.) Complicating matters, each can be moving in opposing directions with differing intensities, so the net impact on yield may be difficult to discern.

Factors Causing Market Price and Yield to Change

Supply and Demand Forces

The competition between those who supply funds and those who demand funds determines the basic "rent" on borrowed money. Changes in their behavior affect the demand and supply of credit and, hence, yields. Major suppliers and demanders of funds are households, businesses, governments, and financial intermediaries. In the United States, businesses and governments are net demanders of funds, whereas households and financial intermediaries are net suppliers.

For example, businesses may increase spending to upgrade plants and equipment. Or a local park district may face a cut in tax revenues, while its spending remains unchanged. In either case, there would be an increased demand for funds. This demand for additional funds leads to higher yields, provided other economic forces remain constant.

On the supply side, household demographics have an impact. For example, households may spend most of their income during their early career years when they are purchasing first homes and starting families. Once careers are established and children raised, spending could be reduced and saving increased. This increase in household saving, other forces remaining constant, increases the supply of funds and leads to lower yields.

Expected Inflation/Deflation

The premium paid the borrower to cover inflationary expectations is a second factor affecting yields. That is, increases in expected inflation lead to higher market yields; decreases in expected inflation lead to reduced market yields.

Because lenders want to be rewarded for lending funds, they build an anticipated inflation premium (or deflation discount) into lending rates. This premium (or discount) is in addition to the basic rent for lending. If the inflation premium was absent, lenders would see their purchasing power erode. Assume a lender agrees to a $1,000 one-year loan at 3 percent. If inflation rises from an anticipated level of 0 percent, say to 7 percent, the lender's $1,000 would not have the same purchasing power as it did a year earlier. In fact, the lender needs to receive $1,070 just to get back the same purchasing power.

The Federal Reserve, U.S. Treasury, and Primary Dealers

Three major participants in the financial markets are the Federal Reserve, the U.S. Treasury Department, and primary dealers. Their roles in the marketplace are essential to the flow of funds from savers to borrowers.

The Federal Reserve System

The Federal Reserve System or Fed is the central bank of the United States. The Fed was created by the Federal Reserve Act, passed by the Congress in 1913 to provide a safer and more flexible banking and monetary system. The Federal Reserve contributes to the attainment of the nation's economic and financial goals through its ability to influence money and credit in the economy. As the nation's central bank, it attempts to ensure long-term growth along with reasonable price stability. In the short run, the Federal Reserve seeks to adapt its policies to combat deflationary or inflationary pressures as they may arise. And as a lender of last resort, it has the responsibility for using the policy instruments available to it in an attempt to forestall national liquidity crises and financial panics. The Federal Reserve also has been entrusted with many supervisory and regulatory functions to promote a sound financial structure

Organization of the Federal Reserve System

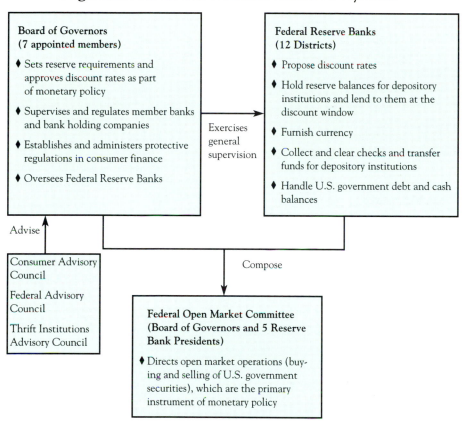

The Federal Reserve System was created in 1913 following the passage of the Federal Reserve Act. The Federal Reserve was formed to provide a safer, more flexible banking and monetary system.

Source: The Federal Reserve System Purposes & Functions, 1984

in the United States. Its responsibilities include regulating the foreign activities of all U.S. banks and the U.S. activities of foreign banks as well as administering the laws that regulate bank holding companies.

The U.S. central bank is a complex organization, comprised of the Board of Governors of the Federal Reserve System, the Federal Open Market Committee, and the Federal Reserve Banks. The 12 regional Federal Reserve Banks operate a check-clearing process, distribute coin and currency, conduct bank examinations, and assist the Treasury at auction time. On a larger scale, the Board of Governors oversees the system with its primary responsibility to formulate monetary policy with its Open Market Committee.

Money Supply

The Federal Reserve has developed different credit measures useful in interpreting monetary conditions, some of which also have served as guides for monetary policy. One such measure is money supply.

Over the years there have been differing opinions as to what constitutes the supply of money. In 1980, following a period of rapid financial innovation and regulatory change, the Federal Reserve redefined money supply to reflect the growing importance of depository institutions, other than commercial banks. Currently, the Fed monitors three different, but related, measures of money supply—M-1, M-2, M-3, with M-1 being the most liquid.

◆ M-1 consists of currency held by the nonbank public, traveler's checks of nonbank issuers, demand deposits (i.e., checking accounts) at commercial banks, and other checkable deposits including NOW accounts, automatic transfer service account balances, credit union share drafts, demand deposits at thrift institutions, and technical adjustments.

◆ M-2 consists of M-1 plus savings and time deposits of less than $100,000 at depository institutions; overnight repurchase agreements at commercial banks; overnight Eurodollar accounts issued to U.S. residents by foreign branches of U.S. banks worldwide; and money market mutual fund accounts.

◆ M-3 consists of M-2 plus large time deposits of more than $100,000 issued by all depository institutions, repurchase agreements with terms greater than overnight, term Eurodollars held by U.S. residents at foreign branches of U.S. banks worldwide, and balances in institution-only money market funds.

The Fed's Monetary Tools: Open Market Operations, Reserve Requirements, Discounting

Open market operations, which involve the Federal Reserve's purchase or sale of U.S. government securities in the secondary market, are the most powerful and flexible monetary policy tool of the Federal Reserve.

Distinguishing the U.S. Treasury from the Federal Reserve

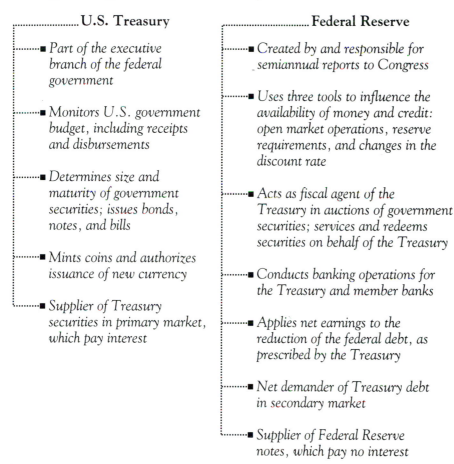

U.S. Treasury

- Part of the executive branch of the federal government

- Monitors U.S. government budget, including receipts and disbursements

- Determines size and maturity of government securities; issues bonds, notes, and bills

- Mints coins and authorizes issuance of new currency

- Supplier of Treasury securities in primary market, which pay interest

Federal Reserve

- Created by and responsible for semiannual reports to Congress

- Uses three tools to influence the availability of money and credit: open market operations, reserve requirements, and changes in the discount rate

- Acts as fiscal agent of the Treasury in auctions of government securities; services and redeems securities on behalf of the Treasury

- Conducts banking operations for the Treasury and member banks

- Applies net earnings to the reduction of the federal debt, as prescribed by the Treasury

- Net demander of Treasury debt in secondary market

- Supplier of Federal Reserve notes, which pay no interest

When the Fed buys securities, it adds to member-bank reserves, increasing the lending capacity of the banking system. As bank lending increases, the supply of money grows. When the Fed sells securities, it collects money from member banks, reducing the banking system's lending capacity. This cutback in lending decreases money supply. As the supply of money changes, so do interest rates. The greater the supply of money, assuming inflationary expectations remain the same, the lower the rates and vice versa. The Federal Open Market Committee (FOMC) determines the Federal Reserve's open market operations and, consequently, is the most important monetary policy-making body of the Federal Reserve System.

In addition to open market operations, the Federal Reserve can change its reserve requirements and the discount rate to influence monetary policy. Even though the Fed has these two tools to stimulate or reign in the economy, its preferred method for injecting or draining reserves from the banking system is open market operations.

By law, depository institutions in the United States are required to have a certain amount of "spare cash" or reserves on hand either in their vaults or on deposit at the Federal Reserve Bank. The higher the reserve requirement, the less lending capacity banks have and the slower the growth in money supply. The lower the reserve requirement, the more lending capacity and the faster the growth in money supply.

Since reserves are noninterest-bearing deposits, banks try to minimize the amount of reserves in excess of the Fed's requirements. Overnight bank lending of excess reserves (federal funds) to banks with insufficient reserves arose as a market solution to provide interest to bank reserve lenders and a source of funds to bank reserve borrowers.

The third monetary tool the Federal Reserve uses is discounting. The Fed uses this tool either by adjusting the amount it's going to lend member banks or changing the discount rate—the interest rate the Fed charges member banks for loans. By cutting the discount rate, the Fed confirms its intention to stimulate bank lending—a clear sign to the marketplace of the Fed's easing monetary policy stance. If the Fed is trying to reign in the economy, it raises the discount rate.

U.S. Treasury

Distinct from the Federal Reserve, the U.S. Treasury is part of the executive branch responsible for administering the financial needs of the federal government.

Among the responsibilities of the Treasury are raising funds to finance the federal deficit (federal tax revenues less government expenditures) through Treasury auctions and handling the repayment of the nation's maturing federal debt (sum of all annual federal deficits and surpluses). Throughout the 1980s, deficits have run into billions of dollars, raising the federal debt as a percent of gross domestic product (GDP).

With the United States running large annual deficits and accumulating huge debts, the Treasury manages its responsibilities by issuing Treasury bills, notes, and bonds. At 1992 levels, this requires the Treasury to issue between $100 billion and $150 billion of new securities monthly.

Primary Dealers

Primary dealers are the third major participant in the Treasury securities market. Representing the core of the cash market for Treasury securities, primary government security dealers consist of approximately 40 banks or bank subsidiaries and brokerage firms, who act as underwriters of new Treasury debt. Primary dealers purchase the bulk of the securities at Treasury auctions.

Once Treasury securities are issued, the dealers maintain an active,

Total Federal Debt as a Percent of GDP

Source: Monetary Trends, June 1992, of the Federal Reserve Bank of St. Louis

liquid secondary market for existing issues. Although some Treasury issues are traded on organized exchanges, almost all the secondary market activity occurs in the over-the-counter dealer market. The secondary market trades more than $100 billion in Treasuries each day. The dealers' willingness to quote continuous firm bids and offers provides the Treasury cash market with unparalleled liquidity.

In addition to primary dealers, approximately 300 to 500 secondary dealers trade in the secondary market. Both primary and secondary dealers generally hold an inventory of U.S. Treasury securities and seek to profit from favorable security price changes, trading for their own account, and commissions. Because the secondary market is so competitive, commissions are slight and bid/ask spreads, reflecting a liquid market, are narrow.

Carrying Treasury securities in inventory can be profitable when the yield curve has a positive slope. A positive yield curve environment implies positive carry—named positive because the coupon income is greater than the short-term cost of financing inventory. Because the majority of the dealers' inventories are financed with short-term loans—*repurchase agreements*—these costs are pivotal in their profit margins.

Using government securities as collateral, a dealer initiates a repurchase agreement, also referred to as *repo* or *RP*, by selling specific securities to receive cash now and simultaneously arranging to buy them back (repurchase them) at a certain price on a specific day in the future—usually the next day. With this repo transaction, the dealer obtains funds via a short-term collateralized loan. The repurchase price is higher than the selling price, reflecting interest expense. Generally, overnight repo rates are slightly lower than the rate for fed funds. There also are term repos, which cover a longer period of time, but rarely more than 30 days.

A *reverse repo*, also called a *matched sale-purchase agreement*, is the opposite side of a repo transaction. With a reverse repo, a dealer buys specific securities and simultaneously agrees to sell them back at a certain price on a specified future date.

The Fed's open market operations often involve repos and reverse repos to supplement outright purchases and sales of government securities. Repos initiated by the Federal Reserve have the opposite meaning of repos initiated by dealers. With Fed-initiated repos, the Federal Reserve buys securities for cash and simultaneously agrees to resell the securities at a certain price by a specific day in the future.

Futures Markets

The Chicago Board of Trade trades a full spectrum of futures and options contracts associated with the U.S. government debt market—Treasury bond, 10-, 5-, and 2-year T-note futures and options, and 30-day fed funds futures. The Chicago Board of Trade also trades municipal bond index futures and options. Treasury bill, Eurodollar, and LIBOR futures and options are traded at the Chicago Mercantile Exchange. The MidAmerica Commodity Exchange trades T-bond futures and options, 10- and 5-year T-note, T-bill, and Eurodollar futures. A division of the New York Cotton Exchange, FINEX®, trades 5- and 2-year T-note futures. Government debt futures are also actively traded at the London International Financial Futures Exchange, Marche a Terme International de France, Deutsche Terminbörse, Singapore International Monetary Exchange, Tokyo International Financial Futures Exchange, Bolsa de Mercadorias & Futuros, Tokyo Stock Exchange, Sydney Futures Exchange, and OM Stockholm.

EQUITY SECURITIES

Bonds, notes, bills, commercial paper, and other debt instruments are some ways companies finance their spending plans. Another major source of funding comes from equity securities. While some companies are privately held, others are publicly held, meaning they sell ownership rights—shares of stock—in their firm to the general public.

These shares of stock are traded on the stock market. In the United States, *the stock market* is generally considered to be the New York Stock Exchange (NYSE), also known as *the Big Board*, which lists more than 2,000 companies having market value in excess of $4 trillion as of December 1992. Also part of the U.S. stock market are the National Association of Securities Dealers Automated Quotation system (NASDAQ) in Washington, D.C., the American Stock Exchange (Amex) in New York, and regional exchanges in Boston, Philadelphia, Cincinnati,

Chicago, San Francisco, and Los Angeles. In addition to these U.S. stock exchanges, there are many exchanges in cities throughout the world, including Hong Kong, Tokyo, London, Frankfurt, Paris, Amsterdam, Madrid, Brussels, Milan, Stockholm, Zurich, Sydney, Taipei, and São Paulo to name a few.

Stock exchanges provide central locations where orders to buy and sell shares of stock are executed for individuals and businesses. In the United States, the NYSE, Amex, and the regional exchanges use a specialist trading system that is different from the open outcry method of trading used in the futures pit. The specialist is an individual or firm having the responsibility to maintain a fair and orderly market in a specific stock. In maintaining fair and orderly markets, specialists are required to buy stock from sellers if there are no other buyers available, or to sell stock to buyers if there are no other sellers. They are not expected to prevent a stock from rising or falling in value. Specialists also are required to announce bid and ask prices regularly.

In addition to these exchanges, which provide physical locations for trading shares of stocks, there is another U.S. market on which stocks are bought and sold: the *over-the-counter* or OTC market. Instead of one central location, the OTC market links buyers and sellers by telephones and other means of communication.

The OTC market is a negotiated market where prices are reached by dealers who bargain with each other when buying or selling securities. The OTC equities market is monitored by the National Association of Securities Dealers (NASD). Currently, 4,700 stocks trade on NASDAQ, which is owned and operated by the NASD. NASDAQ, as well as the New York, the American, and the regional stock exchanges are supervised by the Securities and Exchange Commission (SEC).

The equities markets have changed considerably in recent years with significant growth in trading volume and the number of block trades. In 1975, for example, average daily volume on the New York Stock Exchange totaled 18.5 million shares; block trades of 10,000 shares or more averaged 136 a day. By 1992, average daily volume was 202 million shares and daily block trades averaged 4,468 per day. On the NASDAQ, average daily trading volume increased from 26.4 million shares in 1980 to more than 192 million shares by 1992.

Facilitating this dramatic growth in volume were advances in automation. The Designated Order Turnaround (DOT) system at the NYSE, the Post Execution Reporting (PER) system at the Amex, and the Small Order Execution System (SOES) allow the placement of large volume orders. And the List Order Processing (LIST) program of the DOT system facilitates the trading of entire portfolios by accommodating orders for more than 400 stocks simultaneously in excess of 2,500 shares each.

Another illustration of the change equity markets have undergone is the demographics of the shareholders. In 1950, according to the Federal Reserve, households, personal trusts, and nonprofit corporations accounted

NYSE Average Daily Trading Volume

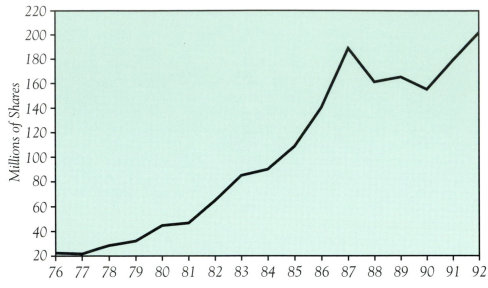

Source: New York Stock Exchange

for more than 91 percent of common stock purchases. By 1991, that percentage declined to 54 percent. Investing in equities in greater numbers are institutions—public and private pension funds, insurance companies, banks, and mutual funds. Institutions increased their share of stock holdings from 6 percent in 1950 to about 43 percent in 1992.

Ownership Rights

Since stockholders are owners in a company, they can take an active role in the firm's management and prosperity. They elect a board of directors and vote on various company resolutions proposed at the annual shareholders' meeting. By comparison, owners of debt instruments are not entitled to any voting rights.

Along with having a voice in the company, shareholders either reap the benefits of a company's success or experience losses if the company falters. Consequently, unlike debt holders who earn a fixed income on their investment, the rewards of owning stock are limited only by the company's profits. Profitability translates into increased stock prices, which owners can realize by selling shares, and larger stock dividends. If the company fails, on the other hand, stockholders are last to receive anything from the firm's dissolution.

Stock Risks and Diversified Portfolios

There are any number of reasons why a company, once profitable, faces a downtrend—the company's visionary dies, the production process the firm uses becomes obsolete, and a change in consumer buying patterns are just a few examples. That is why investors typically do not want to expose all their savings to one firm as they try to avoid risk that is specific to one firm.

Due to firm-specific risk, also referred to as *unsystematic risk*, equity owners often hold a diversified portfolio. Modern portfolio theory suggests diversification achieved by holding as few as 20 different company stocks eliminates most of the firm-specific risk.

Increasingly, individual investors achieve diversification through mutual funds. Mutual funds, first created in the 1920s, pool the funds of individuals or businesses and invest them in a variety of securities to achieve a defined investment objective. Common stock mutual funds offer opportunities to invest in a diversified and professionally managed portfolio of equities with initial investments of as little as $100 or $500 and subsequent contributions of $50 to $100. Common stock funds may be international funds that invest in equities of non-U.S. companies, global funds that invest in securities issued in the United States and in other countries, and sector funds that invest in a particular group of stocks, such as technology, health care, financial services, or other industries.

According to the Investment Company Institute, the group that monitors the mutual fund industry, there were a total of 361 mutual funds with $47.6 billion in assets in 1970. By September 1992, there were 3,662 mutual funds with $1.53 trillion in assets. This includes not only 1,284 stock funds but 2,378 funds specializing in debt securities, including bond and money market funds. Money market mutual funds invest in short-term debt securities that offer stability of principal and current market yields. Bond funds invest in fixed-income securities typically paying higher interest rates than short-term money market instruments.

Stock Indexes

Holding a diversified portfolio helps to manage firm-specific risk, but even the diversified portfolio holder remains exposed to the general volatility of the market, also referred to as *systematic risk*. In many instances, the value of a portfolio is based on how the stock market or a particular group of stocks moves. To track general market direction, several market averages or indexes have emerged to allow continuous monitoring of the stock market's movement. To hedge against overall market risk, portfolio managers have turned to futures and options contracts based on different stock indexes.

There are several stock indexes, but the most familiar are the Dow Jones Industrial Average (DJIA) and the Standard & Poor's 500 (or S&P 500). Others include the Amex Major Market Index, the New York Stock Exchange Composite, the Value Line Index, and the over-the-counter (OTC) or NASDAQ composite. Outside the United States there is the Nikkei 225 Index, the Financial Times Stock Index (or FT-SE, pronounced "footsie"), the Hang Seng Index, and others.

How Indexes Are Constructed

How a particular index tracks the market depends on its composition, that is, the sampling of the stocks, the weighting of the individual stocks, and the method of averaging.

When selecting a sample of stocks for an index, the aim is to choose stocks whose aggregate price movement reflects, as closely as possible, the overall movement of the market or some special market segment. Indexes can be price-weighted in which case the price of all component stocks are added and divided by a divisor. The divisor is used to maintain the comparability of the average over time. By adjusting the divisor, the effects of stock splits, divestitures, mergers, stock dividends, and changes in the component stocks are offset and only the effects of price changes are reflected in the index. Because the index is price-weighted, a 1 percent change in the price of lower-priced stock causes a smaller movement in the average than a 1 percent change in a higher-priced stock.

In recent years, there has been a trend away from price-weighted indexes to capitalization-weighted or market-value-weighted indexes. With capitalization-weighted indexes, the impact of a stock's price change is proportional to its market value as compared with the total market value of all stocks in the index. A stock's market value is the share price times the number of outstanding shares. So, a 1 percent price change of larger capitalization issues has more of an impact on the index than those of smaller capitalization issues.

Another method used to calculate the value of an index is the equally weighted method of calculation. In this method, every stock has equal influence on the movement of the index. Consequently, a 1 percent price change of a lower-priced stock has the same impact on the index as a 1 percent price change of a higher-priced stock. Equally weighted indexes then tend to give secondary stocks more influence than other weighting methods.

Futures Markets

The Kansas City Board of Trade trades Value Line futures and options. The Chicago Mercantile Exchange trades futures and options on the S&P 500, S&P Midcap 400, Russell 2000, FT-SE 100, Major Market Index, and Nikkei Stock Index. The New York Futures Exchange trades NYSE Composite Index futures and options; the Chicago Board of Trade trades Wilshire Small Cap Index futures and options and the Commodity Exchange trades Eurotop 100 futures and options. In addition to these U.S. contracts, stock index futures and/or futures/options are actively trading at the London International Financial Futures Exchange, Singapore International Monetary Exchange, Osaka Securities Exchange, Bolsa de Mercadorias & Futuros, Deutsche Terminbörse, Marche a Terme International de France, MEFF Renta Variable, and Tokyo Stock Exchange.

Stock Indexes

Name of Index	Weighting Method	Futures/Options Contracts on the Index
Dow Jones Industrial Average (DJIA)	Price-weighted average of 30 blue-chip equities	—
American Stock Exchange (Amex) Major Market Index (MMI)	Price-weighted average of 20 blue-chip stocks, 17 of which are also included in DJIA	MMI futures, futures options, & cash options
Standard & Poor's 500 (S&P 500)	Capitalization-weighted index of 500 common stocks, mostly NYSE-listed companies with some Amex and over-the-counter (OTC) stocks	S&P 500 Index futures, futures options, & cash options
New York Stock Exchange (NYSE) Composite	Capitalization-weighted index of more than 2,000 common stocks traded on NYSE	NYSE Composite Index futures, futures options, & cash options
Value Line Arithmetic Index	Equally weighted average of 1,700 stocks traded on NYSE, Amex, and OTC	Value Line futures, futures options, & cash options
NASDAQ-100	Capitalization-weighted index of the 100 largest OTC stocks traded in OTC market via NASDAQ system	—

FOREIGN EXCHANGE

The foreign exchange or *forex* market is the world's largest financial market. Operating virtually around the clock, the forex market trades enormous amounts of money. Estimates range from $600 billion to perhaps as much as $1 trillion traded daily.

Unlike a futures exchange with a central location bringing buyers and sellers together, the forex market is an over-the-counter market where buyers and sellers conduct business linked by telephones, computers, fax machines, and other means of communication. Among its participants are corporations; commercial banks, both money center and regional; pension funds; and investment banking firms.

Foreign exchange is the currency of a country different from one's own country. As individuals or companies from one country trade across borders, the need for foreign currency arises. For example, when a U.S. importer buys French wine, either the importer needs francs to pay the French merchant or the French merchant must accept U.S. dollars and convert them to francs.

Exchange Rates

International trade directly impacts the rate of exchange between currencies—the price of one currency in terms of another. In the cash market, exchange rates between the U.S. dollar and foreign currencies are generally quoted using *European terms*. This method measures the amount of foreign currency needed to buy one U.S. dollar, i.e., foreign currency units per dollar. The other method used to quote exchange rates is the *reciprocal of European terms*—which measures the U.S. dollar value of one foreign currency unit, i.e., dollars per foreign currency unit.

For example, if the European-terms quote is 1.45 Deutsche marks per $1, (1.45 DM/$1), then the reciprocal-of-European-terms quote is $.6897 per Deutsche mark ($1/1.45 DM or $.6897/1 DM). The reciprocal of European terms is the quotation method used by U.S. futures exchanges where foreign currency futures trade. Also, the British pound is usually quoted in reciprocal of European terms.

Knowing whether the rate of exchange is quoted in reciprocal of European terms or European terms is crucial in determining whether the value of one currency has risen or fallen in relation to another. Suppose it takes $1.75 to buy one British pound, but a week later it takes $2 to buy one British pound. Has the value of the dollar risen or fallen?

The dollar has fallen in value because (1) it takes more dollars to buy one British pound—the $/pound ratio rose from $1.75:1 to $2:1, or (2) it takes fewer pounds to buy $1—the pound/$ ratio fell from 0.57143 pounds (1/$1.75) to 0.5 pounds (1/$2). While both statements are correct, the first one is quoting the exchange rate in reciprocal of European terms, and the second is quoting the exchange rate in European terms.

Factors Affecting Exchange Rates

Analyzing exchange rates as the price of a currency suggests competitive market forces—demand and supply—determine exchange rates. This type of free market environment in foreign exchange is often referred to as a *floating-exchange-rate environment*. In a floating-exchange-rate environment, the exchange rate responds to many factors, such as imports and exports, capital flows, and relative inflation rates. Often, limits are placed on exchange-rate fluctuations according to government policies.

One factor affecting the exchange rate between the U.S. dollar and other currencies is the merchandise trade balance. By definition, the merchandise trade balance is the net difference between the value of a country's merchandise imports and exports. As an example, consider the market for Deutsche marks and their rate of exchange. The United States imports products from Germany. To pay for them, Americans need Deutsche marks. On the other hand, Germans desire American-made goods and supply Deutsche marks to the foreign exchange market to acquire U.S. dollars.

The U.S. demand for German goods contributes to the demand for Deutsche marks while German purchases of American goods and services contribute to the supply of Deutsche marks. In this case, the net difference between U.S. purchases of German goods and services and German purchases of American goods and services is the merchandise trade balance between the two countries.

The flow of funds between countries to pay for stock and bond purchases also contributes to the foreign exchange rate. In the near term, these capital flows are greatly influenced by yield differentials. All else being equal, the higher the yield on German securities compared to U.S. securities, for example, the more attractive German securities are relative to U.S. securities and the less attractive U.S. securities are compared to German securities. An increase in German yields would tend to raise the flow of U.S. funds into German securities as well as decrease the outflow of German funds to U.S. securities. Combined, this increased flow of funds into Germany would raise the value of the Deutsche mark, therefore, the $/DM ratio would increase.

The rate of inflation is another factor influencing exchange rates. People try to avoid the eroding effect inflation has on their purchasing power. Consequently, goods from countries with lower inflation become more attractive than the goods from countries with higher inflation. In turn, currency from the lower inflation country rises in value while the currency from the higher inflation country falls in value. If the United States is experiencing lower inflation than its trading partner Germany, for instance, the $/DM ratio falls to reflect the growing price level in Germany relative to the United States. This fact is rooted in the concept of purchasing power parity, which holds that, over the long run, an exchange rate adjusts to reflect the difference in price levels between countries.

Free-Floating Exchange Rates Create Risk

While all these examples illustrate how exchange rates can float in the foreign exchange market, free-floating exchange rates create risk. For example, when a U.S. wine merchant contracts to buy 1,000 cases of French wine, the merchant may agree to pay in French francs, say 600 francs per case, when the vintage is ready for shipment in two years. Over the next two years, the value of the dollar could drop from 20 cents/franc to 40 cents/franc, raising the price of each case from $120 to $240. Pricing the wine in francs exposes the U.S. wine merchant to exchange-rate risk.

Of course, the wine could be priced in dollars at $120 per case. This relieves the U.S. merchant from foreign exchange risk, but now the French wine producer would be hurt if the value of the dollar fell from 20 cents/franc to 40 cents/franc. Instead of receiving 600 francs per case, the producer would receive half as much, or 300 francs per case.

Because of these risks, governments throughout history have intervened to fix exchange rates. In 1944, for example, western world leaders met in Bretton Woods, New Hampshire, to create the International Monetary Fund to cope with world economic and financial problems that occurred following the Great Depression and World War II. As part of the agreement, the value of the U.S. dollar, the world's leading currency at the time, was set at ⅟₃₅ of an ounce of gold. And, world central banks were called to keep the exchange rates of their currencies pegged to the dollar's gold content, with variations limited to plus or minus 1 percent.

Since 1944, there have been several instances when world leaders have met to adjust the fixed-exchange rate and modify the fixed-rate system. But fixed rates have been abandoned over the years, and volatility in the currency market continues. Firms exposed to foreign exchange risk have turned to the forward or forex market, described earlier in this section, and currency futures markets to manage these risks. In the forex market, transactions are customized where the rate of exchange and other terms are agreed upon by both parties. Participation in the forex market is limited to very large customers. With the futures market, contracts are standardized. Futures have a formal clearing process where accounts are settled daily; and they are open to anyone who needs a vehicle to hedge currency risk.

Futures Markets

The Chicago Mercantile Exchange trades Australian dollar, British pound, Canadian dollar, Deutsche mark, Japanese yen, and Swiss franc futures and options, as well as cross-rate futures and options contracts. At the MidAmerica Commodity Exchange, British pound, Canadian dollar, Deutsche mark, Japanese yen, and Swiss franc futures are traded. FINEX®, a division of the New York Cotton Exchange trades European Currency

Unit (ECU) and U.S. Dollar Index® futures and options. The Philadelphia Board of Trade trades futures on Australian dollars, British pounds, Canadian dollars, Deutsche marks, French francs, Japanese yen, Swiss francs, and the ECU.

Poised on the threshold of the 21st century, the futures industry is in a state of change that will impact where and how the world trades futures and options on futures for many years to come.

The accelerated growth of non-U.S. exchanges has had a significant impact on the size and structure of the industry in recent years. And, the hue and cry for increased volume and market share have become a rallying point for both U.S. and non-U.S. exchanges alike. To meet these challenges, exchanges are developing a new breed of contracts designed to attract a larger customer base.

The regulatory environment is also changing with the United States imposing stricter rules and other countries opening up their markets to encourage the growth of new exchanges. In addition, advanced computer technology has all the potential to radically alter futures trading forever.

What impact will these changes have on the future of the futures industry? We can't predict the future, but we can look at some of the industry's most recent trends to gain a better insight into what's ahead.

Growing Internationally

U.S. exchanges currently dominate the world's futures and options on futures markets, but foreign exchanges continue to gain ground each year. In 1984, there were 29 exchanges outside the United States trading futures. By the early 1990s, that number had more than doubled.

THE FUTURE OF THE FUTURES INDUSTRY

Competition, Innovations & Technology

18

Comparison of U.S. to Non-U.S.
Futures and Options Volume*

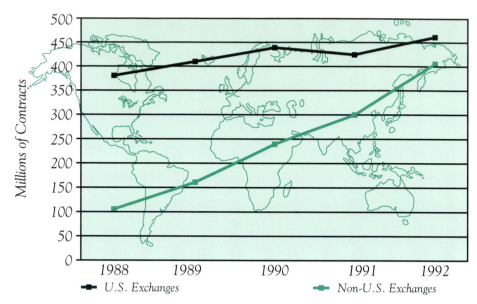

U.S. Exchanges   Non-U.S. Exchanges

*Volume figures include futures, options on futures, and options on stock indexes
and currencies.
Source: Futures Industry Association

Futures and options now are offered on more than 50 futures
exchanges, representing 22 nations in North America, South America,
Europe, and Asia. (Some of the world's largest futures exchanges in trading
volume are listed in the Appendix.)

Many of these exchanges have developed rapidly. The London
International Financial Futures Exchange (LIFFE), for example, opened in
September 1982. Within 10 years it was the world's third largest futures
exchange following the Chicago Board of Trade and Chicago Mercantile
Exchange. LIFFE offers trading in debt instruments, currencies, and other
financial-related futures and options contracts.

The creation and growth of foreign exchanges has been encouraged by
central governments worldwide, eager to establish or further their
reputations as world financial centers. In Europe, the trend gained
momentum as nations prepared for a unified common market and single
European Currency Unit (ECU) in 1992. Financial deregulation and
consolidation also have increased international competitiveness and are
spurring existing exchanges to reexamine how they conduct business. The
Frankfurt Stock Exchange (FSE) is a notable example. In an effort to
become another European financial center, the FSE reached an agreement

in October 1992 with seven smaller, regional exchanges to become a single entity, the Deutsche Borse. The agreement also called for the Frankfurt exchange to acquire that nation's futures exchange, the Deutsche Terminborse.

In Asia, similar developments are underway. As financial deregulation of the Japanese markets occurred during the 1970s and as trading volume and stock prices rose on the Tokyo Stock Exchange (TSE) during the 1980s, the Ministry of Finance began considering the potential benefits of derivative trading. In 1985, the TSE launched Japanese bond futures. Five years later, Nikkei 225 Stock Index futures began trading at the Osaka Stock Exchange.

Other Pacific nations with financial futures exchanges include Australia, Hong Kong, New Zealand, the Philippines, and Singapore. More appear to be on the way. In 1992, Malaysia's Ministry of Finance approved the creation of the Kuala Lumpur Options and Financial Futures Exchange (KLOFFE). In Taiwan, during the summer of 1992, the legislature approved the Financial Futures Trading Act authorizing the creation of futures brokerage firms on the island. Up until the act became effective in January 1993, Taiwanese investors and hedgers could only participate in futures markets overseas using offshore brokers.

Clearly, opportunities to manage risk are no longer limited to the United States. Nor are risk-management opportunities limited to "U.S. only" futures and options contracts. Although U.S. Treasury bond futures traded at the Chicago Board of Trade continue to be the most actively traded contract in the world, the number of high-volume contracts traded on non-U.S. exchanges continues to grow. (The Appendix gives a list of futures and options on futures contracts that traded more than 1 million contracts in 1992.)

Expansion in the industry is not only a result of the growing number of futures exchanges, but also the variety of products offered. In fact, the product mix exchanges consider, develop, and introduce is indispensable for businesses facing global competition and an ever-changing marketplace.

Broadening the Product Mix—More Products, More Customers

Innovative Futures and Options

Between January 1980 and June 1991, 186 new contracts were introduced by U.S. futures exchanges. Nearly half of the total U.S. volume was a result of those 186 contracts during that 10½ year period. Open interest in those same contracts was nearly 70 percent of open interest reported in all U.S. futures contracts as of the end of June 1991.

This dramatic growth encourages exchanges to innovate despite the cost of development and a success rate of 25 to 50 percent for new contracts. Everything from futures on insurance to fertilizer to the environment has been considered. What is particularly interesting is that many of the contracts under consideration are being introduced to businesses that may have never used or, for that matter, even heard of futures before.

One area of continued growth is foreign-denominated debt instruments. According to the Organization for Economic Cooperation and Development (OECD), the growth of debt instruments issued by nations has increased sharply in recent years as many industrialized nations, especially Germany and the United Kingdom, issue increasing amounts of debt to finance their deficits. Since 1987, newly issued, fixed-rate foreign debt doubled from approximately $125 billion to more than $250 billion through September 1992. This explosion presents additional opportunities for exchanges to offer futures contracts on government debt instruments.

Branching out into "nontraditional" products, such as insurance or environmental-type contracts, are other examples of how the futures industry is committed to developing contracts that help businesses meet their risk-management needs. In the case of catastrophic insurance, the Chicago Board of Trade developed a cash market index and a futures contract based on the index to assist the insurance industry in managing its potential liability from natural disasters.

Environmental contracts also represent a brand-new market for the futures industry. As the world's concern over environmental issues rises and governments increase incentives for businesses to cut pollution, an entirely new breed of futures contracts is possible. Take the 1990 U.S. Clean Air Act Amendments, for example, which use market-based incentives to reduce sulfur dioxide (SO_2) emissions. Power plants emitting SO_2 will be issued a set amount of emission allowances equal to half their base-period emissions. Because allowances are fully tradable, utility companies that overcomply with federal regulations will be allowed to sell their allowances to companies that do not meet Federal compliances. In essence, utility companies that do not cut pollution will be forced to pay for emission rights and, thus, penalized for not reducing their emissions. As a result of this legislation, the Chicago Board of Trade plans to introduce the first environmental futures and options contracts—clean air allowance futures and options.

Market Offshoots

The Environmental Protection Agency (EPA) is charged with administering the Clean Air Act and allowance program. However, the EPA can contract with a nongovernmental organization to conduct cash market activities. Consequently, as an outgrowth of its interest to serve the environmental market, the Chicago Board of Trade administered the first Environmental Protection Agency cash auction of sulfur dioxide in March 1993. The exchange also plans to conduct private SO_2 cash market auctions. This is just one example of how exchanges are looking beyond conventional futures and options markets to offer their customers more products and more ways to trade them.

The more revolutionary the market concept, the greater the need for exchanges to educate prospective users and market these concepts for managing risk. These contracts will not likely be overnight successes. It will take time, money, and skill for exchanges to bring these new market concepts to their full economic potential.

Managed Futures

In recent years, another group of customers that have been increasing their participation in the futures markets are institutional investors. These professional money managers include futures in their portfolios by using managed futures to increase portfolio returns and, at the same time, lower portfolio volatility.

Managed futures accounts, like equity mutual funds, enable investors to diversify both geographically and by type of instrument—everything from agricultural commodities and precious metals to interest rates, stock indexes, and foreign currencies. Assets in managed futures accounts have risen dramatically, from less than $1 billion in 1980 to nearly $20 billion by the end of 1992.

Basically, there are two ways to participate in managed futures—a commodity pool or an individually managed account. Commodity pools are organized and administered by Commodity Pool Operators (CPOs) who solicit money from individuals and then pool the funds for investing at a later date. The CPO hires one or more Commodity Trading Advisers (CTAs) whose job is to decide in what markets to invest, when, and in what size. Unlike mutual funds, where initial investments may range from $500 or $1,000, initial investments in managed futures accounts are usually much higher, typically $5,000 to $10,000.

Individually managed accounts, on the other hand, generally require considerably larger initial investments, usually $100,000 or more. Investors in managed accounts include public and private pension funds, retirement funds, and university endowments.

Regulatory Environment

Market regulations within and outside the United States will continue to have a major impact on where customers trade. As a matter of fact, various exchange and governmental officials from the United States and Europe have been working to coordinate regulations to better serve market users around the world. The development of more uniform and compatible regulations among exchanges and nations is a long-term goal of these groups.

Issues such as position limits, margin, taxes, and capital requirements are some of the important considerations of traders who have choices in a competitive market environment. For example, in recent years, the Commodity Futures Trading Commission (CFTC) has raised speculative position limits. This has enticed many fund traders to keep their business in the United States rather than going offshore.

So, while exchanges and governments want to ensure customer protection and the financial integrity of the markets, it becomes a balancing act between market regulation and overregulation. Too little or too much could be detrimental.

CFTC Reauthorization

The Commodity Futures Trading Commission, the federal regulatory agency overseeing U.S. futures trading, was reauthorized in October 1992. The bill contained a number of important provisions addressing new trends and developments in the futures industry. For one, the bill requires exchanges to develop, within three years, automated audit trails so trades can be reconstructed to the nearest minute. Previously, trades were grouped in 30-minute time brackets.

Even before the CFTC reauthorization was signed, the Chicago Board of Trade and Chicago Mercantile Exchange began developing an electronic device that will provide a 100 percent tamperproof audit trail. Traders will use the hand-held electronic trading card, weighing about a pound, in the pit recording trades as soon as they are made. Trades are then automatically transferred to the clearinghouse for processing.

Another provision of the bill expanded the CFTC registration requirement to include floor traders at exchanges. Floor traders join Futures Commission Merchants, Introducing Brokers, Commodity Pool Operators, Commodity Trading Advisers, Associated Persons, and floor brokers who previously were required to register with the CFTC. (See Chapter 5 for details on CFTC registration requirements.)

The bill also gave the Federal Reserve Board margin oversight authority over stock index futures contracts. Before the new law, the exchanges oversaw margin requirements for stock index contracts. The Federal Reserve monitors stock index futures margin changes to make sure they do not create undue risks for the nation's financial system, however, day-to-day responsibility for setting margins remains with the exchanges. Any change in margins or exchange rules in trading stock index futures must be filed with the Federal Reserve. The Fed is free at any time to request a change to levels it deems "appropriate to preserve the financial integrity of the contract market or its clearing system." If an exchange does not consent to a Federal Reserve request, it could change the margin level subject to judicial review.

The legislation also directed the CFTC to work with the Securities and Exchange Commission and the Federal Reserve to conduct a one-year study of the markets, derivatives, and regulatory issues. This study includes a review of whether a single federal agency should regulate the exchange or off-exchange trading of futures, securities, and derivatives.

Technology

Perhaps the most far-reaching change facing the futures industry is the influence of computer technology. In 1990, a CFTC survey listed eight exchanges using electronic systems. As of the end of 1992, there were 27 exchanges worldwide using automated systems for trading futures and options with more exchanges in the process of developing systems.

Exchanges with Electronic Trading Systems
as of the end of 1992

Country	Exchange
Australia	Sydney Futures Exchange
Austria	Osterreichische Termin und Optionenboerse*
Belgium	Belgian Futures and Options Exchange*
Denmark	Copenhagen Stock Exchange*
	Guarantee Fund for Danish Futures and Options*
Finland	Finnish Options Market*
Germany	Deutsche Terminborse*
Ireland	Irish Futures & Options Exchange*
Italy	Mercado Italiano Futures*
Japan	Osaka Grain Exchange*
	Osaka Securities Exchange*
	Osaka Sugar Exchange*
	Tokyo Commodity Exchange*
	Tokyo Grain Exchange*
	Tokyo International Financial Futures Exchange*
	Tokyo Stock Exchange*
	Tokyo Sugar Exchange*
New Zealand	New Zealand Futures & Options Exchange Ltd.*
Singapore	Rubber Association of Singapore Commodity Exchange*
Spain	MEFF Renta Variable
	Mercado Espanol de Futuros Financieros Renta Fija S.A.*
Sweden/U.K.	OM London and OM Sweden*
Switzerland	Swiss Options & Financial Futures Exchange*
United Kingdom	London Futures & Options Exchange
	London International Financial Futures and Options Exchange
United States	Chicago Board of Trade
	Chicago Mercantile Exchange

*Fully automated trading systems
Source: Futures Industry magazine, January/February 1993

Of the 27 exchanges, 21 of them use an electronic system exclusively. The remaining exchanges—Chicago Board of Trade (Project A™), London Futures & Options Exchange, London International Financial Futures Exchange (only for Japanese government bond futures), and MEFF Renta Variable—use their electronic systems along with traditional pit trading/open outcry, during regular pit trading hours. And the Chicago Mercantile Exchange/Chicago Board of Trade (GLOBEX®), LIFFE, and

Sydney Futures Exchange use electronic systems as an after-hours addition to open outcry.

The New Zealand Futures & Options Exchange has the oldest automated system, which began trading in January 1985. The most recent systems are GLOBEX, launched by the Chicago Board of Trade and Chicago Mercantile Exchange in 1992, and the Chicago Board of Trade's Project A, which also came on line in 1992.

Currently, contracts traded on electronic systems tend to be financial in nature—futures on interest rates, debt, stock indexes, and currencies.

The majority of automated systems use a price/time trade-matching system in which orders receive priority based on the best price (highest bid, lowest offer), and among orders of the same price, trades are based on time of order entry.

While each exchange's system has unique features designed to meet the needs of its customers, one of the most revolutionary steps in trading technology is GLOBEX. This system was developed by Reuters Holdings PLC, a worldwide provider of news and market information, the Chicago Board of Trade, and the Chicago Mercantile Exchange.

As the first global electronic trading system open after an exchange's regular trading hours, GLOBEX provides around-the-clock trading of contracts of not one, but many exchanges. As of 1993, the Chicago Board of Trade, Chicago Mercantile Exchange, and MATIF listed several contracts on GLOBEX with more exchanges considering joining the system. GLOBEX terminals are located in Chicago, New York, London, Tokyo, and Paris. And, in the first year of trading, monthly volume grew from 28,349 contracts in July 1992, the first full month of trading, to 209,997 in May 1993. During this time, the Chicago Board of Trade and Chicago Mercantile Exchange not only added more contracts to the system, but MATIF joined GLOBEX.

What's Ahead?

While it may be difficult to determine exactly what's ahead for the futures industry, the trends highlighted in this chapter will, in some way, impact trading in the years to come. But what we can conclude is:

♦ Futures markets will not only continue to offer investors ways to manage risk and provide price information, but will branch out into other business sectors—insurance and utilities, to name a couple—not previously served by futures and options.

♦ The marketplace will continue to be more international in scope.

♦ Regulation will continue to impact the markets. Within a competitive market environment, customers will trade in those markets that best meet their trading objectives and are cost-efficient.

♦ Technology is enhancing open outcry and will continue to impact trading in the years to come.

  History will tell the story.

DIRECTORY OF FUTURES EXCHANGES

For contract specifications and other exchange information, contact the appropriate futures exchange. Listed below are addresses and phone numbers of all U.S. futures exchanges, the Commodity Futures Trading Commission, the National Futures Association, and the top 40 futures exchanges outside the United States according to trading volume as of the end of 1992.

U.S. Futures Exchanges
Chicago Board of Trade (CBOT®)
141 West Jackson Boulevard
Chicago, IL 60604
Tel: 312-435-3500
Fax: 312-341-3329

Chicago Mercantile Exchange (CME)
30 South Wacker Drive
Chicago, IL 60606
Tel: 312-930-1000
Fax: 312-930-3439

Coffee, Sugar & Cocoa Exchange, Inc. (CS&C)
Four World Trade Center
8th Floor
New York, NY 10048
Tel: 212-938-2800
Fax: 212-524-9863

Commodity Exchange, Inc. (COMEX)
Four World Trade Center
New York, NY 10048
Tel: 212-938-2900
Fax: 212-432-1154

Kansas City Board of Trade (KCBOT)
4800 Main Street, Suite 303
Kansas City, MO 64112
Tel: 816-753-7500
Fax: 816-753-5744

MidAmerica Commodity Exchange
(MidAm)
141 West Jackson Boulevard
Chicago, IL 60604
Tel: 312-435-3500
Fax: 312-341-3329

Minneapolis Grain Exchange (MGE)
130 Grain Exchange Building
400 South Fourth Street
Minneapolis, MN 55415
Tel: 612-338-6212
Fax: 612-339-1155

New York Cotton Exchange (NYCE)
Four World Trade Center
New York, NY 10048
Tel: 212-938-2702
Fax: 212-488-8135

New York Futures Exchange (NYFE)
20 Broad Street
New York, NY 10005
Tel: 212-656-4949
Fax: 212-656-2925

New York Mercantile Exchange
(NYMEX)
Four World Trade Center
New York, NY 10048
Tel: 212-938-2222
Fax: 212-938-2985

Philadelphia Board of Trade (PBOT)
1900 Market Street
Philadelphia, PA 19103-3584
Tel: 215-496-5000
Fax: 215-496-5653

U.S. Regulatory Organizations
Commodity Futures Trading
Commission (CFTC)
(U.S. federal regulatory agency)
2033 K Street, N.W.
Washington, DC 20581
Tel: 202-254-6387
Fax: 202-254-3678

National Futures Association (NFA)
(U.S. self-regulatory organization for
futures and options)
200 West Madison Street
Suite 1600
Chicago, IL 60606
Tel: 312-781-1300
Fax: 312-781-1467

Futures Exchanges Outside the U.S.
Australia
Sydney Futures Exchange Limited (SFE)
30-32 Grosvenor Street
Sydney NSW 2000
Australia
Tel: 61-2-256-0555
Fax: 61-2-256-0666

Brazil
Bolsa de Mercadorias & Futuros
(BM&F)
Praca Antonio Prado, 48
São Paulo, SP 01010-901
Brazil
Tel: 55-11-232-5454
Fax: 55-11-239-3531

Canada
The Montreal Exchange (ME)
The Stock Exchange Tower
P.O. Box 61
800 Victoria Square
Montreal, Quebec
H4Z 1A9
Canada
Tel: 514-871-2424
Fax: 514-871-3553

Winnipeg Commodity Exchange (WCE)
500 Commodity Exchange Tower
360 Main Street
Winnipeg, Manitoba
Canada, R3C 3Z4
Tel: 204-949-0495
Fax: 204-943-5448

Denmark
Guarantee Fund for Danish Options
and Futures (FUTOP®)
Kompagnistraede 15, Box 2017
DK-1012 Copenhagen K
Denmark
Tel: 45-33-93-33-11
Fax: 45-33-93-49-80

Finland
Finnish Options Market (FOM)
Keskuskatu 7
3rd Floor, Box 926
SF 00101 Helsinki
Finland
Tel: 358-0-131211
Fax: 358-0-13121211

France
Marche a Terme International de
France (MATIF S.A.)
176, rue Montmartre
75002 Paris
France
Tel: 33-1-40-28-82-72
Fax: 33-1-40-28-81-34

Germany
DTB Deutsche Terminborse
Gruneburgweg 102
Postfach 17 02 03
D-6000 Frankfurt am Main 1
Germany
Tel: 49-69-15303-201
Fax: 49-69-557492

Hong Kong
Hong Kong Futures Exchange Limited
(HKFE)
5/F, Asia Pacific Finance Tower
Citibank Plaza, 3 Garden Road
Hong Kong
Tel: 852-842-9333
Fax: 852-810-5089

Japan
Hokkaido Grain Exchange (HGE)
3 Odori Nishi 5-chome
Chuo-ku, Sapporo
Hokkaido 060
Japan
Tel: 81-11-221-9131
Fax: 81-11-221-4964

Kanmon Commodity Exchange (KCE)
1-5, Nabecho
Shimonoseki-shi
Yamaguchi 750
Japan
Tel: 81-832-31-1313
Fax: 81-832-23-1947

Kobe Grain Exchange (KGE)
2-4-16 Honmachi
Hyogo-ku
Kobe 652
Japan
Tel: 81-78-671-2901
Fax: 81-78-671-3937

Kobe Rubber Exchange (KRE)
49 Harima-cho
Chuo-ku, Kobe 650
Japan
Tel: 81-78-331-4211
Fax: 81-78-332-1622

Maebashi Dried Cocoon Exchange
(Maebashi)
1-49-1 Furuichi-machi 1-chome
Maebashi 371
Japan
Tel: 81-272-521401
Fax: 81-272-518270

Nagoya Grain and Sugar Exchange
(NGSE)
2-3-2 Meieki-Minami
Nakamura-ku
Nagoya 450
Japan
Tel: 81-52-571-8161
Fax: 81-52-581-4653

Nagoya Textile Exchange (NTE)
2-1-5 Nishiki 3
Nakaku, Nagoya 460
Japan
Tel: 81-52-951-2171
Fax: 81-52-961-6407

Osaka Grain Exchange (OGE)
1-10-14 Awaza
Nishi-ku, Osaka 550
Japan
Tel: 81-6-531-7931
Fax: 81-6-541-9343

Osaka Securities Exchange (OSE)
8-16, Kitahama 1-chome
Chuo-ku, Osaka 541
Japan
Tel: 81-6-229-8643
Fax: 81-6-231-2639

Osaka Sugar Exchange (OSuE)
2-5-28 Kyutaro-machi
Chuo-ku, Osaka 541
Japan
Tel: 81-6-245-2266
Fax: 81-6-245-2264

Osaka Textile Exchange (OTE)
2-5-28 Kyutaro-machi
Chuo-ku, Osaka 541
Japan
Tel: 81-6-253-0031
Fax: 81-6-253-0034

The Tokyo Commodity Exchange
(TOCOM)
10-8, Nihonbashi Horidome-cho
1-chome
Chuo-ku, Tokyo 103
Japan
Tel: 81-3-3661-9191
Fax: 81-3-3661-7568

The Tokyo Grain Exchange (TGE)
1-12-5 Kakigara-cho, Nihonbashi
Chuo-ku, Tokyo 103
Japan
Tel: 81-3-3668-9311
Fax: 81-3-3668-9566

The Tokyo International Financial
Futures Exchange (TIFFE)
2-2-2 Otemachi
Chiyoda-ku, Tokyo 100
Japan
Tel: 81-3-3275-2400
Fax: 81-3-3275-2862

Tokyo Stock Exchange (TSE)
2-1, Nihombashi-Kabuto-cho
Chuo-ku, Tokyo 103
Japan
Tel: 81-3-3666-0141
Fax: 81-3-3639-5016

Tokyo Sugar Exchange (TSuE)
9-4 Koami-cho, Nihonbashi
Chuo-ku, Tokyo 103
Japan
Tel: 81-3-3666-0201
Fax: 81-3-3661-4564

Toyohashi Dried Cocoon Exchange
(Toyohashi)
52-2 Ekimae odori
Toyohashi 440
Japan
Tel: 81-532-526231
Fax: 81-532-551529

Yokohama Raw Silk Exchange
(Yokohama)
Silk Center
1 Yamashita-cho
Naka-ku
Yokohama 231
Japan
Tel: 81-45-641-1341
Fax: 81-45-641-1346

Netherlands
Financial Futures Market Amsterdam
(FTA)
Nes 49, 1012 KD Amsterdam
P.O. Box 10220, 1001 EE Amsterdam
Netherlands
Tel: 31-20-550-4555
Fax: 31-20-624-5416

New Zealand
New Zealand Futures & Options
Exchange (NZFOE)
P.O. Box 6734 Wellesley Street
Auckland
New Zealand
Tel: 64-9-309-8308
Fax: 64-9-309-8817

Philippines
Manila International Futures Exchange,
Inc. (MIFE)
7th Floor, Producers Bank Centre
Paseo de Roxas, Makati
Metro Manila 1200
Philippines
Tel: 63-2-8185496 or 8127776
Fax: 63-2-8185529 or 8105763

Singapore
Singapore International Monetary
Exchange Limited (SIMEX)
1 Raffles Place #07-00
OUB Centre
Singapore 0104
Tel: 65-535-7382
Fax: 65-535-7282

South Africa
The South African Futures Exchange
(SAFEX)
32 Diagonal Street, Johannesburg, 2001
P.O. Box 4406, Johannesburg, 2000
South Africa
Tel: 27-11-836-3311
Fax: 27-11-838-4400

Spain
MEFF Sociedad Rectora de Productos
Financieros Derivados de Renta Variable
(MEFF RV)
Torre Picasso, Pl. 26
28020 Madrid
Spain
Tel: 34-1-585-08-00
Fax: 34-1-571-95-42

Mercado de Opciones y Futuros
Financieros, MEFF RENTA FIJA
(MEFF RF)
Via Laietana, 58
08003 Barcelona
Spain
Tel: 34-3-412-11-28
Fax: 34-3-268-47-69

Sweden
OM Stockholm (OM)
Brunkebergstorg 2
Box 16305
103 26 Stockholm
Sweden
Tel: 46-8-700-06-00
Fax: 46-8-723-10-92

Switzerland
Swiss Options and Financial Futures
Exchange Ag (SOFFEX)
Neumattstrasse 7
CH-8953 Dietikon
Zurich
Switzerland
Tel: 41-1-740-30-20
Fax: 41-1-740-1776

United Kingdom
The International Petroleum Exchange
of London Limited (IPE)
International House
1 St. Katharine's Way
London
E1 9UN
England
Tel: 44-71-481-0643
Fax: 44-71-481-8485

The London Commodity Exchange
Limited (London Fox)
1 Commodity Quay
St. Katharine Docks
London
E1 9AX
England
Tel: 44-71-481-2080
Fax: 44-71-702-9923

London International Financial Futures
and Options Exchange (LIFFE)
Cannon Bridge
London EC4R 3XX
England
Tel: 44-71-623-0444
Fax: 44-71-588-3624

The London Metal Exchange Limited
(LME)
E. Wing, 4th Floor
Plantation House
Fenchurch Street
London EC3M 3AP
England
Tel: 44-71-626-3311
Fax: 44-71-626-1703

In addition to the exchanges listed above, there are many other futures exchanges throughout the world. If you need to contact an exchange not listed here, refer to the *Futures and Options Fact Book* published by the Futures Industry Institute, Washington, D.C., or *Directory & Review* published by Futures & Options World, London, England.

TOP-TRADED CONTRACTS

World Futures and Options on Futures Trading Over 1 Million Contracts in 1992

Rank	Contract	Exchange	1992 Volume
1	U.S. Treasury Bond Futures	Chicago Board of Trade (CBOT)	70,003,894*
2	3-Month Eurodollar Futures	Chicago Mercantile Exchange (CME)	60,531,066*
3	French Government Bond Futures	Marche a Terme International de France (MATIF)	31,062,716
4	Crude Oil Futures	New York Mercantile Exchange (NYMEX)	21,109,562
5	U.S. Treasury Bond Options	CBOT	20,258,740*
6	3-Month Euroyen Futures	Tokyo International Financial Futures Exchange (TIFFE)	14,959,373
7	1-Day Interbank Deposits Futures	Bolsa de Mercadorias & Futuros (BM&F)	14,072,749
8	Eurodollar Options	CME	13,762,628*
9	German Government Bond Futures	London International Financial Futures Exchange (LIFFE)	12,616,523
10	S&P 500 Stock Index Futures	CME	12,414,157
11	3-Month Euromark Futures	LIFFE	12,173,431
12	Nikkei 225 Stock Index Futures	Osaka Securities Exchange (OSE)	11,927,329
13	Japanese Government Bond Futures	Tokyo Stock Exchange (TSE)	11,868,127
14	Deutsche Mark Futures	CME	11,593,174*
15	3-Month Sterling Interest Rate Futures	LIFFE	11,296,327
16	10-Year Treasury Note Futures	CBOT	11,217,938*
17	Corn Futures	CBOT	10,356,632

*This number includes the contracts traded on the GLOBEX® system.

Rank	Contract	Exchange	1992 Volume
18	French Government Bond Options	MATIF	10,047,388
19	Soybean Futures	CBOT	9,000,169
20	Long Gilt Futures	LIFFE	8,805,639
21	Aluminum Futures	London Metal Exchange (LME)	8,225,792
22	No. 2 Heating Oil Futures	NYMEX	8,005,462
23	Red Bean Futures	Tokyo Grain Exchange (TGE)	7,804,868
24	Copper (Gr. A) Futures	LME	7,338,242
25	Bovespa Stock Index Futures	BM&F	7,287,054
26	Unleaded Gas Futures	NYMEX	6,674,757
27	Crude Oil Options	NYMEX	6,562,163
28	5-Year T-Note Futures	CBOT	6,441,193
29	3-Month PIBOR Futures	MATIF	6,436,759
30	Deutsche Mark Options	CME	6,354,248
31	Brent Crude Oil Futures	International Petroleum Exchange (IPE)	6,172,156
32	Gold 100-oz. Futures	Commodity Exchange (COMEX)	6,002,009
33	90-Day Bank-Accepted Bill Futures	Sydney Futures Exchange (SFE)	5,697,822
34	3-Month Eurodollar Futures	Singapore International Monetary Exchange (SIMEX)	5,617,972
35	3-Year T-Bond Futures	SFE	5,444,871
36	German Government Bond Futures	Deutsche Terminbörse (DTB)	5,327,846
37	Swiss Franc Futures	CME	5,134,717
38	Platinum Futures	Tokyo Commodity Exchange (TCE)	4,994,307

Rank	Contract	Exchange	1992 Volume
39	Japanese Yen Futures	CME	4,520,356
40	U.S. Dollar Futures	BM&F	4,501,952
41	Soybean Oil Futures	CBOT	4,282,678
42	10-Year T-Bond Futures	SFE	4,255,462
43	Gold Futures	TCE	4,147,868
44	Soybean Meal Futures	CBOT	4,145,397
45	Special High Grade Zinc Futures	LME	4,023,223
46	American Soybean Futures	TGE	4,000,410
47	6-Month T-Bill Futures	OM Stockholm (OM)	3,930,302
48	Italian Government Bond Futures	LIFFE	3,773,105
49	Sugar #11 Futures	Coffee, Sugar & Cocoa Exchange (CS&C)	3,667,481
50	Red Bean Futures	Osaka Grain Exchange (OGE)	3,627,027
51	CAC-40 Stock Index Futures	MATIF	3,601,466
52	Wheat Futures	CBOT	3,498,814
53	Gas Oil Futures	IPE	3,452,643
54	Nikkei Stock Average Futures	SIMEX	3,349,243
55	Live Cattle Futures	CME	3,319,618
56	DAX Stock Index Futures	DTB	3,271,055
57	British Pound Futures	CME	3,053,428
58	Silver 5,000-oz. Futures	COMEX	3,016,339
59	Ibex 35 Index Futures	MEFF Renta Variable (MEFF-RV)	2,898,111
60	German Government Bond Options	LIFFE	2,749,670
61	3-Month PIBOR Options	MATIF	2,659,534

Rank	Contract	Exchange	1992 Volume
62	3-Month Sterling Interest Rate Options	LIFFE	2,648,009
63	FT-SE 100 Futures	LIFFE	2,618,629
64	10-Year T-Note Options	CBOT	2,564,191
65	Euroyen Futures	SIMEX	2,472,931
66	Cotton Yarn Futures	TCE	2,335,431
67	S&P 500 Options	CME	2,209,529
68	Coffee "C" Futures	CS&C	2,152,383
69	3-Month EuroSwiss Franc Futures	LIFFE	1,970,438
70	3-Month Euromark Options	LIFFE	1,964,405
71	Soybean Options	CBOT	1,930,334
72	Corn Options	CBOT	1,833,816
73	Long Gilt Options	LIFFE	1,812,576
74	Imported Soybean Futures	OGE	1,693,998
75	3½-5 Year German Government Bond Futures	DTB	1,667,799
76	Rubber Futures	TCE	1,659,977
77	Live Hog Futures	CME	1,556,092
78	Japanese Yen Options	CME	1,518,409
79	Nickel Futures	LME	1,442,536
80	Cocoa Futures	London Futures and Options Exchange (FOX)	1,397,966
81	Raw Sugar Futures	Tokyo Sugar Exchange (TSuE)	1,387,066
82	Topix Stock Index Futures	TSE	1,358,423

CONTRACT SPECIFICATIONS*

Contract specifications for the top 20 traded futures and options on futures during 1992 follow.

CBOT U.S. Treasury Bond Futures

Trading Unit	$100,000 face value U.S. Treasury bonds
Tick Size	1/32 of a point ($31.25 per contract); par is on the basis of 100 points
Daily Price Limit	Three points ($3,000) per contract above or below the previous day's settlement price (expandable to 4½ points). Limits are lifted the second business day preceding the first day of the delivery month.
Contract Months	March, June, September, December
Trading Hours	7:20 a.m. to 2:00 p.m. (Chicago time), Monday through Friday. Evening trading hours are 5:20 p.m. to 8:05 p.m. (Chicago time), or 6:20 p.m. to 9:05 p.m. (central daylight saving time), Sunday through Thursday. Contract also trades on the GLOBEX® system.
Last Trading Day	Seven business days prior to the last business day of the delivery month
Deliverable Grades	U.S. Treasury bonds maturing at least 15 years from the first business day of the delivery month, if not callable; if callable, not so for at least 15 years from the first day of the delivery month. Coupon based on an 8 percent standard.
Delivery	Federal Reserve book-entry wire-transfer system

*The information in this section is taken from sources believed to be reliable, but it is not guaranteed by the Chicago Board of Trade as to accuracy or completeness, and is intended for purposes of information only. The Rules and Regulations of the individual exchanges should be consulted as the authoritative sources on all current contract specifications.

CME 3-Month Eurodollar Futures

Trading Unit	Eurodollar Time Deposit having a principal value of $1 million with a three-month maturity
Tick Size	.01 ($25 per contract)
Daily Price Limit	No limit
Contract Months	March, June, September, December
Trading Hours	7:20 a.m. to 2:00 p.m. (Chicago time), Monday through Friday, except on the last trading day of an expiring contract, when trading closes at 9:30 a.m. (3:30 p.m. London time). The contract also trades on the GLOBEX® system.
Last Trading Day	The second London bank business day immediately preceding the third Wednesday of the contract month
Delivery	Cash settled

MATIF French Government Bond Futures

Trading Unit	500,000 FF nominal value, French (notional) bond with 10 percent coupon, 7- to 10-year maturity
Tick Size	Two basis points (100 FF per contract)
Daily Price Limit	250 basis points per contract above or below the previous day's settlement price
Contract Months	March, June, September, December
Trading Hours	9:00 a.m. to 4:30 p.m. (Paris time); contract also trades on the GLOBEX® system
Last Trading Day	Fourth business day prior to last business day of delivery month
Delivery	7- to 10-year fixed-income French government bonds, selected from a basket of deliverable bonds

NYMEX Light Crude Oil Futures

Trading Unit	1,000 U.S. barrels (42,000 gallons)
Tick Size	1 cent per barrel ($10 per contract)
Daily Price Limit	$7.50 per barrel ($7,500 per contract) for the first two contract months. Initial back-month limits of $1.50 per barrel rise to $3 per barrel if the previous day's settlement price is at the $1.50 limit. In the event of a $7.50 move in either of the first two contract months, back-month limits are expanded to $7.50 per barrel from the limit in place in the direction of the move.
Contract Months	18 consecutive months plus four long-dated futures that are initially listed 21, 24, 30, and 36 months prior to delivery
Trading Hours	9:45 a.m. to 3:10 p.m. (New York time)
Last Trading Day	Third business day prior to the 25th calendar day of the month preceding the delivery month
Deliverable Grades	Specific crudes with 0.5 percent sulfur by weight or less, not less than 34 degrees API gravity nor more than 45 degrees API gravity. The following crude streams are deliverable: West Texas Intermediate, Mid-Continent Sweet, Low Sweet Mix, New Mexico Sweet, North Texas Sweet, Oklahoma Sweet, South Texas Sweet, Brent Blend, Bonny Light, and Oseberg Blend. Contact the exchange for details on price discounts and premiums.

CBOT U.S. Treasury Bond Options

Trading Unit	One $100,000 face value CBOT U.S. Treasury bond futures contract
Tick Size	1/64 of a point ($15.63 per contract) rounded up to the nearest cent per contract
Strike Prices	One-point strikes ($1,000) for the nearby contract month in a band consisting of the at-the-money, four above, and four below. Two-point ($2,000) strikes are listed outside this band. Back months are also listed in two-point strike price intervals.
Daily Price Limit	Three points ($3,000) per contract above or below the previous day's settlement premium (expandable to 4½ points). Limits are lifted on the last trading day.
Contract Months	Open outcry: the front month of the current quarter plus the next three contracts of the quarterly cycle (March, June, September, December). If the front month is a quarterly contract month, no monthly contract will be listed. The monthly option contract exercises into the current quarterly futures contract. For example, a November option will exercise into a December futures position. Contract months beyond the third quarterly cycle trade on Project A™. When the nearest quarterly contract month expires, the first contract month on Project A moves to open outcry trading on the following business day. For more details, contact the exchange.
Trading Hours	7:20 a.m. to 2:00 p.m. (Chicago time), Monday through Friday. Evening trading hours are 5:20 p.m. to 8:05 p.m. (Chicago time), or 6:20 p.m. to 9:05 p.m. (central daylight saving time), Sunday through Thursday. The contract also trades on the GLOBEX® system.
Last Trading Day	12:00 p.m. (Chicago time) on the last Friday preceding by at least five business days the last business day of the month preceding the option contract month.
Expiration	10:00 a.m. (Chicago time) on the first Saturday following the last day of trading

TIFFE 3-month Euroyen Futures

Trading Unit	100 million yen
Tick Size	.01 or a value of ¥2,500 per tick
Daily Price Limit	None
Contract Months	March, June, September, December (listed on a two-year cycle—eight contract months)
Trading Hours	9:00 a.m. to 12:00 p.m., 1:30 p.m. to 3:30 p.m., and 4:00 p.m. to 6:00 p.m. (Tokyo standard time) On the last trading day hours are 9:00 a.m. to 11:00 a.m.
Last Trading Day	Two business days prior to the third Wednesday of the contract month
Delivery	Cash settled

BM&F 1-Day Interbank Deposits Futures

Trading Unit	Cr$1,000,000,000
Tick Size	Cr$10,000
Daily Price Limit	5 percent on the first contract month
Contract Months	All months
Trading Hours	10:00 a.m. to 1:00 p.m. and 3:00 p.m. to 4:45 p.m. (São Paulo time)
Last Trading Day	Business day preceding the expiration date, which occurs on the first business day of the contract month
Delivery	Cash settled

CME Eurodollar Options

Trading Unit	One Eurodollar Time Deposit futures contract
Tick Size	.01 ($25 per contract)
Strike Prices	.25-point intervals, e.g., 95.00, 95.25
Daily Price Limit	No limit
Contract Months	March, June, September, December and serial month
Trading Hours	7:20 a.m. to 2:00 p.m. (Chicago time), Monday through Friday, except on the last trading day of an expiring contract, when trading closes at 9:30 a.m. (3:30 p.m. London time). The contract also trades on the GLOBEX® trading system.
Last Trading Day	Options in the March quarterly cycle have the same last trading day as the underlying futures contract. Serial options (options not in the March quarterly cycle) stop trading on the Friday immediately preceding the third Wednesday of the contract month.
Delivery	Cash settled

LIFFE German Government Bond (Bund) Futures

Trading Unit	DM 250,000 nominal value notional German government bond with 6 percent coupon
Tick Size	DM .01 (DM 25)
Contract Months	March, June, September, December
Trading Hours	7:30 a.m. to 4:15 p.m. (London time) on the exchange trading floor and 4:20 p.m. to 5:55 p.m. on the APT electronic trading system
Last Trading Day	11:00 a.m. (Frankfurt time) three Frankfurt working days prior to delivery day
Delivery	10th calendar day of delivery month. If such day is not a working day in Frankfurt, then the delivery day will be the next following Frankfurt working day.

CME Standard & Poor's (S&P) 500 Stock Index Futures

Trading Unit	$500 times the Standard & Poor's 500 Stock Index
Tick Size	.05 index points ($25 per contract)
Daily Price Limit	Coordinated with trading halts of the underlying stocks listed for trading in the securities markets. Contact exchange for details of this rule.
Contract Months	March, June, September, December
Trading Hours	8:30 a.m. to 3:15 p.m. (Chicago time). The contract also trades on the GLOBEX® trading system.
Last Trading Day	The business day immediately preceding the day of determination of the final settlement price (normally, the Thursday prior to the third Friday of the contract month)
Delivery	Cash settled

LIFFE 3-Month Eurodeutschmark (Euromark) Interest Rate Futures

Trading Unit	DM 1,000,000
Tick Size	.01 (DM 25)
Contract Months	March, June, September, December
Trading Hours	8:00 a.m. to 4:10 p.m. (London time) on the exchange trading floor and 4:29 p.m. to 5:59 p.m. on the APT electronic trading system
Last Trading Day	11:00 a.m. (London time) two business days prior to the third Wednesday of the delivery month
Delivery	First business day after the last trading day

OSE NIKKEI 225 Stock Index Futures

Trading Unit	¥1,000 times Nikkei stock average
Tick Size	¥10 per Nikkei stock average (minimum value ¥10,000)
Daily Price Limit	Plus or minus 3 percent of the previous day's closing price
Contract Months	March, June, September, December cycle (five contract months traded at all times)
Trading Hours	9:00 a.m. to 11:00 a.m. and 12:30 p.m. to 3:00 p.m. (Osaka time)
Last Trading Day	The business day before the second Friday of each contract month
Delivery	Cash settled

TSE Japanese Government Bond Futures

Trading Unit	Standard 6 percent, 10-year Japanese government bond ¥100 million face value
Tick Size	$\frac{1}{100}$ of a point per 100 points (¥10,000 per contract)
Daily Price Limit	Two points upward or downward (¥2 million per contract)
Contract Months	March, June, September, December cycle (five contract months traded at all times)
Trading Hours	9:00 a.m. to 11:00 a.m. and 12:30 p.m. to 3:00 p.m. (Tokyo time)
Last Trading Day	The ninth business day prior to each delivery date
Deliverable Grades	Exchange-listed Japanese government bonds having maturity of 7 years or more but less than 11 years

CME Deutsche Mark Futures

Trading Unit	DM 125,000
Tick Size	.0001 per mark ($12.50 per contract)
Daily Price Limit	Opening limit between 7:20 a.m. to 7:35 a.m. (Chicago time) of 200 points. GLOBEX® price limits of 200 points. After the opening price limit has expired, a schedule of sequential expanded daily price limits will be effective for 15-minute intervals. Contact the exchange for details.
Contract Months	January, March, April, June, July, September, October, December, spot month
Trading Hours	7:20 a.m. to 2:00 p.m. (Chicago time), Monday through Friday, except on the last trading day of an expiring contract, when trading closes at 9:16 a.m. The contract also trades on the GLOBEX® system.
Last Trading Day	Second business day immediately preceding the third Wednesday of the contract month
Delivery	Third Wednesday of the contract month

LIFFE 3-Month Sterling Interest Rate Futures

Trading Unit	£500,000
Tick Size	0.01 (£12.50)
Daily Price Limit	None
Contract Months	March, June, September, December
Trading Hours	8:05 a.m. to 4:02 p.m. (London time) on the exchange trading floor and 4:27 p.m. to 5:57 p.m. on the APT electronic trading system.
Last Trading Day	11:00 a.m. (London time) on the third Wednesday of the delivery month
Delivery	First business day after the last trading day

CBOT 10-Year Treasury Note Futures

Trading Unit	$100,000 face value U.S. Treasury notes
Tick Size	$\frac{1}{32}$ of a point ($31.25 per contract); par is on the basis of 100 points
Daily Price Limit	Three points ($3,000) per contract above or below the previous day's settlement price
Contract Months	March, June, September, December
Trading Hours	7:20 a.m. to 2:00 p.m. (Chicago time), Monday through Friday. Evening trading hours are 5:20 p.m. to 8:05 p.m. (Chicago time), or 6:20 p.m. to 9:05 p.m. (central daylight saving time), Sunday through Thursday. Contract also trades on the GLOBEX® system.
Last Trading Day	Seven business days prior to the last business day of the delivery month
Deliverable Grades	U.S. Treasury notes maturing at least 6½ years, but not more than 10 years, from the first business day of the delivery month. Coupon based on an 8 percent standard.
Delivery	Federal Reserve book-entry wire-transfer system

CBOT Corn Futures

Trading Unit	5,000 bushels
Tick Size	¼ cent per bushel ($12.50 per contract)
Daily Price Limit	12 cents per bushel ($600 per contract) above or below the previous day's settlement price (expandable to 18 cents per bushel). No limit in the spot month.
Contract Months	December, March, May, July, September
Trading Hours	9:30 a.m. to 1:15 p.m. (Chicago time), Monday through Friday. Trading in expiring contracts closes at noon on the last trading day.
Last Trading Day	Seventh business day preceding the last business day of the delivery month
Deliverable Grades	No. 2 Yellow at par and substitution at differentials established by the exchange

MATIF French Government Bond Options

Trading Unit	One French (notional) bond futures contract
Tick Size	One basis point
Strike Prices	Expressed in integer multiples of 100 basis points, 9 at least bracketing the at-the-money price
Daily Price Limit	None
Contract Months	One front month plus four successive quarterly maturities from March, June, September, December (if the front month is a quarterly contract month, no monthly contract will be listed). The monthly option contract exercises into the subsequent quarterly futures contract.
Trading Hours	9:05 a.m. to 4:30 p.m. (Paris time). Contract also trades on the GLOBEX® system.
Last Trading Day	Last Thursday of the month preceding the notional bond delivery month
Delivery	Notional bond futures contract

CBOT Soybean Futures

Trading Unit	5,000 bushels
Tick Size	¼ cent per bushel ($12.50 per contract)
Daily Price Limit	30 cents per bushel ($1,500 per contract) above or below the previous day's settlement price (expandable to 45 cents per bushel). No limit in the spot month.
Contract Months	September, November, January, March, May, July, August
Trading Hours	9:30 a.m. to 1:15 p.m. (Chicago time), Monday through Friday. Trading in expiring contracts closes at noon on the last trading day.
Last Trading Day	Seventh business day preceding the last business day of the delivery month
Deliverable Grades	No. 2 Yellow at par and substitution at differentials established by the exchange

LIFFE Long Gilt Futures

Trading Unit	£50,000 nominal value notional gilt with 9 percent coupon
Tick Size	£¹⁄₃₂ (£15.625)
Daily Price Limit	None
Contract Months	March, June, September, December
Trading Hours	8:30 a.m. to 4:15 p.m. (London time) on the exchange trading floor and 4:30 p.m. to 6:00 p.m. on the APT electronic trading system
Last Trading Day	11:00 a.m. (London time) two business days prior to last business day in delivery month
Delivery	Any business day in delivery month

Sources of Information*

The following list includes just a few of the many possible resources on futures and options on futures trading. Many of the books and periodicals listed are available directly from the publisher or the library system.

Book
Hieronymus, Thomas A. *Economics of Futures Trading for Commercial and Personal Profit*, 2nd ed. New York: Commodity Research Bureau, 1977.

Chicago Board of Trade Publication
Market Development Department:
Action in the Marketplace, 1993.

Books
Goss, Barry A., and B.S. Yamey, eds. *Economics of Futures Trading*. New York: John Wiley & Sons, 1976.

Peck, Anne E., ed. *Futures Markets: Their Economic Role*. Washington, DC: American Enterprise Institute for Public Policy Research, 1985.

Stoll, Hans R., and Robert E. Whaley. *Futures and Options: Theory and Applications*. Cincinnati: South-Western Publishing, 1993.

Williams, Jeffrey. *The Economic Function of Futures Markets*. New York: Cambridge University Press, 1986.

Books
Marasco, M.C., ed. *The Complete Commodity Futures Directory*, 3rd ed. rev. Frankfort, IL: Christopher Resources.

Futures and Fact Book. Washington, DC: Futures Industry Institute, 1993.

Book
Maxwell, Joseph R., Sr. *Commodity Futures Trading Orders*. Red Bluff, CA: Speer Books, 1975.

*The sources listed in this section are believed to be accurate as of the date of publication but are not guaranteed or endorsed by the Chicago Board of Trade as to accuracy or completeness. The textbooks, periodicals, and other sources are given for information and education purposes only.

Chapter 1

Chapter 2

Chapter 3

Chapter 5

Pamphlets
Regulatory Guide for Commodity Pool Operators and Commodity Trading Advisors. Chicago: National Futures Association, 1993.

Regulatory Guide for Futures Commission Merchants and Introducing Brokers. Chicago: National Futures Association, 1993.

Chicago Board of Trade Publications
Market Development Department:
Margins for Options on T-Bond & T-Note Futures, 1987.

Secretary's Office:
Board of Trade of the City of Chicago Rules and Regulations.

Chapter 6

Book
MidAmerica Institute. *Margins & Market Integrity: State of the Art Research on the Impact of Margins in Stocks and Futures Markets.* Chicago: Probus Publishing, 1991.

Chicago Board of Trade Publications
Market Development Department:
MidAm Rough Rice Delivery Manual, 1988.

The Delivery Process in Brief: Treasury Bond and Treasury Note Futures, 1987.

Chapter 7

Book
Peck, Anne E., ed. *Futures Markets: Regulatory Issues.* Washington, DC: American Enterprise Institute for Public Policy Research, 1985.

Pamphlet
An Introduction to the National Futures Association. Chicago: National Futures Association, 1991.

Chicago Board of Trade Publication
Secretary's Office:
Board of Trade of the City of Chicago Rules and Regulations.

Chapter 8

Books
Figlewski, Stephen, et al. *Hedging with Financial Futures for Institutional Investors: From Theory to Practice.* Cambridge, MA: Ballinger Publishing, 1985.

Fischer, Donald E., ed. *Options and Futures: New Route to Risk-Return Management.* Homewood, IL: Dow Jones-Irwin, 1984.

McKinzie, Jeff L., and Keith Schap. *Hedging Financial Instruments: A Guide to Basis Trading for Bankers, Treasurers, and Portfolio Managers.* Chicago: Probus Publishing, 1988.

Noddings, Thomas C. *Super Hedging.* Chicago: Probus Publishing, 1985.

Platt, Robert B. *Controlling Interest Rate Risk: New Techniques and Applications for Money Management.* New York: John Wiley & Sons, 1986.

Sennholz, Lyn M., et al. *Interest Rate Futures Hedging Course.* Spring Mills, PA: Center for Futures Education, 1984.

————. *Livestock Hedging Course.* Spring Mills, PA: Center for Futures Education, 1984.

Siegel, Daniel R., and Diane F. Siegel. *Futures Markets: Arbitrage, Risk Management and Portfolio Strategies.* New York: McGraw-Hill, 1990.

————. *Stock Index Futures Hedging Course.* Spring Mills, PA: Center for Futures Education, 1983.

Vince, Ralph. *Portfolio Management Formulas.* New York: John Wiley & Sons, 1990.

Chicago Board of Trade Publications

Market Development Department:
Basis Trading for Cash Merchandisers, 1993.

Chicago Board of Trade Conversion Factors, rev. ed. Boston: Financial Publishing, 1991.

Financial Instruments Markets: An Advanced Study of Cash-Futures Relationships, 1986.

Introduction to Agricultural Hedging: A Home Study Course, 1988.

Understanding Basis: The Economics of Where and When, 1990.

Books

Ainsworth, Ralph M. *Basic Principles of Successful Commodity Futures Speculation.* Albuquerque, NM: Institute for Economics and Financial Research, 1983.

Belveal, L. Dee. *Speculation in Commodity Contracts and Options,* 2nd ed. Homewood, IL: Dow Jones-Irwin, 1985.

Epstein, Ira, and David Garfield, M.D. *Psychology of Smart Investing: Meeting the 6 Mental Challenges.* New York: John Wiley & Sons, 1992.

Ghosh, S., et al. *Stabilizing Speculative Commodity Markets.* Miami Beach, FL: Oxford Press, 1987.

Harper, Henry H. *The Psychology of Speculation: The Human Element in Stock Market Transactions.* Burlington, VT: Fraser Publishing, 1978.

Chapter 9

Huff, Charles, and Barbara Marinacci. *Commodity Speculation for Beginners: A Guide to the Futures Market.* New York: McGraw-Hill, 1982.

Schwager, Jack D. *Market Wizards: Interviews with Top Traders.* New York: New York Institute of Finance, 1989.

_____. *New Market Wizards: Conversations with America's Top Traders.* New York: HarperBusiness, 1992.

Weiss, David M. *Traders: Jobs, Products, Markets.* New York: New York Institute of Finance, 1990.

Chapter 10

Books

Arnold, Curtis M. *Timing the Market: How to Profit in Bull and Bear Markets with Technical Analysis.* Chicago: Probus Publishing, 1986.

Beckman, Robert C. *Powertiming: Using the Elliott Wave System to Anticipate and Time Market Turns.* Chicago: Probus Publishing, 1992.

Bernstein, Jacob. *Handbook of Commodity Cycles: A Window on Time.* New York: John Wiley & Sons, 1982.

_____. *Short-Term Trading in Futures: A Manual of Systems, Strategies and Techniques.* Chicago: Probus Publishing, 1987.

_____. *Strategic Futures Trading: Contemporary Trading Systems to Maximize Profits.* Chicago: Probus Publishing, 1992.

Cadogan, Georges. *Kondratieff and the Mastery of the Future Through the Theory of Cycles.* Albuquerque, NM: Institute for Economic and Financial Research, 1983.

Edwards, Robert D., and John Magee. *Technical Analysis of Stock Trends,* 6th ed. New York: New York Institute of Finance, 1992.

Ehlers, John F. *MESA and Trading Market Cycles.* New York: John Wiley & Sons, 1992.

Elliot, Ralph N. *The Wave Principle.* Albuquerque, NM: Institute for Economic and Political World Strategic Studies, 1979.

Eng, William F. *Day Trader's Manual: Theory, Art, and Science of Profitable Short-Term Investing.* New York: John Wiley & Sons, 1993.

_____. *Technical Analysis of Stocks, Options and Futures.* Chicago: Probus Publishing, 1988.

Frost, Alfred J., and Robert R. Prechter. *Elliot Wave Principle: Key to Stock Market Profits,* 5th ed. Chappaqua, NY: New Classics Library, 1985.

Grushcow, Jack, and Courtney Smith. *Profits Through Seasonal Trading.* New York: John Wiley & Sons, 1980.

Hadady, R. Earl. *Contrary Opinion: How to Use It for Profit in Trading Commodity Futures*. Pasadena, CA: Key Books Press, 1983.

Hill, John R. *Stock and Commodity Market Trend Trading by Advanced Technical Analysis*. Hendersonville, NC: Commodity Research Institute, 1977.

Hurst, J.M. *The Profit Magic of Stock Transaction Timing*. Englewood Cliffs, NJ: Prentice-Hall, 1970.

Kaufman, Perry J. *New Commodity Trading Systems and Methods*. New York: John Wiley & Sons, 1987.

_____, ed. *Technical Analysis in Commodities*. New York: John Wiley & Sons, 1980.

LeBeau, Charles, and David W. Lucas. *Technical Traders Guide to Computer Analysis of the Futures Market*. Homewood, IL: Business One Irwin, 1992.

Maxwell, Joseph R. *Commodity Futures Trading with Moving Averages*. Red Bluff, CA: Speer Books, 1975.

_____. *Commodity Futures Trading with Point and Figure Charts*. Red Bluff, CA: Speer Books, 1978.

Murphy, John J. *Study Guide for Technical Analysis of the Futures Markets: A Self-Training Manual*. New York: New York Institute of Finance, 1987.

_____. *Technical Analysis of the Futures Markets: A Comprehensive Guide to Trading Methods and Applications*. New York: New York Institute of Finance, 1986.

Pring, Martin J., ed. *Historical Chart Book, Vol. 1*. Washington Depot, CT: International Institute for Economic Research, 1986.

_____. *Technical Analysis Explained: The Successful Investor's Guide to Spotting Investment Trends and Turning Points*. New York: McGraw-Hill, 1986.

Schwager, Jack D. *A Complete Guide to the Futures Markets: Fundamental Analysis, Technical Analysis, Trading, Spreads, and Options*. New York: John Wiley & Sons, 1984.

Schwarz, Edward W., Joanne M. Hill, and Thomas Schneeweis. *Financial Futures: Fundamentals, Strategies, and Applications*. Homewood, IL: Dow Jones-Irwin, 1986.

Shaleen, Kenneth H. *Technical Analysis and Options Strategies*. Chicago: Probus Publishing, 1992.

_____. *Volume and Open Interest*. Chicago: Probus Publishing, 1991.

Sklarew, Arthur. *Techniques of a Professional Commodity Chart Analyst*, rev. ed. New York: Commodity Research Bureau, 1980.

Smith, Courtney. *Seasonal Charts for Futures Traders: A Sourcebook.* New York: John Wiley & Sons, 1987.

Taylor, William T. *Trader's and Investor's Guide to Commodity Trading Systems, Software, and Data Bases.* Chicago: Probus Publishing, 1986.

Chapter 11	**Books**

Bernstein, Jacob. *How to Profit from Seasonal Commodity Spreads: A Complete Guide.* New York: John Wiley & Sons, 1983.

Goldberg, Harold. *Advanced Commodity Spread Trading.* Brightwaters, NY: Windsor Books, 1985.

Hadady, R. Earl. *Historical Commodity Spread Charts.* Pasadena, CA: Key Books Press, 1984.

Kallard, Thomas. *Commodity Spreads: Year-Round Trading Strategies to Beat Inflation and Build Capital.* New York: Optosonic Press, 1982.

————. *Fortune Building Commodity Spreads for the '90s.* Brightwaters, NY: Windsor Books, 1991.

Schwager, Jack D. *A Complete Guide to the Futures Markets: Fundamental Analysis, Technical Analysis, Trading, Spreads, and Options.* New York: John Wiley & Sons, 1984.

Smith, Courtney. *Commodity Spreads: Techniques and Methods for Spreading Financial Futures, Grains, Meats, and Other Commodities.* New York: John Wiley & Sons, 1982.

Weisweiller, Rudi, ed. *Arbitrage: Opportunities and Techniques in the Financial and Commodity Markets.* New York: John Wiley & Sons, 1986.

Williams, Jeffrey C., and Brian D. Wright. *Storage and Commodity Markets.* New York: Cambridge University Press, 1991.

Chicago Board of Trade Publications
Market Development Department:
Agricultural Spreads for Cash Merchandisers, 1993.

CBOT Financial Instruments Guide, 1991.

CBOT Handbook Series on Agricultural Spreads: July/November Soybean Spread 1982-1992, 1993; *July/December Corn Spread 1982-1992*, 1993; *Wheat/Corn Spread 1982-1992*, 1993; *December Corn/Oat Spread 1982-1992*, 1993; *July Soybean/Wheat Spread 1982-1992*, 1993; *November/December Soybean Crush Spread 1982-1992*, 1993.

CBOT Handbook Series on Metals Markets: Gold/Silver Ratio Spread, 1988.

Books

Angell, George. *Agricultural Options: Trading Puts and Calls in the New Grain and Livestock Futures Market.* New York: AMACOM, 1986.

Ansbacher, Max G. *The New Options Market.* New York: Walker, 1987.

Bobin, Christopher. *Agricultural Options.* New York: John Wiley & Sons, 1990.

Bookstaber, Richard M. *Option Pricing and Strategies in Investing.* Chicago: Probus Publishing, 1987.

Catania, Patrick J., et al. *Agricultural Options: A Primer for Producers.* Bloomington, MN: Doane Information Services, 1984.

Cleeton, Claud Edwin. *Strategies for the Options Trader.* New York: John Wiley & Sons, 1979.

Fischer, Donald E., ed. *Options and Futures: New Route to Risk-Return Management.* Homewood, IL: Dow Jones-Irwin, 1984.

Gastineau, Gary. *The Options Manual,* 3rd ed. New York: McGraw-Hill, 1988.

Kramer, Samuel L., et al. *Options Hedging Handbook.* Spring Mills, PA: Center for Futures Education, 1985.

Labuszewski, John W., and Jeanne Cairns Sinquefield. *Inside the Commodity Option Markets.* New York: John Wiley & Sons, 1985.

Labuszewski, John W., and John E. Nyhoff. *Trading Options on Futures.* New York: John Wiley & Sons, 1988.

Mayer, Terry S. *Commodity Options: A User's Guide to Speculating and Hedging.* New York: New York Institute of Finance, 1983.

McMillan, Lawrence G. *Options as a Strategic Investment: A Comprehensive Analysis of Listed Option Strategies,* 3rd ed. New York: New York Institute of Finance, 1980.

Natenberg, Sheldon. *Option Volatility and Pricing Strategies: Advanced Trading Techniques for Professionals.* Chicago: Probus Publishing, 1988.

Schiller, Jon. *The Insider's Automatic Options Strategy: How to Win on Better Than 9 Out of 10 Trades with Extremely Low Risk.* New York: Windsor Books, 1992.

Trester, Kenneth R. *The Compleat Option Player: Winning Strategy and Tactics in the New Options Game,* 2nd ed. Costa Mesa, CA: Investrek Publishing, 1981.

Chapter 12

Chicago Board of Trade Publications
Market Development Department:
Flexible Choice, 1990.

Options on Agricultural Futures: A Home Study Course, 1989.

Options on U.S. Treasury Bond Futures for Institutional Investors, 1987.

Strategies for Buying and Writing Options on Treasury Bond Futures, 1987.

Chapter 13

Books

Aldrich, Samuel R., and Walter O. Scott. *Modern Soybean Production,* 2nd ed. Champaign, IL: S&A Publications, 1983.

Aldrich, Samuel R., Robert G. Hoeft, and Walter O. Scott. *Modern Corn Production,* 3rd ed. Champaign, IL: S&A Publications, 1986.

Atkin, Michael. *International Grain Trade.* Cambridge, England: Woodhead Publishing, 1992.

Broehl, Wayne G., Jr. *Cargill: Trading the World's Grain.* Hanover, NH: University Press of New England, 1992.

Ensminger, M.E. *Beef Cattle Science,* 6th ed. Danville, IL: Interstate Printers & Publishers, 1987.

Ferris, William G. *The Grain Traders: The Story of the Chicago Board of Trade.* East Lansing, MI: Michigan State University Press, 1988.

From Wheat to Flour. Washington DC: Wheat Flour Institute, 1976.

Fussell, Betty. *The Story of Corn.* New York: Alfred A. Knopf, 1992.

Galston, William A. *A Tough Row to Hoe: The 1985 Farm Bill and Beyond.* Washington, DC: Hamilton Press, 1985.

Glaser, Leverne K. *Provisions of the Food Security Act of 1985.* Washington, DC: U.S. Department of Agriculture, 1985.

Libby, Ronald T. *Protecting Markets: U.S. Policy and the World Grain Trade.* New York: Cornell University Press, 1992.

McCoy, John H. *Livestock and Meat Marketing,* 3rd ed. Westport, CT: AVI, 1979.

Morgan, Daniel. *Merchants of Grain.* New York: Penguin Books, 1980.

Nosker, Dean. *Futures Handbook for Farmers.* Bloomington, MN: Doane Information Services, 1980.

Prior-Willeard, Christopher. *Farming Futures: A Guide to the Agricultural Commodity Futures Markets.* Wolfeboro, NH: Longwood Publishing Group, 1985.

Sennholz, Lyn M., et al. *Livestock Hedging Course*. Spring Mills, PA: Center for Futures Education, 1984.

Teweles, Richard J., and Frank J. Jones. *The Commodity Futures Game: Who Wins? Who Loses? Why?*, 2nd ed. New York: McGraw-Hill, 1987.

Timmer, C. Peter. *Getting Prices Right: The Scope and Limits of Agricultural Price Policy*. Ithaca, NY: Cornell University Press, 1986.

Wills, Walter J. *An Introduction to Grain Marketing*. Danville, IL: Interstate Printers & Publishers, 1972.

Government Publications
U.S. Department of Agriculture:
  Cattle
  Crop Production
  Grain Stocks
  Hogs and Pigs
  Livestock and Poultry Situation and Outlook
  Livestock Slaughter
  Oil Crops
  Outlook for U.S. Agricultural Exports
  Rice Situation and Outlook
  Rice Stocks
  Wheat Situation and Outlook

USDA Foreign Agricultural Service:
  World Oilseed Situation and Outlook

U.S. Agricultural Marketing Service:
  Grain and Feed Market News

U.S. Department of Commerce:
  Fats and Oils
  Oilseed Crushings

Chicago Board of Trade Publications
Market Development Department:
CBOT Handbook Series on Agricultural Markets: *Weather and the Corn Market; Weather and the Soybean Market; Weather and the Wheat Market*, 1993.

Grains: Production, Processing, Marketing, rev. ed., 1992.

Books
Bernstein, Jacob. *An Investor's Guide to Using Cycles in the Precious Metals and Copper*. New York: John Wiley & Sons, 1985.

Rapson, W.S., and T. Groenewald. *Gold Usage*. New York: Academic Press, 1978.

Chapter 14

Teweles, Richard J., and Frank J. Jones. *The Commodity Futures Game: Who Wins? Who Loses? Why?*, 2nd ed. New York: McGraw-Hill, 1987.

Periodicals and Reports

Metals Week. New York: McGraw-Hill.

The Silver Market. New York: Handy and Harman.

Government Publications

U.S. Bureau of Mines:
    Mineral Industry Surveys, Copper
    Mineral Industry Surveys, Gold and Silver Monthly
    Mineral Industry Surveys, Platinum-Group Metals
    Minerals Yearbook

Chapter 15

Books

Dean, William, and David S. Evans, eds. *Terms of the Trade: A Handbook for the Forest Products Industry*. Eugene, OR: Random Lengths Publications, 1978.

Duerr, William A., ed. *Timber! Problems, Prospects, Policies*. Ames, IA: Iowa State University, 1973.

Savaiko, Bernard C. *Trading in Soft Commodity Futures*. New York: John Wiley & Sons, 1986.

Teweles, Richard J., and Frank J. Jones. *The Commodity Futures Game: Who Wins? Who Loses? Why?*, 2nd ed. New York: McGraw-Hill, 1987.

Periodicals and Reports

Crow's Weekly Letter. Portland, OR: C.C. Crow Publications.

Florida Agricultural Statistics: Citrus Summary. Florida Crop and Livestock Reporting Service.

Statistical Annual. Portland, OR: Western Wood Products Association.

Government Publications

U.S. Bureau of the Census:
    Housing Starts
    Lumber Production and Mill Stocks

U.S. Department of Agriculture:
    Cold Storage
    Cotton and Wool Situation and Outlook
    Crop Production
    Fruit and Tree Nuts Situation and Outlook
    Sugar and Sweetener Situation and Outlook

USDA Foreign Agricultural Service:
  World Cocoa Situation
  World Coffee Situation
  World Sugar and Molasses Situation and Outlook

Books

Brown, Stewart L., and Steven Errera. *Trading Energy Futures: A Manual for Energy Industry Professionals.* Westport, CT: Quorum Books, 1987.

Prast, William G., and Howard L. Lax. *Oil-Futures Markets: An Introduction.* Lexington, MA: Lexington Books, 1983.

Stobaugh, Robert, and Daniel Yergin, eds. *Energy Futures: The Report of the Harvard Business School Energy Project.* New York: Random House, 1982.

Teweles, Richard J., and Frank J. Jones. *The Commodity Futures Game: Who Wins? Who Loses? Why?*, 2nd ed. New York: McGraw-Hill, 1987.

Treat, John E. *Energy Futures Trading Opportunities for the 1980s.* Tulsa, OK: PennWell Books, 1984.

Periodical

Oil and Gas Journal. Tulsa, OK: PennWell Publishing.

Government Publications

U.S. Department of Energy:
  Monthly Energy Review
  Petroleum Supply Monthly
  Weekly Petroleum Status Report

Books

Aliber, Robert Z. *The International Money Game,* 5th ed. New York: Basic Books, 1987.

Ansbacher, Max G. *The New Stock-Index Market, Strategies for Profit in Stock Index Futures and Options.* New York: Walker, 1983.

Beaumont, Perry H. *Fixed Income Synthetic Assets.* New York. John Wiley & Sons, 1992.

Bookstaber, Richard. *The Complete Investment Book: Trading Stocks, Bonds and Options with Computer Applications.* Glenview, IL: Scott Foresman, 1985.

Burghardt, Galen, Morton Lane, and John Papa. *Treasury Bond Basis.* Chicago: Probus Publishing, 1989.

Chapter 16

Chapter 17

Burghardt, Galen, Terry Belton, Morton Lane, Geoffrey Luce, and Richard McVey. *Eurodollar Futures and Options: Controlling Money Market Risk.* Chicago: Probus Publishing, 1992.

Cooner, James J. *Investing in Municipal Bonds: Balancing Risks and Rewards.* New York: John Wiley and Sons, 1987.

Crawford, Richard D., and William W. Sihler. *Troubled Money Business.* New York: HarperBusiness, 1991.

Daigler, Robert T. *Financial Futures Markets: Concepts, Evidence, and Applications.* New York: HarperCollins, 1993.

Darst, David. *The Complete Bond Book: A Guide to All Types of Fixed Income Securities.* New York: McGraw-Hill, 1975.

————. *The Handbook of the Bond and Money Markets.* New York: McGraw-Hill, 1981.

DeRosa, David F. *Managing Foreign Exchange Risk.* Chicago: Probus Publishing, 1991.

Downes, John, and Jordan Elliot Goodman. *Dictionary of Finance and Investment Terms.* Woodbury, NY: Barron's, 1985.

Dubofsky, David A. *Options and Financial Futures: Valuation and Users.* New York: McGraw-Hill, 1992.

Fabozzi, Frank J., ed. *Handbook of Mortgage-Backed Securities,* rev. ed. Chicago: Probus Publishing, 1988.

————, and Irving M. Pollack, eds. *Handbook of Fixed Income Securities,* 2nd ed. Homewood, IL: Dow Jones-Irwin, 1986.

Federal Reserve System: Purposes and Functions, 7th ed. Washington, DC: Board of Governors of the Federal Reserve System, 1984.

Feldstein, Sylvan G., and Frank J. Fabozzi. *The Dow Jones-Irwin Guide to Municipal Bonds.* Homewood, IL: Dow Jones-Irwin, 1986.

Figgie, Harry E., Jr., and Gerald J. Swanson, Ph.D. *Bankruptcy 1995: The Coming Collapse of America and How to Stop It.* Boston: Little, Brown and Company, 1992.

Figlewski, Stephen, et al. *Hedging with Financial Futures for Institutional Investors: From Theory to Practice.* Cambridge, MA: Ballinger Publishing, 1985.

Gastineau, Gary L. *Dictionary of Financial Risk Management.* Chicago: Probus Publishing, 1992.

Grant, James. *Money of the Mind: Borrowing and Lending in America from the Civil War to Michael Milken.* New York: Farrar Straus Giroux, 1992.

Greider, William. *Secrets of the Temple: How the Federal Reserve Runs the Country*. New York: Simon & Schuster, 1987.

————. *Who Will Tell the People: The Betrayal of American Democracy*. New York: Simon & Schuster, 1992.

Homer, Sidney, and Richard Sylla. *A History of Interest Rates*, 3rd ed. New Brunswick, Canada: Rutgers University Press, 1991.

Hull, John. *Options, Futures, and Other Derivative Securities, 2nd ed.* Englewood Cliffs, NJ: Prentice Hall, 1993.

Kawaller, Ira G. *Financial Futures and Options: Managing Risk in the Interest Rate, Currency and Equity Markets*. Chicago: Probus Publishing, 1992.

Kolb, Robert W. *Financial Instruments Markets Reader*. 2nd ed. Miami: Kolb Publishing, 1993.

Krieger, Andrew J. *Money Bazaar: Inside the Trillion-Dollar World of Currency Trading*. New York: Times Books, 1992.

Lloyd, Humphrey E.D. *The RSL Market Timing System: How to Pinpoint Market Turns in Mutual Funds, Futures and Options*. Brightwaters, NY: Windsor Books, 1991.

Loosigian, Allan M. *Interest Rate Futures*. Homewood, IL: Dow Jones-Irwin, 1980.

Lorie, James H., and Mary T. Hamilton. *The Stock Market: Theories and Evidence*, 2nd ed. Homewood, IL: Dow Jones-Irwin, 1985.

Luskin, Donald L. *Index Options and Futures: The Complete Guide*. New York: John Wiley & Sons, 1987.

Marlin, George J., and Joe Mysak. *The Guidebook to Municipal Bonds: The History, The Industry, The Mechanics*. New York: American Banker/Bond Buyer, 1991.

Peters, Edgar E. *Chaos and Order in the Capital Markets*. New York: John Wiley & Sons, 1991.

Petzel, Todd E. *Financial Futures & Options*. New York: Quorum Books, 1989.

Pitts, Mark, and Frank J. Fabozzi. *Interest Rate Futures and Options*. Chicago: Probus Publishing, 1990.

Platt, Robert B. *Controlling Interest Rate Risk: Techniques and Applications for Money Management*. New York: John Wiley & Sons, 1986.

Powers, Mark, and Mark Castelino. *Inside the Financial Futures Market*, 3rd ed. New York: John Wiley & Sons, 1991.

Ray, Christina I. *The Bond Market: Trading and Risk Management.* Homewood, IL: Business One Irwin, 1992.

Rebell, Arthur L., and Gail Gordon. *Financial Futures and Investment Strategy.* Homewood, IL: Dow Jones-Irwin, 1984.

Ritter, Lawrence S., and William L. Silber. *Principles of Money, Banking, and Financial Markets.* New York: Basic Books, 1991.

Rothstein, Nancy, and James M. Little. *The Handbook of Financial Futures: A Guide for Investors and Professional Financial Managers.* New York: McGraw-Hill, 1983.

Schwarz, Edward W., Joanne M. Hill, and Thomas Schneeweis. *Financial Futures: Fundamentals, Strategies, and Applications.* Homewood, IL: Business One Irwin, 1986.

Sennholz, Lyn M., et al. *Interest Rate Futures Hedging Course.* Spring Mills, PA: Center for Futures Education, 1984.

————. *Stock Index Futures Hedging Course.* Spring Mills, PA: Center for Futures Education, 1983.

Stigum, Marcia. *The Money Market,* 3rd ed. Homewood, IL: Dow Jones-Irwin, 1990.

Van Horne, James C. *Financial Market Rates and Flows,* 2nd ed. Englewood Cliffs, NJ: Prentice-Hall, 1984.

Volcker, Paul, and Toyoo Gyohten. *Changing Fortunes: The World's Money and the Threat to American Leadership.* New York: Times Books, 1992.

Weiner, Neil S. *Stock Index Futures: A Guide for Traders, Investors, and Analysts.* New York: John Wiley & Sons, 1983.

Periodicals and Reports

American Banker. New York: American Banker.

Bank Credit Analyst. Hamilton, Bermuda: Monetary Research.

Bank Credit Analyst Interest Rate Forecast. Hamilton, Bermuda: Monetary Research.

Euromoney. London, U.K.: Euromoney Publications.

Federal Reserve Bulletin. Washington, DC: U.S. Board of Governors of the Federal Reserve System.

International Bank Credit Analyst. Hamilton, Bermuda: Monetary Research.

Real Estate Review. Boston: Warren Gorham Lamont.

Government Publication
U.S. Treasury Department:
  Treasury Bulletin

Chicago Board of Trade Publications
Market Development Department:
CBOT *Financial Instruments Guide,* 1991.

Chicago Board of Trade Treasury Bond Futures Yield Calculator.

Chicago Board of Trade 5-Year Treasury Note Futures Yield Calculator.

Chicago Board of Trade 7-, 10-Year Treasury Note Futures Yield Calculator.

Financial Instruments Markets: An Advanced Study of Cash-Futures Relationships, 1986.

Treasury Futures for Institutional Investors, 1990.

Books
Peters, Carl C., ed. *Managed Futures: Performance, Evaluation and Analysis of Commodity Funds, Pools and Accounts.* Chicago: Probus Publishing, 1992.

Books
Edwards, Franklin R., and Cindy W. Ma. *Futures and Options.* New York: McGraw-Hill, 1992.

Erickson, Rosemary, and George Steinbeck. *Language of Commodities: A Commodity Glossary.* New York: New York Institute of Finance, 1985.

Geczi, Michael L. *Futures, the Anti-inflation Investment.* New York: Avon Books, 1980.

Gold, Gerald. *Modern Commodity Futures Trading,* 7th ed. New York: Commodity Research Bureau, 1975.

Herbst, Anthony F. *Commodity Futures: Markets, Methods of Analysis, and Management of Risk.* New York: John Wiley & Sons, 1986.

Horn, Frederick F., and Victor W. Farah. *Trading in Commodity Futures,* 2nd ed. New York: New York Institute of Finance, 1979.

Hull, John. *Introduction to Futures and Options Markets.* Englewood Cliffs, NJ: Prentice Hall, 1991.

Kaufman, Perry J. *Handbook of Futures Markets: Commodity, Financial, Stock Index and Options.* New York: John Wiley & Sons, 1984.

Kolb, Robert W. *Understanding Futures Markets,* 3rd ed. Miami: Kolb Publishing, 1991.

Chapter 18

General

Kroll, Stanley, and Michael J. Paulenoff. *Business One Irwin Guide to the Futures Markets*. Homewood, IL: Business One Irwin, 1993.

Leuthold, Raymond M., Joan C. Junkus, and Jean E. Cordier. *Theory and Practice of Futures Markets*. Lexington, MA: Lexington Books, 1989.

Luft, Carl F. *Understanding and Trading Futures*. Chicago: Probus Publishing, 1991.

Powers, Mark J. *Getting Started in Commodity Futures Trading*. Waterloo, IA: Investor Publications, 1983.

Teweles, Richard J., and Frank J. Jones. *The Commodity Futures Game: Who Wins? Who Loses? Why?*, 2nd ed. New York: McGraw-Hill, 1987.

Williams, Larry. *Definitive Guide to Futures Trading, Vol. 1*. Brightwaters, NY: Windsor Books, 1988.

Periodicals and Reports
Commitments of Traders in Futures. Commodity Futures Trading Commission.

CRB Commodity Yearbook. New York: Commodity Research Bureau.

Journal of Futures Markets. New York: John Wiley & Sons.

Government Publications
U.S. Bureau of the Census:
  Statistical Abstract of the United States

U.S. Printing Office:
  Catalog of U.S. Government Publications

Chicago Board of Trade Publications
Market Development Department:
Readings in Futures Markets, Book 1: Selected Writings of Holbrook Working. Anne E. Peck, ed. 1977.

Readings in Futures Markets, Vol. 2: Selected Writings on Futures Markets: Basic Research in Commodity Markets. Anne E. Peck, ed. 1983.

Readings in Futures Markets, Book 3: Views from the Trade. Anne E. Peck, ed. 1978.

Readings in Futures Markets, Book 4: Selected Writings on Futures Markets: Research Directions in Commodity Markets, 1970-1980. Anne E. Peck, ed. 1984.

Readings in Futures Markets, Book 5: Selected Writings on Futures Markets: Explorations in Financial Futures Markets. Anne E. Peck, ed. 1985.

Readings in Futures Markets, Book 6: Selected Writings on Futures Markets: Interrelations Among Futures, Option, and Futures Option Markets. R.E. Whaley, ed. 1992.

Review of Research in Futures Markets, Vols. 1-10, 1982-1993.

Note: Chicago Board of Trade publications listed in the Sources of Information are generally available from the exchange. For more information on ordering specific publications, contact the appropriate Chicago Board of Trade departments.

GLOSSARY

Accrued Interest: Interest earned between the most recent interest payment and the present date but not yet paid to the lender.

Actuals: See **Cash Commodity.**

Add-on Method: A method of paying interest where the interest is added onto the principal at maturity or interest payment dates.

Adjusted Futures Price: The cash-price equivalent reflected in the current futures price. This is calculated by taking the futures price times the conversion factor for the particular financial instrument (e.g., bond or note) being delivered.

Against Actuals: See **Exchange For Physicals.**

Arbitrage: The simultaneous purchase and sale of similar commodities in different markets to take advantage of a price discrepancy.

Arbitration: The procedure of settling disputes between members, or between members and customers.

Assign: To make an option seller perform his obligation to assume a short futures position (as a seller of a call option) or a long futures position (as a seller of a put option).

Associated Person (AP): An individual who solicits orders, customers, or customer funds (or who supervises persons performing such duties) on behalf of a Futures Commission Merchant, an Introducing Broker, a Commodity Trading Adviser, or a Commodity Pool Operator.

Associate Membership (CBOT): A Chicago Board of Trade membership that allows an individual to trade financial instrument futures and other designated markets.

At-the-Money Option: An option with a strike price that is equal, or approximately equal, to the current market price of the underlying futures contract.

A

Balance of Payment: A summary of the international transactions of a country over a period of time including commodity and service transactions, capital transactions, and gold movements.

Bar Chart: A chart that graphs the high, low, and settlement prices for a specific trading session over a given period of time.

Basis: The difference between the current cash price and the futures price of the same commodity. Unless otherwise specified, the price of the nearby futures contract month is generally used to calculate the basis.

Bear: Someone who thinks market prices will decline.

Bear Market: A period of declining market prices.

Bear Spread: In most commodities and financial instruments, the term refers to selling the nearby contract month, and buying the deferred contract, to profit from a change in the price relationship.

B

Bid: An expression indicating a desire to buy a commodity at a given price; opposite of offer.

Board of Trade Clearing Corporation: An independent corporation that settles all trades made at the Chicago Board of Trade acting as a guarantor for all trades cleared by it, reconciles all clearing member firm accounts each day to ensure that all gains have been credited and all losses have been collected, and sets and adjusts clearing member firm margins for changing market conditions. Also referred to as **clearing corporation.** See **Clearinghouse.**

Book Entry Securities: Electronically recorded securities that include each creditor's name, address, Social Security or tax identification number, and dollar amount loaned, (i.e., no certificates are issued to bond holders, instead, the transfer agent electronically credits interest payments to each creditor's bank account on a designated date).

Broker: A company or individual that executes futures and options orders on behalf of financial and commercial institutions and/or the general public.

Brokerage Fee: See **Commission Fee.**

Brokerage House: See **Futures Commission Merchant.**

Bull: Someone who thinks market prices will rise.

Bull Market: A period of rising market prices.

Bull Spread: In most commodities and financial instruments, the term refers to buying the nearby month, and selling the deferred month, to profit from the change in the price relationship.

Butterfly Spread: The placing of two interdelivery spreads in opposite directions with the center delivery month common to both spreads.

Buying Hedge: See **Purchasing Hedge.**

C

Calendar Spread: See **Interdelivery Spread** and **Horizontal Spread.**

Call Option: An option that gives the buyer the right, but not the obligation, to purchase (go "long") the underlying futures contract at the strike price on or before the expiration date.

Canceling Order: An order that deletes a customer's previous order.

Carrying Charge: For physical commodities such as grains and metals, the cost of storage space, insurance, and finance charges incurred by holding a physical commodity. In interest rate futures markets, it refers to the differential between the yield on a cash instrument and the cost of funds necessary to buy the instrument. Also referred to as **cost of carry** or **carry.**

Carryover: Grain and oilseed commodities not consumed during the marketing year and remaining in storage at year's end. These stocks are "carried over" into the next marketing year and added to the stocks produced during that crop year.

Cash Commodity: An actual physical commodity someone is buying or selling, e.g., soybeans, corn, gold, silver, Treasury bonds, etc. Also referred to as **actuals.**

Cash Contract: A sales agreement for either immediate or future delivery of the actual product.

Cash Market: A place where people buy and sell the actual commodities, i.e., grain elevator, bank, etc. See **Spot** and **Forward Contract.**

Cash Settlement: Transactions generally involving index-based futures contracts that are settled in cash based on the actual value of the index on the last trading day, in contrast to those that specify the delivery of a commodity or financial instrument.

Certificate of Deposit (CD): A time deposit with a specific maturity evidenced by a certificate.

Charting: The use of charts to analyze market behavior and anticipate future price movements. Those who use charting as a trading method plot such factors as high, low, and settlement prices; average price movements; volume; and open interest. Two basic price charts are bar charts and point-and-figure charts. See **Technical Analysis.**

Cheap: Colloquialism implying that a commodity is underpriced.

Cheapest to Deliver: A method to determine which particular cash debt instrument is most profitable to deliver against a futures contract.

Clear: The process by which a clearinghouse maintains records of all trades and settles margin flow on a daily mark-to-market basis for its clearing member.

Clearing Corporation: See **Board of Trade Clearing Corporation.**

Clearinghouse: An agency or separate corporation of a futures exchange that is responsible for settling trading accounts, clearing trades, collecting and maintaining margin monies, regulating delivery, and reporting trading data. Clearinghouses act as third parties to all futures and options contracts—acting as a buyer to every clearing member seller and a seller to every clearing member buyer.

Clearing Margin: Financial safeguards to ensure that clearing members (usually companies or corporations) perform on their customers' open futures and options contracts. Clearing margins are distinct from customer margins that individual buyers and sellers of futures and options contracts are required to deposit with brokers. See **Customer Margin.**

Clearing Member: A member of an exchange clearinghouse. Memberships in clearing organizations are usually held by companies. Clearing members are responsible for the financial commitments of customers that clear through their firm.

Closing Price: See **Settlement Price.**

Closing Range: A range of prices at which buy and sell transactions took place during the market close.

COM Membership (CBOT): A Chicago Board of Trade membership that allows an individual to trade contracts listed in the commodity options market category.

Commission Fee: A fee charged by a broker for executing a transaction. Also referred to as **brokerage fee.**

Commission House: See **Futures Commission Merchant (FCM).**

Commodity: An article of commerce or a product that can be used for commerce. In a narrow sense, products traded on an authorized commodity exchange. The types of commodities include agricultural products, metals, petroleum, foreign currencies, and financial instruments and indexes, to name a few.

Commodity Credit Corporation (CCC): A branch of the U.S. Department of Agriculture, established in 1933, that supervises the government's farm loan and subsidy programs.

Commodity Futures Trading Commission (CFTC): A federal regulatory agency established under the Commodity Futures Trading Commission Act, as amended in 1974, that oversees futures trading in the United States. The commission is comprised of five commissioners, one of whom is designated as chairman, all appointed by the President subject to Senate confirmation, and is independent of all cabinet departments.

Commodity Pool: An enterprise in which funds contributed by a number of persons are combined for the purpose of trading futures contracts or commodity options.

Commodity Pool Operator (CPO): An individual or organization that operates or solicits funds for a commodity pool.

Commodity Trading Adviser (CTA): A person who, for compensation or profit, directly or indirectly advises others as to the value or the advisability of buying or selling futures contracts or commodity options. Advising indirectly includes exercising trading authority over a customer's account as well as providing recommendations through written publications or other media.

Computerized Trading Reconstruction (CTR) System: A Chicago Board of Trade computerized surveillance program that pinpoints in any trade the traders, the contract, the quantity, the price, and time of execution to the nearest minute.

Concurrent Indicators: See **Lagging Indicators.**

Consumer Price Index (CPI): A major inflation measure computed by the U.S. Department of Commerce. It measures the change in prices of a fixed market basket of some 385 goods and services in the previous month.

Contract Grades: See **Deliverable Grades.**

Contract Month: See **Delivery Month.**

Controlled Account: See **Discretionary Account.**

Convergence: A term referring to cash and futures prices tending to come together (i.e., the basis approaches zero) as the futures contract nears expiration.

Conversion Factor: A factor used to equate the price of T-bond and T-note futures contracts with the various cash T-bonds and T-notes eligible for delivery. This factor is based on the relationship of the cash-instrument coupon to the required 8 percent deliverable grade of a futures contract as well as taking into account the cash instrument's maturity or call.

Cost of Carry (or **Carry**): See **Carrying Charge.**

Coupon: The interest rate on a debt instrument expressed in terms of a percent on an annualized basis that the issuer guarantees to pay the holder until maturity.

Crop (Marketing) Year: The time span from harvest to harvest for agricultural commodities. The crop marketing year varies slightly with each ag commodity, but it tends to begin at harvest and end before the next year's harvest, e.g., the marketing year for soybeans begins September 1 and ends August 31. The futures contract month of November represents the first major new-crop marketing month, and the contract month of July represents the last major old-crop marketing month for soybeans.

Crop Reports: Reports compiled by the U.S. Department of Agriculture on various ag commodities that are released throughout the year. Information in the reports includes estimates on planted acreage, yield, and expected production, as well as comparison of production from previous years.

Cross-Hedging: Hedging a cash commodity using a different but related futures contract when there is no futures contract for the cash commodity being hedged and the cash and futures markets follow similar price trends (e.g., using soybean meal futures to hedge fish meal).

Crush Spread: The purchase of soybean futures and the simultaneous sale of soybean oil and meal futures. See **Reverse Crush.**

Current Yield: The ratio of the coupon to the current market price of the debt instrument.

Customer Margin: Within the futures industry, financial guarantees required of both buyers and sellers of futures contracts and sellers of options contracts to ensure fulfillment of contract obligations. FCMs are responsible for overseeing customer margin accounts. Margins are determined on the basis of market risk and contract value. Also referred to as **performance-bond margin.** See **Clearing Margin.**

D

Daily Trading Limit: The maximum price range set by the exchange each day for a contract.

Day Traders: Speculators who take positions in futures or options contracts and liquidate them prior to the close of the same trading day.

Deferred (Delivery) Month: The more distant month(s) in which futures trading is taking place, as distinguished from the nearby (delivery) month.

Deliverable Grades: The standard grades of commodities or instruments listed in the rules of the exchanges that must be met when delivering cash commodities against futures contracts. Grades are often accompanied by a schedule of discounts and premiums allowable for delivery of commodities of lesser or greater quality than the standard called for by the exchange. Also referred to as **contract grades.**

Delivery: The transfer of the cash commodity from the seller of a futures contract to the buyer of a futures contract. Each futures exchange has specific procedures for delivery of a cash commodity. Some futures contracts, such as stock index contracts, are cash settled.

Delivery Day: The third day in the delivery process at the Chicago Board of Trade, when the buyer's clearing firm presents the delivery notice with a certified check for the amount due at the office of the seller's clearing firm.

Delivery Month: A specific month in which delivery may take place under the terms of a futures contract. Also referred to as **contract month.**

Delivery Points: The locations and facilities designated by a futures exchange where stocks of a commodity may be delivered in fulfillment of a futures contract, under procedures established by the exchange.

Delta: A measure of how much an option premium changes, given a unit change in the underlying futures price. Delta often is interpreted as the probability that the option will be in-the-money by expiration.

Demand, Law of: The relationship between product demand and price.

Differentials: Price differences between classes, grades, and delivery locations of various stocks of the same commodity.

Discount Method: A method of paying interest by issuing a security at less than par and repaying par value at maturity. The difference between the higher par value and the lower purchase price is the interest.

Discount Rate: The interest rate charged on loans by the Federal Reserve to member banks.

Discretionary Account: An arrangement by which the holder of the account gives written power of attorney to another person, often his broker, to make trading decisions. Also known as a **controlled** or **managed account.**

E

Econometrics: The application of statistical and mathematical methods in the field of economics to test and quantify economic theories and the solutions to economic problems.

Equilibrium Price: The market price at which the quantity supplied of a commodity equals the quantity demanded.

Eurodollars: U.S. dollars on deposit with a bank outside of the United States and, consequently, outside the jurisdiction of the United States. The bank could be either a foreign bank or a subsidiary of a U.S. bank.

European Terms: A method of quoting exchange rates, which measures the amount of foreign currency needed to buy one U.S. dollar, i.e., foreign currency unit per dollar. See **Reciprocal of European Terms.**

Exchange For Physicals (EFP): A transaction generally used by two hedgers who want to exchange futures for cash positions. Also referred to as **against actuals** or **versus cash.**

Exercise: The action taken by the holder of a call option if he wishes to purchase the underlying futures contract or by the holder of a put option if he wishes to sell the underlying futures contract.

Exercise Price: See **Strike Price.**

Expanded Trading Hours: Additional trading hours of specific futures and options contracts at the Chicago Board of Trade that overlap with business hours in other time zones.

Expiration Date: Options on futures generally expire on a specific date during the month preceding the futures contract delivery month. For example, an option on a March futures contract expires in February but is referred to as a March option because its exercise would result in a March futures contract position.

Extrinsic Value: See **Time Value.**

Face Value: The amount of money printed on the face of the certificate of a security; the original dollar amount of indebtedness incurred.

Federal Funds: Member bank deposits at the Federal Reserve; these funds are loaned by member banks to other member banks.

Federal Funds Rate: The rate of interest charged for the use of federal funds.

Federal Housing Administration (FHA): A division of the U.S. Department of Housing and Urban Development that insures residential mortgage loans and sets construction standards.

Federal Reserve System: A central banking system in the United States, created by the Federal Reserve Act in 1913, designed to assist the nation in attaining its economic and financial goals. The structure of the Federal Reserve System includes a Board of Governors, the Federal Open Market Committee, and 12 Federal Reserve Banks.

Feed Ratio: A ratio used to express the relationship of feeding costs to the dollar value of livestock. See **Hog/Corn Ratio** and **Steer/Corn Ratio.**

Fill-or-Kill: A customer order that is a price limit order that must be filled immediately or canceled.

Financial Analysis Auditing Compliance Tracking System (FACTS): The National Futures Association's computerized system of maintaining financial records of its member firms and monitoring their financial conditions.

Financial Instrument: There are two basic types: (1) a debt instrument, which is a loan with an agreement to pay back funds with interest; (2) an equity security, which is a share or stock in a company.

First Notice Day: According to Chicago Board of Trade rules, the first day on which a notice of intent to deliver a commodity in fulfillment of a given month's futures contract can be made by the clearinghouse to a buyer. The clearinghouse also informs the sellers who they have been matched up with.

Floor Broker (FB): An individual who executes orders for the purchase or sale of any commodity futures or options contract on any contract market for any other person.

Floor Trader (FT): An individual who executes trades for the purchase or sale of any commodity futures or options contract on any contract market for such individual's own account.

Foreign Exchange Market: See **Forex Market.**

Forex Market: An over-the-counter market where buyers and sellers conduct foreign exchange business by telephone and other means of communication. Also referred to as **foreign exchange market.**

Forward (Cash) Contract: A cash contract in which a seller agrees to deliver a specific cash commodity to a buyer sometime in the future. Forward contracts, in contrast to futures contracts, are privately negotiated and are not standardized.

Full Carrying Charge Market: A futures market where the price difference between delivery months reflects the total costs of interest, insurance, and storage.

Full Membership (CBOT): A Chicago Board of Trade membership that allows an individual to trade all futures and options contracts listed by the exchange.

Fundamental Analysis: A method of anticipating future price movement using supply and demand information.

Futures Commission Merchant (FCM): An individual or organization that solicits or accepts orders to buy or sell futures contracts or options on futures and accepts money or other assets from customers to support such orders. Also referred to as **commission house** or **wire house.**

Futures Contract: A legally binding agreement, made on the trading floor of a futures exchange, to buy or sell a commodity or financial instrument sometime in the future. Futures contracts are standardized according to the quality, quantity, and delivery time and location for each commodity. The only variable is price, which is discovered on an exchange trading floor.

Futures Exchange: A central marketplace with established rules and regulations where buyers and sellers meet to trade futures and options on futures contracts.

G

Gamma: A measurement of how fast delta changes, given a unit change in the underlying futures price.

GIM Membership (CBOT): A Chicago Board of Trade membership that allows an individual to trade all futures contracts listed in the government instrument market category.

GLOBEX®: A global after-hours electronic trading system.

Grain Terminal: Large grain elevator facility with the capacity to ship grain by rail and/or barge to domestic or foreign markets.

Gross Domestic Product (GDP): The value of all final goods and services produced by an economy over a particular time period, normally a year.

Gross National Product (GNP): Gross Domestic Product plus the income accruing to domestic residents as a result of investments abroad less income earned in domestic markets accruing to foreigners abroad.

Gross Processing Margin (GPM): The difference between the cost of soybeans and the combined sales income of the processed soybean oil and meal.

Hedger: An individual or company owning or planning to own a cash commodity—corn, soybeans, wheat, U.S. Treasury bonds, notes, bills, etc.—and concerned that the cost of the commodity may change before either buying or selling it in the cash market. A hedger achieves protection against changing cash prices by purchasing (selling) futures contracts of the same or similar commodity and later offsetting that position by selling (purchasing) futures contracts of the same quantity and type as the initial transaction.

Hedging: The practice of offsetting the price risk inherent in any cash market position by taking an equal but opposite position in the futures market. Hedgers use the futures markets to protect their businesses from adverse price changes. See **Selling (Short) Hedge** and **Purchasing (Long) Hedge.**

High: The highest price of the day for a particular futures contract.

Hog/Corn Ratio: The relationship of feeding costs to the dollar value of hogs. It is measured by dividing the price of hogs ($/hundredweight) by the price of corn ($/bushel). When corn prices are high relative to pork prices, fewer units of corn equal the dollar value of 100 pounds of pork. Conversely, when corn prices are low in relation to pork prices, more units of corn are required to equal the value of 100 pounds of pork. See **Feed Ratio.**

Holder: See **Option Buyer.**

Horizontal Spread: The purchase of either a call or put option and the simultaneous sale of the same type of option with typically the same strike price but with a different expiration month. Also referred to as a **calendar spread.**

IDEM Membership (CBOT): A Chicago Board of Trade membership of trading privileges for futures contracts in the index, debt, and energy markets category (gold, municipal bond index, 30-day fed funds, and stock index futures).

Initial Margin: See **Original Margin.**

Intercommodity Spread: The purchase of a given delivery month of one futures market and the simultaneous sale of the same delivery month of a different, but related, futures market.

Interdelivery Spread: The purchase of one delivery month of a given futures contract and simultaneous sale of another delivery month of the same commodity on the same exchange. Also referred to as an **intramarket** or **calendar spread.**

Intermarket Spread: The sale of a given delivery month of a futures contract on one exchange and the simultaneous purchase of the same delivery month and futures contract on another exchange.

In-the-Money Option: An option having intrinsic value. A call option is in-the-money if its strike price is below the current price of the underlying futures contract. A put option is in-the-money if its strike price is above the current price of the underlying futures contract. See **Intrinsic Value.**

Intramarket Spread: See **Interdelivery Spread.**

Intrinsic Value: The amount by which an option is in-the-money. See **In-the-Money Option.**

Introducing Broker (IB): A person or organization that solicits or accepts orders to buy or sell futures contracts or commodity options but does not accept money or other assets from customers to support such orders.

Inverted Market: A futures market in which the relationship between two delivery months of the same commodity is abnormal.

Invisible Supply: Uncounted stocks of a commodity in the hands of wholesalers, manufacturers, and producers that cannot be identified accurately; stocks outside commercial channels but theoretically available to the market.

L

Lagging Indicators: Market indicators showing the general direction of the economy and confirming or denying the trend implied by the leading indicators. Also referred to as **concurrent indicators.**

Last Trading Day: According to the Chicago Board of Trade rules, the final day when trading may occur in a given futures or options contract month. Futures contracts outstanding at the end of the last trading day must be settled by delivery of the underlying commodity or securities or by agreement for monetary settlement (in some cases by EFPs).

Leading Indicators: Market indicators that signal the state of the economy for the coming months. Some of the leading indicators include: average manufacturing workweek, initial claims for unemployment insurance, orders for consumer goods and material, percentage of companies reporting slower deliveries, change in manufacturers' unfilled orders for durable goods, plant and equipment orders, new building permits, index of consumer expectations, change in material prices, prices of stocks, change in money supply.

Leverage: The ability to control large dollar amounts of a commodity with a comparatively small amount of capital.

Limit Order: An order in which the customer sets a limit on the price and/or time of execution.

Limits: See **Position Limit, Price Limit, Variable Limit.**

Linkage: The ability to buy (sell) contracts on one exchange (such as the Chicago Mercantile Exchange) and later sell (buy) them on another exchange (such as the Singapore International Monetary Exchange).

Liquid: A characteristic of a security or commodity market with enough units outstanding to allow large transactions without a substantial change in price. Institutional investors are inclined to seek out liquid investments so that their trading activity will not influence the market price.

Liquidate: Selling (or purchasing) futures contracts of the same delivery month purchased (or sold) during an earlier transaction or making (or taking) delivery of the cash commodity represented by the futures contract. See **Offset.**

Liquidity Data Bank® (LDB®): A computerized profile of CBOT market activity, used by technical traders to analyze price trends and develop trading strategies. There is a specialized display of daily volume data and time distribution of prices for every commodity traded on the Chicago Board of Trade.

Loan Program: A federal program in which the government lends money at preannounced rates to farmers and allows them to use the crops they plant for the upcoming crop year as collateral. Default on these loans is the primary method by which the government acquires stocks of agricultural commodities.

Loan Rate: The amount lent per unit of a commodity to farmers.

Long: One who has bought futures contracts or owns a cash commodity.

Long Hedge: See **Purchasing Hedge.**

Low: The lowest price of the day for a particular futures contract.

M

Maintenance Margin: A set minimum margin (per outstanding futures contract) that a customer must maintain in his margin account.

Managed Account: See **Discretionary Account.**

Managed Futures: Represents an industry comprised of professional money managers known as commodity trading advisors who manage client assets on a discretionary basis, using global futures markets as an investment medium.

Margin: See **Clearing Margin** and **Customer Margin.**

Margin Call: A call from a clearinghouse to a clearing member, or from a brokerage firm to a customer, to bring margin deposits up to a required minimum level.

Market Information Data Inquiry System (MIDIS): Historical Chicago Board of Trade price, volume, open interest data and other market information accessible by computers within the Chicago Board of Trade building.

Market Order: An order to buy or sell a futures contract of a given delivery month to be filled at the best possible price and as soon as possible.

Market Price Reporting and Information System (MPRIS): The Chicago Board of Trade's computerized price-reporting system.

Market Profile®: A Chicago Board of Trade information service that helps technical traders analyze price trends. Market Profile consists of the Time and Sales ticker and the Liquidity Data Bank®.

Market Reporter: A person employed by the exchange and located in or near the trading pit who records prices as they occur during trading.

Marking-to-Market: To debit or credit on a daily basis a margin account based on the close of that day's trading session. In this way, buyers and sellers are protected against the possibility of contract default.

Minimum Price Fluctuation: See **Tick.**

Money Supply: The amount of money in the economy, consisting primarily of currency in circulation plus deposits in banks: **M-1**—U.S. money supply consisting of currency held by the public, traveler's checks, checking account funds, NOW and super-NOW accounts, automatic transfer service accounts, and balances in credit unions. **M-2**—U.S. money supply consisting of M-1 plus savings and small time deposits (less than $100,000) at depository institutions, overnight repurchase agreements at commercial banks, and money market mutual fund accounts. **M-3**—U.S. money supply consisting of M-2 plus large time deposits ($100,000 or more) at depository institutions, repurchase agreements with maturities longer than one day at commercial banks, and institutional money market accounts.

Moving-Average Charts: A statistical price analysis method of recognizing different price trends. A moving average is calculated by adding the prices for a predetermined number of days and then dividing by the number of days.

Municipal Bonds: Debt securities issued by state and local governments, and special districts and counties.

N

National Futures Association (NFA): An industrywide, industry-supported, self-regulatory organization for futures and options markets. The primary responsibilities of the NFA are to enforce ethical standards and customer protection rules, screen futures professionals for membership, audit and monitor professionals for financial and general compliance rules, and provide for arbitration of futures-related disputes.

Nearby (Delivery) Month: The futures contract month closest to expiration. Also referred to as **spot month.**

Negative Yield Curve: See **Yield Curve.**

Notice Day: According to Chicago Board of Trade rules, the second day of the three-day delivery process when the clearing corporation matches the buyer with the oldest reported long position to the delivering seller and notifies both parties. See **First Notice Day.**

O

Offer: An expression indicating one's desire to sell a commodity at a given price; opposite of bid.

Offset: Taking a second futures or options position opposite to the initial or opening position. See **Liquidate.**

OPEC: Organization of Petroleum Exporting Countries, emerged as the major petroleum pricing power in 1973, when the ownership of oil production in the Middle East transferred from the operating companies to the governments of the producing countries or to their national oil companies. Members are: Algeria, Ecuador, Gabon, Indonesia, Iran, Iraq, Kuwait, Libya, Nigeria, Qatar, Saudi Arabia, the United Arab Emirates, and Venezuela.

Opening Range: A range of prices at which buy and sell transactions took place during the opening of the market.

Open Interest: The total number of futures or options contracts of a given commodity that have not yet been offset by an opposite futures or option transaction nor fulfilled by delivery of the commodity or option exercise. Each open transaction has a buyer and a seller, but for calculation of open interest, only one side of the contract is counted.

Open Market Operation: The buying and selling of government securities—Treasury bills, notes, and bonds—by the Federal Reserve.

Open Outcry: Method of public auction for making verbal bids and offers in the trading pits or rings of futures exchanges.

Option: A contract that conveys the right, but not the obligation, to buy or sell a particular item at a certain price for a limited time. Only the seller of the option is obligated to perform.

Option Buyer: The purchaser of either a call or put option. Option buyers receive the right, but not the obligation, to assume a futures position. Also referred to as the **holder.**

Option Premium: The price of an option—the sum of money that the option buyer pays and the option seller receives for the rights granted by the option.

Option Seller: The person who sells an option in return for a premium and is obligated to perform when the holder exercises his right under the option contract. Also referred to as the **writer.**

Option Spread: The simultaneous purchase and sale of one or more options contracts, futures, and/or cash positions.

Option Writer: See **Option Seller.**

Original Margin: The amount a futures market participant must deposit into his margin account at the time he places an order to buy or sell a futures contract. Also referred to as **initial margin.**

Out-of-the-Money Option: An option with no intrinsic value, i.e., a call whose strike price is above the current futures price or a put whose strike price is below the current futures price.

Over-the-Counter (OTC) Market: A market where products such as stocks, foreign currencies, and other cash items are bought and sold by telephone and other means of communication.

P&S (Purchase and Sale) Statement: A statement sent by a commission house to a customer when his futures or options on futures position has changed, showing the number of contracts bought or sold, the prices at which the contracts were bought or sold, the gross profit or loss, the commission charges, and the net profit or loss on the transactions.

Par: The face value of a security. For example, a bond selling at par is

P

worth the same dollar amount it was issued for or at which it will be redeemed at maturity.

Payment-In-Kind (PIK) Program: A government program in which farmers who comply with a voluntary acreage-control program and set aside an additional percentage of acreage specified by the government receive certificates that can be redeemed for government-owned stocks of grain.

Performance Bond Margin: The amount of money deposited by both a buyer and seller of a futures contract or an options seller to ensure performance of the term of the contract. Margin in commodities is not a payment of equity or down payment on the commodity itself, but rather it is a security deposit. See **Customer Margin** and **Clearing Margin.**

Pit: The area on the trading floor where futures and options on futures contracts are bought and sold. Pits are usually raised octagonal platforms with steps descending on the inside that permit buyers and sellers of contracts to see each other.

Point-and-Figure Charts: Charts that show price changes of a minimum amount regardless of the time period involved.

Position: A market commitment. A buyer of a futures contract is said to have a long position and, conversely, a seller of futures contracts is said to have a short position.

Position Day: According to the Chicago Board of Trade rules, the first day in the process of making or taking delivery of the actual commodity on a futures contract. The clearing firm representing the seller notifies the Board of Trade Clearing Corporation that its short customers want to deliver on a futures contract.

Position Limit: The maximum number of speculative futures contracts one can hold as determined by the Commodity Futures Trading Commission and/or the exchange upon which the contract is traded. Also referred to as **trading limit.**

Position Trader: An approach to trading in which the trader either buys or sells contracts and holds them for an extended period of time.

Positive Yield Curve: See **Yield Curve.**

Premium: (1) The additional payment allowed by exchange regulation for delivery of higher-than-required standards or grades of a commodity against a futures contract. (2) In speaking of price relationships between different delivery months of a given commodity, one is said to be "trading at a premium" over another when its price is greater than that of the other. (3) In financial instruments, the dollar amount by which a security trades above its principal value. See **Option Premium.**

Price Discovery: The generation of information about "future" cash market prices through the futures markets.

Price Limit: The maximum advance or decline—from the previous day's settlement price—permitted for a contract in one trading session by the rules of the exchange. See also **Variable Limit.**

Price Limit Order: A customer order that specifies the price at which a trade can be executed.

Primary Dealer: A designation given by the Federal Reserve System to commercial banks or broker/dealers who meet specific criteria. Among the criteria are capital requirements and meaningful participation in the Treasury auctions.

Primary Market: Market of new issues of securities.

Prime Rate: Interest rate charged by major banks to their most creditworthy customers.

Producer Price Index (PPI): An index that shows the cost of resources needed to produce manufactured goods during the previous month.

Pulpit: A raised structure adjacent to, or in the center of, the pit or ring at a futures exchange where market reporters, employed by the exchange, record price changes as they occur in the trading pit.

Purchasing Hedge (or **Long Hedge**)**:** Buying futures contracts to protect against a possible price increase of cash commodities that will be purchased in the future. At the time the cash commodities are bought, the open futures position is closed by selling an equal number and type of futures contracts as those that were initially purchased. Also referred to as a **buying hedge. See Hedging.**

Put Option: An option that gives the option buyer the right but not the obligation to sell (go "short") the underlying futures contract at the strike price on or before the expiration date.

Range (Price): The price span during a given trading session, week, month, year, etc.

Reciprocal of European Terms: One method of quoting exchange rates, which measures the U.S. dollar value of one foreign currency unit, i.e., U.S. dollars per foreign units. See **European Terms.**

Repurchase Agreements (or **Repo**)**:** An agreement between a seller and a buyer, usually in U.S. government securities, in which the seller agrees to buy back the security at a later date.

Reserve Requirements: The minimum amount of cash and liquid assets as a percentage of demand deposits and time deposits that member banks of the Federal Reserve are required to maintain.

Resistance: A level above which prices have had difficulty penetrating.

Resumption: The reopening the following day of specific futures and options markets that also trade during the evening session at the Chicago Board of Trade.

Reverse Crush Spread: The sale of soybean futures and the simultaneous purchase of soybean oil and meal futures. See **Crush Spread.**

R

Runners: Messengers who rush orders received by phone clerks to brokers for execution in the pit.

Scalper: A trader who trades for small, short-term profits during the course of a trading session, rarely carrying a position overnight.

Secondary Market: Market where previously issued securities are bought and sold.

Security: Common or preferred stock; a bond of a corporation, government, or quasi-government body.

Selling Hedge (or **Short Hedge):** Selling futures contracts to protect against possible declining prices of commodities that will be sold in the future. At the time the cash commodities are sold, the open futures position is closed by purchasing an equal number and type of futures contracts as those that were initially sold. See **Hedging.**

Settle: See **Settlement Price.**

Settlement Price: The last price paid for a commodity on any trading day. The exchange clearinghouse determines a firm's net gains or losses, margin requirements, and the next day's price limits, based on each futures and options contract settlement price. If there is a closing range of prices, the settlement price is determined by averaging those prices. Also referred to as **settle** or **closing price.**

Short: *(noun)* One who has sold futures contracts or plans to purchase a cash commodity. *(verb)* Selling futures contracts or initiating a cash forward contract sale without offsetting a particular market position.

Short Hedge: See **Selling Hedge.**

Simulation Analysis of Financial Exposure (SAFE): A sophisticated computer risk-analysis program that monitors the risk of clearing members and large-volume traders at the Chicago Board of Trade. It calculates the risk of change in market prices or volatility to a firm carrying open positions.

Speculator: A market participant who tries to profit from buying and selling futures and options contracts by anticipating future price movements. Speculators assume market price risk and add liquidity and capital to the futures markets.

Spot: Usually refers to a cash market price for a physical commodity that is available for immediate delivery.

Spot Month: See **Nearby (Delivery) Month**

Spread: The price difference between two related markets or commodities.

Spreading: The simultaneous buying and selling of two related markets in the expectation that a profit will be made when the position is offset. Examples include: buying one futures contract and selling another futures contract of the same commodity but different delivery month; buying and selling the same delivery month of the same commodity on different futures exchanges; buying a given delivery month of one futures market and selling the same delivery month of a different, but related, futures market.

Steer/Corn Ratio: The relationship of cattle prices to feeding costs. It is measured by dividing the price of cattle ($/hundredweight) by the price of corn ($/bushel). When corn prices are high relative to cattle prices, fewer units of corn equal the dollar value of 100 pounds of cattle. Conversely, when corn prices are low in relation to cattle prices, more units of corn are required to equal the value of 100 pounds of beef. See **Feed Ratio.**

Stock Index: An indicator used to measure and report value changes in a selected group of stocks. How a particular stock index tracks the market depends on its composition—the sampling of stocks, the weighting of individual stocks, and the method of averaging used to establish an index.

Stock Market: A market in which shares of stock are bought and sold.

Stop-Limit Order: A variation of a stop order in which a trade must be executed at the exact price or better. If the order cannot be executed, it is held until the stated price or better is reached again.

Stop Order: An order to buy or sell when the market reaches a specified point. A stop order to buy becomes a market order when the futures contract trades (or is bid) at or above the stop price. A stop order to sell becomes a market order when the futures contract trades (or is offered) at or below the stop price.

Strike Price: The price at which the futures contract underlying a call or put option can be purchased (if a call) or sold (if a put). Also referred to as **exercise price.**

Supply, Law of: The relationship between product supply and its price.

Support: The place on a chart where the buying of futures contracts is sufficient to halt a price decline.

Suspension: The end of the evening session for specific futures and options markets traded at the Chicago Board of Trade.

Technical Analysis: Anticipating future price movement using historical prices, trading volume, open interest, and other trading data to study price patterns.

Tick: The smallest allowable increment of price movement for a contract. Also referred to as **minimum price fluctuation.**

Time Limit Order: A customer order that designates the time during which it can be executed.

Time and Sales Ticker: Part of the Chicago Board of Trade Market Profile® system consisting of an on-line graphic service that transmits price and time information throughout the day.

Time-Stamped: Part of the order-routing process in which the time of day is stamped on an order. An order is time-stamped when it is (1) received on the trading floor, and (2) completed.

T

Time Value: The amount of money option buyers are willing to pay for an option in the anticipation that, over time, a change in the underlying futures price will cause the option to increase in value. In general, an option premium is the sum of time value and intrinsic value. Any amount by which an option premium exceeds the option's intrinsic value can be considered time value. Also referred to as **extrinsic value.**

Trade Balance: The difference between a nation's imports and exports of merchandise.

Trading Limit: See **Position Limit.**

Treasury Bill: See **U.S. Treasury Bill.**

Treasury Bond: See **U.S. Treasury Bond.**

Treasury Note: See **U.S. Treasury Note.**

U

Underlying Futures Contract: The specific futures contract that is bought or sold by exercising an option.

U.S. Treasury Bill: A short-term U.S. government debt instrument with an original maturity of one year or less. Bills are sold at a discount from par with the interest earned being the difference between the face value received at maturity and the price paid.

U.S. Treasury Bond: Government-debt security with a coupon and original maturity of more than 10 years. Interest is paid semiannually.

U.S. Treasury Note: Government-debt security with a coupon and original maturity of one to 10 years.

V

Variable Limit: According to the Chicago Board of Trade rules, an expanded allowable price range set during volatile markets.

Variation Margin: During periods of great market volatility or in the case of high-risk accounts, additional margin deposited by a clearing member firm to an exchange clearinghouse.

Versus Cash: See **Exchange For Physicals.**

Vertical Spread: Buying and selling puts or calls of the same expiration month but different strike prices.

Volatility: A measurement of the change in price over a given time period. It is often expressed as a percentage and computed as the annualized standard deviation of percentage change in daily price.

Volume: The number of purchases or sales of a commodity futures contract made during a specified period of time, often the total transactions for one trading day.

W

Warehouse Receipt: Document guaranteeing the existence and availability of a given quantity and quality of a commodity in storage; commonly used as the instrument of transfer of ownership in both cash and futures transactions.

Wire House: See **Futures Commission Merchant (FCM).**
Writer: See **Option Seller.**

Y

Yield: A measure of the annual return on an investment.
Yield Curve: A chart in which the yield level is plotted on the vertical axis and the term to maturity of debt instruments of similar creditworthiness is plotted on the horizontal axis. The yield curve is positive when long-term rates are higher than short-term rates. However, when short-term rates are higher than yields on long-term investments, the yield curve is negative or inverted.
Yield to Maturity: The rate of return an investor receives if a fixed-income security is held to maturity.

INDEX